The Letters of

Wolfgang Amadeus Mozart

By Wolfgang Amadeus Mozart

The Letters of Wolfgang Amadeus Mozart

Layout and Cover Copyright ©2014
All Rights Reserved
Printed in the USA

Translated by Lady Wallace

Table of Contents

PREFACE 9

FIRST PART. ITALY, VIENNA, MUNICH. 1770 TO 1776. 13
1. Salzburg, 1769. 15
2. Verona, Jan. 1770. 16
3. Milan, Jan. 26, 1770. 18
4. Milan, Feb. 10, 1770. 19
5. Milan, Feb. 17, 1770. 19
6. Milan, Carnival, Erchtag. 20
7. Milan, March 3, 1770. 20
8. Bologna, March 24, 1770. 21
9. Rome, April 14, 1770. 21
10. Rome, April 2l, l770. 22
11. Rome, April 25, 1770. 23
12. Naples, May 19, 1770. 24
13. Naples, May 29, 1770. 25
14. Naples, June 5, 1770. 26
15. Naples, June 16, 1770. 27
16. Rome, July 7, 1770. 27
17. Bologna, July 21, 1770. 27
18. 28
19. Bologna, August 4, 1770. 28

20. Bologna, August 21, 1770. 29

21. Bologna, Sept. 8, 1770. 29

22. 30

23. Bologna, Sept. 29, 1770. 30

24. Bologna, Oct. 6, 1770. 30

25. Milan, Oct. 20, 1770. 31

26. Milan, Oct. 27, 1770. 31

27. Milan, Nov. 3, 1770. 32

28. Milan, Dec. 1, 1770. 32

29. 33

30. Venice, Feb 15, 1771 33

31. Venice, Feb. 20, 1771. 34

32. Verona, August 18, 1771. 34

33. Milan, August 23, 1771. 35

34. Milan, August 31, 1771. 35

35. Milan, Sept. 13, 1771. 36

36. Milan, Sept. 21, 1771. 36

37. Milan, Oct. 5, 1771. 36

38. Milan, Oct. 26, 1771. 37

39. Milan, Nov. 2, 1771. 37

40. Milan, Nov. 24,1771. 37

41. Milan, Nov. 30, 1771. 38

42. Bologna, Oct. 28, 1772. 38

43. Milan, Nov. 7,1772. 38

44. 39

45. Milan, Nov. 21, 1772. 40

46. Milan, Nov. 28,1772. 40
47. Milan, Dec. 5,1772. 40
48. Milan, Dec. 18,1772. 41
49. 42
50. Vienna, August 14,1773. 43
51. Vienna, August 21,1773. 43
52. Vienna, Sept. 15,1773. 44
53. Munich, Dec. 28,1774. 44
54. Munich, Dec. 30, 1774. 45
55. Munich, Jan. 11,1775. 45
56. Munich, Jan. 14,1775. 46
57. 47
58. 47

SECOND PART. MUNICH, AUGSBURG, MANNHEIM. SEPTEMBER 1771 TO MARCH 1778. 51
59. Wasserburg, Sept. 23, l777. 51
60. Munich, Sept. 26,1777. 53
61. Munich, Sept. 29, 1777. 55
62. Munich, Oct. 2,1777. 57
63. Munich, Oct. 6, 1777. 60
64. Munich, Oct. 11, 1777. 62
65. Augsburg, Oct. 14, 1777. 65
66. Augsburg, Oct. 17, 1777. 67
67. Augsburg, Oct. 17, 1777. 72
68. Augsburg, Oct. 23, 1777. 74

69. Augsburg, Oct. 25, 1777. ... 77
70. Mannheim, Oct. 30, 1777. ... 78
71. Mannheim, Nov. 4, 1777. ... 79
72. Mannheim, Nov. 5, 1777. ... 81
73. Mannheim, Nov. 8, 1777. ... 82
74. Mannheim, Nov. 13, 1777. ... 84
75. Mannheim, Nov. 13, 1777. ... 87
76. Mannheim, Nov. 14-16, 1777. ... 87
77. Mannheim, Nov. 20, 1777. ... 90
78. Mannheim, Nov. 22, 1777. ... 91
79. Mannheim, Nov. 26, 1777. ... 93
80. Mannheim, Nov. 29, 1777. ... 94
81. Mannheim, Dec. 3, 1777. ... 97
82. Mannheim, Dec. 6, 1777. ... 99
83. Mannheim, Dec. 10, 1777. ... 100
84. Mannheim, Dec. 14, 1777. ... 103
85. Mannheim, Dec. 18, 1777. ... 103
86. Mannheim, Dec. 20, 1777. ... 104
87. Mannheim, Dec. 27, 1777. ... 105
88. Mannheim, Jan. 7, 1778. ... 106
89. Mannheim, Jan 10,1778 ... 107
90. Mannheim, Jan. 17, 1778. ... 108
91. Mannheim, Feb.2 1778 ... 110
92. Mannheim, Feb. 7, 1778. ... 113
93. Mannheim, Feb. 14, 1778. ... 114
94. Mannheim, Feb. 19, 1778. ... 116

95. Mannheim, Feb. 22, 1778. 118

96. Mannheim, Feb. 28, 1778. 119

97. Mannheim, Feb. 28,1778. 122

98. Mannheim, March 7,1778. 124

99. Mannheim, March. 11, 1778. 124

THIRD PART. PARIS. MARCH 1778 TO JANUARY 1779. 126

100. Paris, March 24, 1778. 126

101. Paris, April 5, 1778. 129

102. Paris, May 1, 1778. 130

103. Paris, May 14, 1778. 133

104. Paris, May 29,1778. 134

105. Paris, June 12, 1778. 135

106. Paris, July 3, 1778. 137

107. Paris, July 3, 1778. 138

108. Paris, July 9, 1778. 141

109. Paris, July 18,1778. 147

110. Paris, July 31, 1778. 152

111. Paris, August 7, 1778. 157

112. St. Germains, August 27, 1778. 161

113. Paris, Sept. 11, 1778. 163

114. Nancy, Oct. 3, 1778. 167

115. Strassburg, Oct. 15, l778. 169

116. Strassburg, Oct. 20, 1778. 171

117. Mannheim, November 12, 1778. 174

118. Mannheim, Nov. 24, 1778. 177

119. Mannheim, Dec. 3, l778. 178

120. Kaisersheim, Dec. 18, 1778. 179

121. Kaisersheim, Dec. 23, 1778. 182

122. Munich, Dec. 29, 1778. 183

123. Munich, Dec. 31, 1778. 184

124. Munich, Jan. 8, 1779. 185

125. Salzburg, May 10, 1779. 187

FORTH PART. MUNICH.—IDOMENEO. NOVEMBER 1780 TO JANUARY 1781. 189

126. Munich, Nov. 8, 1780. 189

127. Munich, Nov. 13, 1780. 191

128. Munich, Nov. 15, 1780. 192

129. Munich, Nov. 22, 1780. 193

130. Munich, Nov. 24, 1780. 195

131. Munich, Dec. l, 1780. 198

132. Munich, Dec. 5,1780. 199

133. Munich, Dec. 13, 1780. 200

134. Munich, Dec. 16, 1780. 201

135. Munich, Dec. 19, 1780. 203

136. Munich, Dec 27, 1780. 204

137. Munich, Dec. 30. 1780. 206

138. Munich, Jan. 3, 1780. 207

139. Munich, Jan. 10,1780. 208

140. Munich, Jan. 18, 1780. 209

PREFACE

A full and authentic edition of Mozart's Letters ought to require no special apology; for, though their essential substance has already been made known by quotations from biographies by Nissen, Jahn, and myself, taken from the originals, still in these three works the letters are necessarily not only very imperfectly given, but in some parts so fragmentary, that the peculiar charm of this correspondence—namely, the familiar and confidential mood in which it was written at the time—is entirely destroyed. It was only possible to restore, and to enable others to enjoy this charm—a charm so novel, even to those already conversant with Mozart's life, that the most familiar incidents acquire fresh zest from it—by an ungarbled edition of these letters. This is what I now offer, feeling convinced that it will be welcome not only to the mass of Mozart's admirers, but also to professional musicians; for in them alone is strikingly set forth how Mozart lived and labored, enjoyed and suffered, and this with a degree of vivid and graphic reality which no biography, however complete, could ever succeed in giving. Who does not know the varied riches of Mozart's life? All that agitated the minds of men in that day—nay, all that now moves, and ever will move, the heart of man—vibrated with fresh pulsation, and under the most manifold forms, in his sensitive soul, and mirrored itself in a series of letters, which indeed rather resemble a journal than a correspondence.

This artist, Nature had gifted in all respects with the most clear and vigorous intellect that ever man possessed. Even in a language which he had not so fully mastered as to acquire the facility of giving expression to his ideas, he contrived to relate to others all that he saw and heard, and felt and thought, with surprising clearness and the most charming sprightliness, combined with talent and good feeling. Above all, in his letters to his father when travelling, we meet with the most minute delineations of countries and people, of the progress of the fine arts, especially in the theatres and in music; we also see the impulses of his own heart and a hundred other things which, in fascination, and universal as well as artistic interest, have scarcely a parallel in our literature. The style may fail to a certain degree in polish, that is, in definite purpose in expressing what he wished to say in an attractive or congenial form,—an art, however, which Mozart so thoroughly understood in his music. His mode of writing, especially in the later letters from Vienna, is often very slovenly, evidencing how averse the Maestro was to the task. Still these letters are manifestly the unconstrained, natural, and simple outpourings of his heart, delightfully recalling to our minds all the sweetness and pathos, the spirit and grace, which have a thousand times enchanted us in the music of Mozart. The accounts of his visit to Paris may, indeed, lay claim to a certain aesthetic value, for they are written throughout with visible zest in his own descriptions, and also with wit, and charm, and characteristic energy. As these combined merits can only become apparent by an ungarbled series of the letters, I have resolved, after many long years of zealous research in collecting them, to undertake the work,—that is, to publish the letters entire that have come to my knowledge.

It now only remains for me to give some words of explanation as to the method I have pursued in editing them.

In the first place, this edition, (being transcribed closely from the originals,) if compared with the letters already published, will prove that the latter are open to many corrections, both in trivial and more important respects. I have forborne, however, attracting attention to the deviations from the original text, either in Nissen or Jahn. I have no wish to he punctilious about trifles, where, as in the case of Jahn, the principal points are correct. Further, by this faithful production of the letters, (nothing being omitted but the constant repetition of forms of greeting and subscription,) we find many an additional feature in the Maestro's life, and chiefly various facts with regard to the creation and publication of his works, which may serve to complete and to amend various statements in Dr. Ludwig Ritter von Kochel's "Chronological Thematic Catalogue of the Musical Compositions of W. A. Mozart," (Leipzig, Breitkopf and Hartel). This will be effected not only by the hitherto unpublished letters, though comparatively few in number, but also by passages being given in full, which have been hitherto suppressed as of no consequence. I have referred to Nissen and Jahn only when, in spite of all my inquiries, I could not discover the proprietor of the original, or procure a correct copy.

I must also remark that all letters without a special address are written to his father. I have only adhered to Mozart's defective orthography in his few letters of early date, and in the rest adopted the more modern fashion. I did so for this simple reason, that these defects form a charm in his juvenile letters, from being in accordance with their boyish contents, while, with regard to the others, they only tend to distract the attention from the substance of the letters, instead of imparting additional interest to them. Biographers can, and ought always to render faithfully the original writing, because quotations alternate with the text of the biographer; but in a regular and uninterrupted series of letters this attraction must be very sparingly used, or it will have a pernicious effect.

The explanatory remarks, and also the supplementary Lexicon, in which I have availed myself of Jahn's catalogue, will make the letters more intelligible to the world at large. The Index, too, has been most carefully prepared to facilitate references.

Lastly, I return my best thanks to the keeper of the Archives of the Mozarteum in Salzburg, to Herr Jellinck, and to all the librarians and collectors of autographs who have assisted me in my task, either by furnishing me with copies of their Mozart letters, or by letting me know where I could procure them. I would also earnestly request all who may possess any Mozart letters to send me an exact transcript of them in the interest of Art; for those here given allude to many still unknown, which are no doubt scattered about here and there, waiting to be brought to light.

With respect to myself, the best reward I aspire to in return for the many sacrifices this collection has cost me, is, that my readers may do justice to the purpose which chiefly guided me throughout this publication,—my desire being not merely to benefit science, and to give a graphic description of the amiability and purity of heart which so distinguished this attractive man, (for such was my aim in my "Life of Mozart,") but above all to draw attention afresh to the unremitting zeal with which Mozart did homage to every advance in Art, striving to make music more and more the interpreter of man's innermost being. I also wished to show how much his course was impeded by the sluggishness and stupidity of the multitude, though partly sustained by the sympathy of kindred souls, till the glorious victory was won over routine and imbecility. Amidst all the fatiguing process of copying and collating letters already so familiar to me, these considerations moved me more vividly than ever; and no work on the Maestro can ever bring them with such force before the intelligent reader as this connected succession of letters, containing his own details of his unwearied artistic struggles and productions. May these letters, then, kindle fresh zeal in our artists of the present day, both in youthful genius and in laurel-crowned Maestri!—

especially may they have the happiest influence on those who devote themselves to that phase of Art in which Mozart attained the highest renown!—may they impart that energetic courage which is derived from the experience that incessant efforts for the progress of Art and its appliances enlarge the limits of human intellect, and can alone insure an immortal crown!

    LUDWIG NOHL.
    MUNICH, October 1, 1864.

FIRST PART. ITALY, VIENNA, MUNICH. 1770 TO 1776.

Wolfgang Amadeus Mozart was born in Salzburg on the 17th January, 1756. His father, Leopold Mozart, belonged to a respectable tradesman's family in the free city of Augsburg. Conscious of being gifted with no small portion of intellectual endowments, he followed the impulse that led him to aim at a higher position in life, and went to the then celebrated University of Salzburg in order to study jurisprudence. As he did not, however, at once succeed in procuring employment in this profession, he was forced, from his straitened means, to enter the service of Canon Count Thun as valet. Subsequently, however, his talents, and that thorough knowledge of music by which he had already (according to the custom of many students) gained some part of his livelihood, obtained for him a better position. In the year 1743 he was received into the band (Kapelle) of the Salzburg cathedral by Archbishop Sigismund; and as his capabilities and fame as a violinist increased, the same Prince shortly afterwards promoted him to the situation of Hof-Componist (Court Composer) and leader of the orchestra, and in 1762 he was appointed Hof-Kapellmeister (conductor of the Court music).

In 1747 Leopold Mozart married Anna Maria Pertlin, a foster-child of the Convent of St. Gilgen. The fruits of this marriage were seven children, two of whom alone survived,—Maria Anna, (the fourth), called Nannerl, born in 1751; and the youngest, Wolfgang Amadeus Johannes Chrysostomus. The daughter at a very early age displayed a most remarkable talent for music, and when her father began to give her instructions in it, an inborn and passionate love of this art was soon evident in her little brother of three years old, who at once gave tokens of a degree of genius far surpassing all experience, and really bordering on the marvellous. In his fourth year he could play all sorts of little pieces on the piano. He only required half an hour to learn a minuet, and one hour for a longer movement; and in his fifth year he actually composed some pretty short pieces, several of which are still extant.

[Footnote: The Grand Duchess Helene Paulowna, a few weeks ago, made a present to the Mozarteum of the music-book from which Mozart learned music, and in which he wrote down his first compositions.]

The wonderful acquirements of both these children, to which Wolfgang soon added skilful playing on the violin and organ, induced their father to travel with them. In January, 1702, when the boy was just six years old, they went first to Munich, and in the autumn to Vienna, the children everywhere on their journey exciting the greatest sensation, and being handsomely remunerated. Leopold Mozart, therefore, soon afterwards resolved to undertake a longer journey, accompanied by his whole family. This lasted more than three years, extending from the smaller towns in West Germany to Paris and London, while they visited, on their way back, Holland, France, and Switzerland. The careful musical instruction which the father perseveringly bestowed on his son, went hand in hand with the most admirable education, and the boy was soon as universally beloved for his amiable disposition and natural simplicity and candor, as admired for his rare gifts and acquirements.

After nearly a year passed at home in unremitting musical instruction, and practice of various instruments as well as composition, the father once more set off with all his family to Vienna,—on this occasion with a view to Wolfgang paving the way to Italy by the composition of an opera, (Italy, at that time, being the Eldorado of music.) He succeeded in procuring the scrittura of an opera buffa, "La Finta semplice;" but, when finished, although the Emperor himself had intrusted the composition to the boy, the cabals of envious singers effectually prevented its being performed. But a German operetta which the lad of twelve also wrote at that time, "Bastien und Bastienne," was given in private, at the summer residence of the Mesmer family, in the suburb called Landstrasse. The father, too, had some compensation by the Emperor commissioning his son to compose a solemn mass for the consecration of the new Waisenhaus church, which Wolfgang himself directed with the conductor's baton, in presence of the Imperial Family, on the 7th December, 1768.

Immediately on their return home, the young virtuoso was appointed archiepiscopal Concertmeister. He passed almost the whole of the year 1769 in Salzburg, chiefly engaged in the composition of masses. We also see him at that time eagerly occupied in improving his knowledge of Latin, although two years previously he had composed a comedy in that language,—"Apollo et Hyacinthus." From this study proceeds the first letter which is still extant from his hand:—

1. Salzburg, 1769.

MY DEAR YOUNG LADY,—

I beg you will pardon the liberty I take in plaguing you with these few lines, but as you said yesterday that there was nothing you could not understand in Latin, and I might write what I chose in that language, I could not resist the bold impulse to write you a few Latin lines. When you have deciphered these, be so good as to send me the answer by one of Hagenauer's servants, for my messenger cannot wait; remember, you must answer this by a letter.

[Footnote: By a messenger of the Hagenauer family, in whose house, opposite the inn of "Den drei Allurten," Mozart was born, and with whom his family were on the most intimate terms.]

"Cuperem scire, de qua causa, a quam plurimis adolescentibus ottium usque adeo oestimetur, ut ipsi se nec verbis, nec verberibus ad hoc sinant abduci."

[Footnote: "I should like to know the reason why indolence is so highly prized by very many young men, that neither by words nor blows will they suffer themselves to be roused from it."]

WOLFGANG MOZART.

The father's plan to go to Italy, there to lay the foundation of a European reputation for his son, was realized in the beginning of December, 1769, and during the journey, the boy, who was at that time just entering his fifteenth year, subjoined to his father's reports scraps of his own writing, in which, in true boyish fashion, he had recourse to all kinds of languages and witticisms, but always exhibiting in his opinions on music the closest observation, the gravest thought, and the most acute judgment.

2. Verona, Jan. 1770.

MY VERY DEAREST SISTER,—

I have at last got a letter a span long after hoping so much for an answer that I lost patience; and I had good cause to do so before receiving yours at last. The German blockhead having said his say, now the Italian one begins. Lei e piu franca nella lingua italiana di quel che mi ho immaginato. Lei mi dica la cagione perche lei non fu nella commedia che hanno giocata i Cavalieri. Adesso sentiamo sempre una opera titolata Il Ruggiero. Oronte, il padre di Bradamante, e un principe (il Signor Afferi) bravo cantante, un baritono,

[Footnote: "You are more versed in the Italian language than I believed. Tell me why you were not one of the actors in the comedy performed by the Cavaliers. We are now hearing an opera called 'Il Ruggiero.' Oronte, the father of Bradamante, is a Prince (acted by Afferi, a good singer, a baritone)."]

but very affected when he speaks out a falsetto, but not quite so much so as Tibaldi in Vienna. Bradamante innamorata di Ruggiero (ma [Footnote: "Bradamante is enamored of Ruggiero, but"]—she is to marry Leone, but will not) fa una povera Baronessa, che ha avuto una gran disgrazia, ma non so la quale; recita [Footnote: "Pretends to be a poor Baroness who has met with some great misfortune, but what it is I don't know, she performs"] under an assumed name, but the name I forget; ha una voce passabile, e la statura non sarebbe male, ma distuona come il diavolo. Ruggiero, un ricco principe innamorato di Bradamante, e un musico; canta un poco Manzuolisch [Footnote: Manzuoli was a celebrated soprano, from whom Mozart had lessons in singing when in London.] ed ha una bellissima voce forte ed e gia vecchio; ha 55 anni, ed ha una [Footnote: "She has a tolerable voice, and her appearance is in her favor, but she sings out of tune like a devil Ruggiero, a rich Prince enamored of Bradamante, is a musico, and sings rather in Manzuoli's style, and has a fine powerful voice, though quite old; he is fifty-five, and has a"] flexible voice. Leone is to marry Bradamante—richississimo e, [Footnote: "Immensely rich."] but whether he is rich off the stage I can't say. La moglie di Afferi, che ha una bellissima voce, ma e tanto susurro nel teatro che non si sente niente. Irene fa una sorella di Lolli, del gran

2. Verona, Jan. 1770.

violinista che habbiamo sentito a Vienna, a una [Footnote: "Afferi's wife has a most beautiful voice, but sings so softly on the stage that you really hear nothing at all. A sister of Lolli, the great violinist whom we heard at Vienna, acts Irene; she has a"] very harsh voce, e canta sempre [Footnote: "Voice, and always sings"] a quaver too tardi o troppo a buon' ora. Granno fa un signore, che non so come si chiame; e la prima volta che lui recita. [Footnote: "Slow or too fast. Ganno is acted by a gentleman whose name I never heard. It is his first appearance on the stage."] There is a ballet between each act. We have a good dancer here called Roessler. He is a German, and dances right well. The very last time we were at the opera (but not, I hope, the very last time we ever shall be there) we got M. Roessler to come up to our palco, (for M. Carlotti gives us his box, of which we have the key,) and conversed with him. Apropos, every one is now in maschera, and one great convenience is, that if you fasten your mask on your hat you have the privilege of not taking off your hat when any one speaks to you; and you never address them by name, but always as "Servitore umilissimo, Signora Maschera." Cospetto di Bacco! that is fun! The most strange of all is that we go to bed at half-past seven! Se lei indovinasse questo, io diro certamente che lei sia la madre di tutti gli indovini. [Footnote: "If you guess this, I shall say that you are the mother of all guessers."] Kiss mamma's hand for me, and to yourself I send a thousand kisses, and assure you that I shall always be your affectionate brother.

Portez-vous bien, et aimez-moi toujours.

3. Milan, Jan. 26, 1770.

I REJOICE in my heart that you were so well amused at the sledging party you write to me about, and I wish you a thousand opportunities of pleasure, so that you may pass your life merrily. But one thing vexes me, which is, that you allowed Herr von Molk [an admirer of this pretty young girl of eighteen] to sigh and sentimentalize, and that you did not go with him in his sledge, that he might have upset you. What a lot of pocket- handkerchiefs he must have used that day to dry the tears he shed for you! He no doubt, too, swallowed at least three ounces of cream of tartar to drive away the horrid evil humors in his body. I know nothing new except that Herr Gellert, the Leipzig poet, [Footnote: Old Mozart prized Gellert's poems so highly, that on one occasion he wrote to him expressing his admiration.] is dead, and has written no more poetry since his death. Just before beginning this letter I composed an air from the "Demetrio" of Metastasio, which begins thus, "Misero tu non sei."

The opera at Mantua was very good. They gave "Demetrio." The prima donna sings well, but is inanimate, and if you did not see her acting, but only singing, you might suppose she was not singing at all, for she can't open her mouth, and whines out everything; but this is nothing new to us. The seconda donna looks like a grenadier, and has a very powerful voice; she really does not sing badly, considering that this is her first appearance. Il primo uomo, il musico, sings beautifully, but his voice is uneven; his name is Caselli. Il secondo uomo is quite old, and does not at all please me. The tenor's name is Ottini; he does not sing unpleasingly, but with effort, like all Italian tenors. We know him very well. The name of the second I don't know; he is still young, but nothing at all remarkable. Primo ballerino good; prima ballerina good, and people say pretty, but I have not seen her near. There is a grotesco who jumps cleverly, but cannot write as I do—just as pigs grunt. The orchestra is tolerable. In Cremona, the orchestra is good, and Spagnoletta is the name of the first violinist there. Prima donna very passable- -rather ancient, I fancy, and as ugly as sin. She does not sing as well as she acts, and is the wife of a violin-player at the opera. Her name is Masci. The opera was the "Clemenza di Tito." Seconda donna not ugly on the stage, young, but nothing superior. Primo uomo, un musico, Cicognani, a fine voice, and a beautiful cantabile. The other two musici young and passable. The tenor's name is non lo so [I don't know what]. He has a pleasing exterior, and resembles Le Roi at Vienna. Ballerino primo good, but an ugly dog. There was a ballerina who danced far from badly, and, what is a capo d'opera, she is anything but plain, either on the stage or off it. The rest were the usual average. I cannot write much about the Milan opera, for we did not go there, but we heard that it was not successful. Primo uomo, Aprile, who sings well, and has a fine even voice; we heard him at a grand church festival. Madame Piccinelli, from Paris, who sang at one of our concerts, acts at the opera. Herr Pick, who danced at Vienna, is now dancing here. The opera is "Didone abbandonata," but it is not to be given much longer. Signer Piccini, who is writing the next opera, is here. I am told that the title is to be "Cesare in Egitto."

WOLFGANG DE MOZART,
Noble of Hohenthal and attached to the Exchequer.

4. Milan, Feb. 10, 1770.

SPEAK of the wolf, and you see his ears! I am quite well, and impatiently expecting an answer from you. I kiss mamma's hand, and send you a little note and a little kiss; and remain, as before, your—— What? Your aforesaid merry-andrew brother, Wolfgang in Germany, Amadeo in Italy.

DE MORZANTINI.

5. Milan, Feb. 17, 1770.

Now I am in for it! My Mariandel! I am so glad that you were so tremendously merry. Say to nurse Urserl that I still think I sent back all her songs, but if, engrossed by high and mighty thoughts of Italy, I carried one off with me, I shall not fail, if I find it, to enclose it in one of my letters. Addio, my children, farewell! I kiss mamma's hands a thousand times, and send you a thousand kisses and salutes on your queer monkey face. Per fare il fine, I am yours,

6. Milan, Carnival, Erchtag.

MANY kisses to mamma and to you. I am fairly crazed with so much business, [Footnote: Concerts and compositions of every kind occupied Mozart. The principal result of his stay in Milan was, that the young maestro got the scrittura of an opera for the ensuing season. As the libretto was to be sent to them, they could first make a journey through Italy with easy minds. The opera was "Mitridate, Re di Ponto."] so I can't possibly write any more.

7. Milan, March 3, 1770.

CARA SORELLA MIA,—

I am heartily glad that you have had so much amusement. Perhaps you may think that I have not been as merry as you; but, indeed, I cannot sum up all we have done. I think we have been at least six or seven times at the opera and the feste di ballo, which, as in Vienna, begin after the opera, but with this difference, that at Vienna the dancing is more orderly. We also saw the facchinata and chiccherata. The first is a masquerade, an amusing sight, because the men go as facchini, or porters; there was also a barca filled with people, and a great number on foot besides; and five or six sets of trumpets and kettledrums, besides several bands of violins and other instruments. The chiccherata is also a masquerade. What the people of Milan call chiccere, we call petits maitres, or fops. They were all on horseback, which was a pretty sight. I am as happy now to hear that Herr von Aman [Footnote: The father had written in a previous letter, "Herr von Aman's accident, of which you wrote to us, not only distressed us very much, but cost Wolfgang many tears. You know how sensitive he is"] is better, as I was grieved when you mentioned that he had met with an accident. What kind of mask did Madame Rosa wear, and Herr von Molk, and Herr von Schiedenhofen? Pray write this to me, if you know it; your doing so will oblige me very much. Kiss mamma's hands for me a thousand million times, and a thousand to yourself from "Catch him who can!" Why, here he is!

8. Bologna, March 24, 1770.

Oh, you busy creature!

Having been so long idle, I thought it would do me no harm to set to work again for a short time. On the post-days, when the German letters come, all that I eat and drink tastes better than usual. I beg you will let me know who are to sing in the oratorio, and also its title. Let me hear how you like the Haydn minuets, and whether they are better than the first. From my heart I rejoice to hear that Herr von Aman is now quite recovered; pray say to him that he must take great care of himself and beware of any unusual exertion. Be sure you tell him this. I intend shortly to send you a minuet that Herr Pick danced on the stage, and which every one in Milan was dancing at the feste di ballo, only that you may see by it how slowly people dance. The minuet itself is beautiful. Of course it comes from Vienna, so no doubt it is either Teller's or Starzer's. It has a great many notes. Why? Because it is a theatrical minuet, which is in slow time. The Milan and Italian minuets, however, have a vast number of notes, and are slow and with a quantity of bars; for instance, the first part has sixteen, the second twenty, and even twenty-four.

We made the acquaintance of a singer in Parma, and also heard her to great advantage in her own house—I mean the far-famed Bastardella. She has, first, a fine voice; second, a flexible organ; third, an incredibly high compass. She sang the following notes and passages in my presence.

[Here, Mozart illustrates with about 20 measures of music]

9. Rome, April 14, 1770.

I AM thankful to say that my stupid pen and I are all right, so we send a thousand kisses to you both. I wish that my sister were in Rome, for this city would assuredly delight her, because St. Peter's is symmetrical, and many other things in Rome are also symmetrical. Papa has just told me that the loveliest flowers are being carried past at this moment. That I am no wiseacre is pretty well known.

Oh! I have one annoyance—there is only a single bed in our lodgings, so mamma may easily imagine that I get no rest beside papa. I rejoice at the thoughts of a new lodging. I have just finished sketching St. Peter with his keys, St. Paul with his sword, and St. Luke with—my sister, I had the honor of kissing St. Peter's foot at San Pietro, and as I have the misfortune to be so short, your good old

WOLFGANG MOZART
was lifted up!

10. Rome, April 21, 1770.

CARA SORELLA MIA,—

Pray try to find the "Art of Ciphering" which you copied out, but I have lost it, and know nothing about it. So pray do write it out again for me, with some other copies of sums, and send them to me here.

Manzuoli has entered into a contract with the Milanese to sing in my opera [see Nos. 2-6]. For this reason he sang four or five arias to me in Florence, and also some of my own, which I was obliged to compose in Milan (none of my theatrical things having been heard there) to prove that I was capable of writing an opera. Manzuoli asks 1000 ducats. It is not yet quite certain whether Gabrielli will come. Some say Madame de' Amicis will sing in it; we shall see her in Naples. I wish that she and Manzuoli could act together; we should then be sure of two good friends. The libretto is not yet chosen. I recommended one of Metastasio's to Don Ferdinando [Count Firmiani's steward, in Milan] and to Herr von Troyer. I am at this moment at work on the aria "Se ardore e speranza."

11. Rome, April 25, 1770.

CARA SORELLA MIA,—

Io vi accerto che io aspetto con una incredibile premura tutte le giornate di posta qualche lettere di Salisburgo. Jeri fummo a S. Lorenzo e sentimmo il Vespero, e oggi matina la messa cantata, e la sera poi il secondo vespero, perche era la festa della Madonna del Buonconsiglio. Questi giorni fummi nel Campidoglio e viddemmo varie belle cose. Se io volessi scrivere tutto quel che viddi, non bastarebbe questo foglietto. In due Accademie suonai, e domani suonero anche in una.—Subito dopo pranzo giuochiamo a Potsch [Boccia]. Questo e un giuoco che imparai qui, quando verro a casa, ve l'imparero. Finita questa lettera finiro una sinfonia mia, che comminciai. L'aria e finita, una sinfonia e dal copista (il quale e il mio padre) perche noi non la vogliamo dar via per copiarla; altrimente ella sarebbe rubata.
WOLFGANGO in Germania. AMADEO MOZART in Italia.
Roma caput mundi il 25 Aprile anno 1770 nell' anno venture 1771.

[Footnote: "DEAREST SISTER,—"I assure you that I always expect with intense eagerness my letters from Salzburg on post-days. Yesterday we were at S. Lorenzo and heard vespers, and to-day at the chanted mass, and in the evening at the second vespers, because it was the Feast of the Madonna del Buonconsiglio. A few days ago we were at the Campidoglio, where we saw a great many fine things. If I tried to write you an account of all I saw, this sheet would not suffice. I played at two concerts, and to- morrow I am to play at another. After dinner we played at Potsch [Boccia]. This is a game I have learnt, and when I come home, I will teach it to you. When I have finished this letter, I am going to complete a symphony that I have begun. The aria is finished. The copyist (who is my father) has the symphony, because we do not choose it to be copied by any one else, or it might be stolen.

"WOLFGANGO in Germany.
"AMADKEO MOZAKT in Italy.
"Rome, mistress of the world: April 25,1770."]

12. Naples, May 19, 1770.

CARA SORELLA MIA,—

Vi prego di scrivermi presto e tutti i giorni di posta. Io vi ringrazio di avermi mandata questi "Art of Ciphering," [FOOTNOTE: "I beg you will write to me soon, indeed every post-day. I thank you for having sent me the 'Art of Ciphering.'"] e vi prego, se mai volete avere mal di testa, di mandarmi ancora un poco di questi "books." [FOOTNOTE: "And I beg if you ever want to have a headache, that you will send me some more."] Perdonate mi che scrivo si malamente, ma la razione e perche anche io ebbi un poco mal di testa. [FOOTNOTE: "of the same kind. Excuse my writing so badly, but the reason is that I have a bit of a headache myself."]

Haydn's twelfth minuet, which you sent me, pleases me very much; you have composed an inimitable bass for it, and without the slightest fault. I do beg that you will often exercise yourself in such things. Mamma must not forget to see that the guns are both polished up. Tell me how Master Canary is? Does he still sing? and still whistle? Do you know why I am thinking about the canary? Because we have one in our ante-room that chirps out a G sharp just like ours. [Footnote: Mozart was extremely fond of animals, and later in life had always birds in his room.] A propos, Herr Johannes [Hagenauer], no doubt, received the letter of congratulation which we intended to write to him? But if he has not got it, I will tell him myself, when we meet in Salzburg, what ought to have been in it. Yesterday we wore our new clothes; we were as handsome as angels. My kind regards to Nandl; she must not fail to pray diligently for me.

Jomelli's opera is to be given on the 30th. We saw the king and queen at mass in the court chapel at Portici, and we also saw Vesuvius. Naples is beautiful, but as crowded with people as Vienna or Paris. As for London and Naples, I think that in point of insolence on the part of the people Naples almost surpasses London; because here the lazzaroni have their regular head or leader, who receives twenty-five ducati d'argento monthly from the king for keeping the lazzaroni in order.

Madame de' Amicis sings in the opera—we were there. Caffaro is to compose the second opera, Ciccio di Majo the third, but who is to compose the fourth is not yet known. Be sure you go regularly to Mirabell, to hear the Litanies, and listen to the "Regina Coeli" or the "Salve Regina," and sleep sound, and take care to have no evil dreams. My most transcendent regards to Herr von Schiedenhofen—tralaliera! tralaliera! Tell him to learn the repetition minuet on the piano, to be sure to DO so, and DO not let him forget it. He must DO this in order to DO me the favor to let me accompany him some day or other. DO give my best compliments to all my friends, and DO continue to live happily, and DO not die, but DO live on, that you may be able to DO another letter for me, and I DO one for you, and thus we shall go on DOING till we can DO something worth DOING; but I am one of those who will go on DOING till all DOINGS are at an end. In the mean time I DO subscribe myself

Your W. M.

13. Naples, May 29, 1770.

Jeri l'altro fummo nella prova dell' opera del Sign. Jomelli, la quale e una opera che e ben scritta e che me piace veramente. Il Sign. Jomelli ci ha parlato ed era molto civile. E fummo anche in una chiesa a sentir una Musica la quale fu del Sign. Ciccio di Majo, ed era una bellissima Musica. Anche lui ci parlci ed era molto compito. La Signora de' Amicis canto a meraviglia. Stiamo Dio grazia assai bene di salute, particolarmente io, quando viene una lettera di Salisburgo. Vi prego di scrivermi tutti giorni di posta, e se anche non avete niente da scrivermi, solamente vorrei averlo per aver qualche lettera tutti giorni di posta. Egli non sarebbe mal fatto, se voi mi scriveste qualche volta una letterina italiana.

[FOOTNOTE: "The other day we attended the rehearsal of Signer Jomelli's opera, which is well written and pleases me exceedingly. Signor Jomelli spoke to us and was very civil. We also went to a church to hear a mass by Signor Ciccio di Majo, and it was most beautiful music. Signora de' Amicus sang incomparably. We are, thank God, very well, and I feel particularly so when a letter from Salzburg arrives. I beg you will write to me every post-day, even if you have nothing to write about, for I should like to have a letter by every post. It would not be a bad idea to write me a little letter in Italian."]

14. Naples, June 5, 1770.

Vesuvius is smoking fiercely! Thunder and lightning and blazes! Haid homa gfresa beim Herr Doll. Das is a deutscha Compositor, und a browa Mo. [Footnote: "Today we dined with Herr Doll, he is a good composer and a worthy man" [Vienna Patois]] Now I begin to describe my course of life.—Alle 9 ore, qualche volta anche alle dieci mi svelgio, e poi andiamo fuor di casa, e poi pranziamo da un trattore, e dopo pranzo scriviamo, e poi sortiamo, e indi ceniamo, ma che cosa? Al giorno di grasso, un mezzo pollo ovvero un piccolo boccone d'arrosto; al giorno di magro un piccolo pesce; e di poi andiamo a dormire. Est-ce que vous avez compris?- -Redma dafir Soisburgarisch, don as is gschaida. Wir sand Gottlob gesund da Voda und i. [Footnote: "I rise generally every morning at 9 o'clock, but sometimes not till 10, when we go out. We dine at a restaurateur's, after dinner I write, and then we go out again, and afterwards sup, but on what? on jours gras, half a fowl, or a small slice of roast meat, on jours maigres a little fish, and then we go to sleep. Do you understand? Let us talk Salzburgisch, for that is more sensible. Thank God, my father and I are well" [Patois]] I hope you and mamma are so also. Naples and Rome are two drowsy cities. A scheni Schrift! net wor?

[Footnote: "Fine writing, is it not?" [Patois.]] Write to me, and do not be so lazy. Altrimente avrete qualche bastonate di me. Quel plaisir! Je te casserai la tete. [Footnote: "Otherwise I will cudgel you soundly. What a pleasure—to break your head!"] I am delighted with the thoughts of the portraits [of his mother and sister, wno had promised to have their likenesses taken], und i bi korios wias da gleich sieht; wons ma gfoin, so los i mi und den Vodan a so macho. Maidli, lass Da saga, wo list dan gwesa he? [Footnote: "And I am anxious to see what they are like, and then I will have my father and myself also taken. Fair maiden, say, where have you been, eh?" [Patois.]] The opera here is Jomelli's; it is fine, but too grave and old-fashioned for this stage. Madame de' Amicis sings incomparably, and so does Aprile, who used to sing at Milan. The dancing is miserably pretentious. The theatre beautiful. The King has been brought up in the rough Neapolitan fashion, and at the opera always stands on a stool, so that he may look a little taller than the Queen, who is beautiful and so gracious, for she bowed to me in the most condescending manner no less than six times on the Molo.

15. Naples, June 16, 1770.

I AM well and lively and happy as ever, and as glad to travel. I made an excursion on the Mediterranean. I kiss mamma's hand and Nannerl's a thousand times, and am your son, Steffl, and your brother, Hansl.

16. Rome, July 7, 1770.

CARA SORELLA MIA,—
I am really surprised that you can compose so charmingly. In a word, the song is beautiful. Often try something similar. Send me soon the other six minuets of Haydn. Mademoiselle, j'ai l'honneur d'etre votre tres-humble serviteur et frere,

CHEVALIER DE MOZART.
[He had received from the Pope the cross of the Order of the Golden Spur.]

17. Bologna, July 21, 1770.

I WISH mamma joy of her name-day, and hope that she may live for many hundred years to come and retain good health, which I always ask of God, and pray to Him for you both every day. I cannot do honor to the occasion except with some Loretto bells, and wax tapers, and caps, and gauze when I return. In the mean time, good-bye, mamma. I kiss your hand a thousand times, and remain, till death, your attached son.

18.

Io vi auguro d'Iddio, vi dia sempre salute, e vi lasci vivere ancora cent' anni e vi faccia morire quando avrete mille anni. Spero che voi impararete meglio conoscermi ni avvenire e che poi ne giudicherete come ch' egli vi piace. Il tempo non mi permette di scriver motto. La penna non vale un corno, ne pure quello che la dirigge. Il titolo dell' opera che ho da comporre a Milano, non si sa ancora.

[Footnote: "My prayer to God is, that He may grant you health, and allow you to live to be a hundred, and not to die till you are a thousand years old. I hope that you will learn to know me better in future, and that you will then judge of me as you please. Time does not permit me to write much. My pen is not worth a pin, nor the hand that guides it. I don't yet know the title of the opera that I am to compose at Milan."]

My landlady at Rome made me a present of the "Thousand and One Nights" in Italian; it is most amusing to read.

19. Bologna, August 4, 1770.

I GRIEVE from my heart to hear that Jungfrau Marthe is still so ill, and I pray every day that she may recover. Tell her from me that she must beware of much fatigue and eat only what is strongly salted [she was consumptive]. A propos, did you give my letter to Robinsiegerl? [Sigismund Robinig, a friend of his]. You did not mention it when you wrote. I beg that when you see him you will tell him he is not quite to forget me. I can't possibly write better, for my pen is only fit to write music and not a letter. My violin has been newly strung, and I play every day. I only mention this because mamma wished to know whether I still played the violin. I have had the honor to go at least six times by myself into the churches to attend their splendid ceremonies. In the mean time I have composed four Italian symphonies [overtures], besides five or six arias, and also a motett.

Does Herr Deibl often come to see you? Does he still honor you by his amusing conversation? And the noble Herr Carl von Vogt, does he still deign to listen to your tiresome voices? Herr von Schiedenhofen must assist you often in writing minuets, otherwise he shall have no sugar-plums.

If time permitted, it would be my duty to trouble Herr von Molk and Herr von Schiedenhofen with a few lines; but as that most indispensable of all things is wanting, I hope they will forgive my neglect, and consider me henceforth absolved from this honor. I have begun various cassations [a kind of divertimento], so I have thus responded to your desire. I don't think the piece in question can be one of mine, for who would venture to publish as his own composition what is, in reality, written by the son of the Capellmeister, and whose mother and sister are in the same town? Addio—farewell! My sole recreations consist in dancing English hornpipes and cutting capers. Italy is a land of sleep; I am always drowsy here. Addio—good-bye!

20. Bologna, August 21, 1770.

I AM not only still alive, but in capital spirits. To-day I took a fancy to ride a donkey, for such is the custom in Italy, so I thought that I too must give it a trial. We have the honor to associate with a certain Dominican who is considered a very pious ascetic. I somehow don't quite think so, for he constantly takes a cup of chocolate for breakfast, and immediately afterwards a large glass of strong Spanish wine; and I have myself had the privilege of dining with this holy man, when he drank a lot of wine at dinner and a full glass of very strong wine afterwards, two large slices of melons, some peaches and pears for dessert, five cups of coffee, a whole plateful of nuts, and two dishes of milk and lemons. This he may perhaps do out of bravado, but I don't think so—at all events, it is far too much; and he eats a great deal also at his afternoon collation.

21. Bologna, Sept. 8, 1770.

NOT to fail in my duty, I must write a few words. I wish you would tell me in your next letter to what brotherhoods I belong, and also let me know the prayers I am bound to offer up for them. I am now reading "Telemachus," and am already in the second volume. Good-bye for the present! Love to mamma.

22.

I HOPE that mamma and you are both well, but I wish you would answer my letters more punctually in time to come; indeed, it is far easier to answer than to originate. I like these six minuets far better than the first twelve; we often played them to the Countess [Pallivicini, at whose country-seat, near Bologna, father and son spent some months]. We only wish we could succeed in introducing a taste for German minuets into Italy, as their minuets last nearly as long as entire symphonies. Forgive my bad writing; I could write better, but I am in such a hurry.

23. Bologna, Sept. 29, 1770.

IN order to fill up papa's letter, I intend to add a few words. I grieve deeply to hear of Jungfrau Marthe's long-continued illness, which the poor girl bears, too, with such patience. I hope, please God, she may still recover. If not, we must not grieve too much, for the will of God is always best, and God certainly knows better than we do whether it is most for our good to be in this world or in the next. But it will cheer her to enjoy this fine weather once more after all the rain.

24. Bologna, Oct. 6, 1770.

I AM heartily glad that you have been so gay; I only wish I had been with you. I hope Jungfrau Marthe is better. To-day I played the organ at the Dominicans. Congratulate the .... from me, and say that I sincerely wish they may live to see the fiftieth anniversary of Father Dominikus's saying mass, and that we may all once more have a happy meeting.

[Footnote: Jahn observes that he probably alludes to their intimate friends, the merchant Hagenauer's family, with whom old Mozart had many pecuniary transactions for the purpose of his travels, and whose son entered the church in 1764.]

My best wishes to all Thereserls, and compliments to all my friends in the house and out of the house. I wish I were likely soon to hear the Berchtesgadner symphonies, and perhaps blow a trumpet or play a fife in one myself. I saw and heard the great festival of St. Petronius in Bologna. It was fine, but long. The trumpeters came from Lucca to make the proper flourish of honor, but their trumpeting was detestable.

25. Milan, Oct. 20, 1770.

MY DEAR MAMMA,—

I cannot write much, for my fingers ache from writing out such a quantity of recitative. I hope you will pray for me that my opera ["Mitridate Re di Ponto"] may go off well, and that we soon may have a joyful meeting. I kiss your hands a thousand times, and have a great deal to say to my sister; but what? That is known only to God and myself. Please God, I hope soon to be able to confide it to her verbally; in the mean time, I send her a thousand kisses. My compliments to all kind friends. We have lost our good Martherl, but we hope that by the mercy of God she is now in a state of blessedness.

26. Milan, Oct. 27, 1770.

MY VERY DEAREST SISTER,—

You know that I am a great talker, and was so when I left you. At present I replace this very much by signs, for the son of this family is deaf and dumb. I must now set to work at my opera. I regret very much that I cannot send you the minuet you wish to have, but, God willing, perhaps about Easter you may see both it and me. I can write no more.— Farewell! and pray for me.

27. Milan, Nov. 3, 1770.

MY VERY DEARLY LOVED SISTER,—

I thank you and mamma for your sincere good wishes; my most ardent desire is to see you both soon in Salzburg. In reference to your congratulations, I may say that I believe Herr Martinelli suggested your Italian project. My dear sister, you are always so very clever, and contrived it all so charmingly that, just underneath your congratulations in Italian, followed M. Martini's compliments in the same style of penmanship, so that I could not possibly find you out; nor did I do so, and I immediately said to papa, "Oh! how I do wish I were as clever and witty as she is!" Then papa answered, "Indeed, that is true enough." On which I rejoined, "Oh! I am so sleepy;" so he merely replied, "Then stop writing." Addio! Pray to God that my opera may be successful. I am your brother,

W. M.,
whose fingers are weary from writing.

28. Milan, Dec. 1, 1770.

DEAREST SISTER,—

As it is so long since I wrote to you, I thought that I might perhaps pacify your just wrath and indignation by these lines. I have now a great deal to work at, and to write for my opera. I trust all will go well, with the help of God. Addio! As ever, your faithful brother,

WOLFGANG MOZART.

29.

MY DARLING SISTER,—

It is long since I have written to you, having been so much occupied with my opera. As I have now more time, I shall attend better to my duty. My opera, thank God, is popular, as the theatre is full every evening, which causes great surprise, for many say that during all the time they have lived in Milan they never saw any first opera so crowded as on this occasion. I am thankful to say that both papa and I are quite well, and I hope at Easter to have an opportunity of relating everything to mamma and you. Addio! A propos, the copyist was with us yesterday, and said that he was at that moment engaged in transcribing my opera for the Lisbon court. Good-bye, my dear Madlle. sister,

Always and ever your attached brother.

30. Venice, Feb 15, 1771

MY VERY DEAR SISTER,—

You have, no doubt, heard from papa that I am well. I have nothing to write about, except my love and kisses to mamma. Give the enclosed—Al sig. Giovanni. La signora perla ricono la riverisce tanto come anche tutte le altre perle, e li assicuro che tutte sono inamorata di lei, e che sperano che lei prendera per moglie tutte, come i Turchi per contenar tutte sei. Questo scrivo in casa di Sign. Wider, il quale e un galant' uomo come lei melo scrisse, ed jeri abbiamo finito il carnavale da lui, cenardo da lui e poi ballammo ed andammo colle perle in compagnie nel ridotto nuovo, che mi piacque assai. Quando sto dal Sign. Wider e guardando fuori della finestra vedo la casa dove lei abito quando lei fu in Venezia. Il nuovo non so niente. Venezia mi piace assai. Il mio complimento al Sign., suo padre e madre, sorelle, fratelli, e a tutti i miei amici ed amiche. Addio!

[Footnote: "To Herr Johannes [Hagenauer] The fair 'pearl' has the same high opinion of you that all the other 'pearls' here have. I assure you that they are all in love with you, and their hope is that you will marry them all (like the Turks), and so please them every one. I write this in the house of Signor Wider, who is an excellent man and exactly what you wrote to me, yesterday we finished the Carnival in his house. We supped there and then danced, and went afterwards, in company with the 'pearls,' to the new masquerade, which amused me immensely. When I look out of the window at Signor Wider's, I see the house that you inhabited in Venice. I have no news. I like Venice very well. My compliments to your father and mother, brothers and sisters, and all my friends. Adieu!"]

31. Venice, Feb. 20, 1771.

I AM still well, and, thank God, in the land of the living. Madame de' Amicis has been singing at S. Benedetto. Say to Herr Johannes that the Widerischen Berlein family are constantly speaking of him (particularly Madlle. Catherine), so he must soon return to Vienna to encounter the attacca—that is, in order to become a true Venetian, you must allow yourself to be bumped down on the ground. They wished to do this to me also, but though seven women tried it, the whole seven together did not succeed in throwing me down. Addio!

The travellers arrived again at home towards the end of March, 1771. The marriage of the Archduke Ferdinand with the Princess of Modena, which took place in the October of that year, was attended with great festivities, and recalled the father and son to Italy in the course of a few months, Wolfgang having received a command from the Empress Maria Theresa to compose a dramatic serenata in honor of these nuptials.

32. Verona, August 18, 1771.

DEAREST SISTER,—

I have not slept more than half an hour, for I don't like to sleep after eating. You may hope, believe, think, be of opinion, cherish the expectation, desire, imagine, conceive, and confidently suppose, that we are in good health; but I can tell you so to a certainty. Wish Herr von

Heffner a happy journey from me, and ask him if he has seen Annamindl?

[Wolfgang, who was then fifteen, had taken advantage of his leisure during their short stay in Salzburg to fall in love for the first time. We shall find frequent allusions to this subject. See also No. 25.]

33. Milan, August 23, 1771.

MY VERY DEAR SISTER,—

We suffered much from heat in the course of our journey, and the dust constantly dried us up so impertinently that we should have been choked, or died of thirst, if we had not been too sensible for that. For a whole month past (say the Milanese) there has been no rain here; to-day a slight drizzle began, but the sun has now come out again, and it is once more very warm. What you promised me (you well know my meaning, you kind creature!) don't fail to perform, I entreat. I shall be indeed very grateful to you. I am at this moment actually panting from the heat—I tear open my waistcoat! Addio—good-bye!

WOLFGANG.

Above us we have a violinist, below us is another, next to us a singing-master, who gives lessons, and, in the room opposite, a hautboy-player. This is famous for a composer—it inspires so many fine thoughts.

34. Milan, August 31, 1771.

MY DEAREST SISTER,—

We are quite well, thank God! I have been eating quantities of fine pears, peaches, and melons in your place. My greatest amusement is to talk by signs to the dumb, which I can do to perfection. Herr Hasse [the celebrated opera composer] arrived here yesterday, and to-day we are going to pay him a visit. We only received the book of the Serenata last Thursday. [Footnote: It was "Ascanio in Alba" that Wolfgang got to compose for Milan; and it was this music which made Hasse exclaim, "This boy will cause us all to be forgotten."] I have very little to write about. Do not, I entreat, forget about THE ONE OTHER, where no other can ever be. You understand me, I know.

35. Milan, Sept. 13, 1771.

DEAR SISTER,—

I write only for writing's sake. It is indeed very inconvenient, because I have a severe cold. Say to Fraulein W. von Molk that I rejoice at the thoughts of Salzburg, in the hope that I may again receive the same kind of present for the minuets which was bestowed on me at a similar concert. She knows all about it.

36. Milan, Sept. 21, 1771.

I AM well, God be praised! I can't write much. 1st, I have nothing to say. 2d, my fingers ache from writing. I often whistle an air, but no one responds. Only two arias of the Serenata are still wanting, and then it will be finished. I have no longer any fancy for Salzburg; I am afraid I might go mad too. [He had heard that several persons there had lost their reason.]

37. Milan, Oct. 5, 1771.

I AM in good health, but always sleepy. Papa has snatched from my pen all that I had to write about, which is, that he has already written everything. Signora Gabrielli is here, and we are soon going to see her, as we wish to become acquainted with all distinguished singers.

38. Milan, Oct. 26, 1771.

MY work being now completed, I have more time to write, but have nothing to say, as papa has written you all I could have said. I am well, thank God! but have no news, except that in the lottery the numbers 35, 59, 60, 61, and 62 have turned up prizes, so if we had selected these we should have won; but as we did not put in at all we neither won nor lost, but only laughed at those who did the latter. The two arias encored in the Serenata were those of Manzuoli, and Girelli, the prima donna, I hope you may be well amused in Triebenbach with shooting, and (weather permitting) with walking.

39. Milan, Nov. 2, 1771.

Papa says that Herr Kerschbaumer travels with profit and observation, and we can testify that he conducts himself very judiciously; at all events he can give a more satisfactory account of his journey than some of his friends, one of whom said that he could not see Paris properly because the houses there were too high. To-day Hasse's opera is to be given; as papa, however, is not going, I can't go either. [FOOTNOTE: Hasse had also a festal opera to compose, but Leopold Mozart writes, "I am sorry to say that Wolfgang's Serenata has totally eclipsed Hasse's opera."] Fortunately I know all the airs thoroughly by heart, so I can see and hear them in my own thoughts at home.

40. Milan, Nov. 24, 1771.

DEAREST SISTER,—

Herr Manzuoli, the musico, who has always been considered and esteemed as the best of his class, has in his old age given a proof of his folly and arrogance. He was engaged at the opera for the sum of 500 gigliati (ducats), but as no mention was made in the contract of the Serenata, he demanded 500 ducats more for singing in it, making 1000. The court only sent him 700 and a gold box, (and enough too, I think,) but he returned the 700 ducats and the box, and went away without anything. I don't know what the result of this history will be—a bad one, I fear!

41. Milan, Nov. 30, 1771.

That you may not suppose I am ill, I write you a few lines. I saw four fellows hanged in the Dom Platz. They hang here just as they do in Lyons.

We now find the father and son once more in Salzburg, in the middle of December, 1771. Archbishop Sigismund died, and on the 14th of March, 1772, Archbishop Hieronymus was elected, who was destined to cause much sorrow to Mozart. Soon after, in honor of the procession and homage of the new prince, he composed the allegorical azione teatrale "Il sogno di Scipione." In October he resumed his travels, having undertaken the scrittura for the approaching Carnivals both at Milan and at Venice.

42. Bologna, Oct. 28, 1772.

We have got to Botzen already. Already? rather not till now. I am hungry, thirsty, sleepy, and lazy, but I am quite well. We saw the monastery in Hall, and I played the organ there. When you see Nadernannerl, tell her I spoke to Herr Brindl (her lover), and he charged me to give her his regards. I hope that you kept your promise and went last Sunday to D——N——[in cipher]. Farewell! write me some news. Botzen—a pig-sty!

43. Milan, Nov. 7, 1772.

Don't be startled at seeing my writing instead of papa's. These are the reasons: first, we are at Herr von Oste's, and the Herr Baron Christiani is also here, and they have so much to talk about, that papa cannot possibly find time to write; and, secondly, he is too lazy. We arrived here at 4 o'clock this afternoon, and are both well. All our good friends are in the country or at Mantua, except Herr von Taste and his wife, who send you and my sister their compliments. Herr Misliweczeck [a young composer of operas from Paris] is still here. There is not a word of truth either in the Italian war, which is so eagerly discussed in Germany, or in the castles here being fortified. Forgive my bad writing.

Address your letters direct to us, for it is not the custom here, as in Germany, to carry the letters round; we are obliged to go ourselves to fetch them on post-days. There is nothing new here; we expect news from Salzburg.

Not having a word more to say, I must conclude. Our kind regards to all our friends. We kiss mamma 1,000,000,000 times (I have no room for more noughts); and as for my sister, I would rather embrace her in persona than in imagination.

44.

CARISSIMA SOREILA,—

Spero che voi sarete stata dalla Signora, che voi gia sapete. Vi prego, se la videte di farla un Complimento da parte mia. Spero e non dubito punto che voi starete bene di salute. Mi son scordato di darvi nuova, che abbiamo qui trovato quel Sign. Belardo, ballerina, che abbiamo conosciuto in Haye ed in Amsterdam, quello che attaco colla spada il ballerino, il Sign. Neri, perche credeva che lui fosse cagione che non ebbe la permission di ballar in teatro. Addio, non scordarvi di me, io sono sempre il vostro fidele fratello.

[FOOTNOTE: "DEAREST SISTFR,—"I hope you have been to see the lady—you know who. I beg that when you see her you will give her my compliments. I hope, and do not doubt, that you are in good health. I forgot to tell you that we found Signor Belardo here, a dancer whom we knew at the Hague and at Amsterdam—the same person who attacked Signor Neri with a sword, because he thought he was the cause of his not obtaining permission to dance in the theatre. Adieu! Do not forget me, always your faithful brother."]

45. Milan, Nov. 21, 1772.

I thank you exceedingly—you know for what. I cannot possibly write to Herr von Heffner. When you see him, make him read aloud what follows. I hope he will be satisfied with it:—

"I am not to take it amiss that my unworthy friend has not answered my letter; as soon as he has more leisure, he will certainly, beyond all doubt, positively and punctually send me a reply."

46. Milan, Nov. 28, 1772.

We both send our congratulations to Herr von Aman; tell him from me that, owing to his having all along made a mystery of the affair, I feel much annoyed, for I fear I may have said more than I ought about his bride. I thought he had been more straightforward. One thing more. Say to Herr von Aman that, if he wishes to have a right merry wedding, he must be so kind as to wait till we return, so that what he promised me may come to pass, namely, that I was to dance at his wedding. Tell Herr Leitgeb [a horn-player in the Archbishop's orchestra] that he must come straight to Milan, for he is sure to succeed well here; but he must come soon. Pray let him know this, for I am anxious about it.

47. Milan, Dec. 5, 1772.

I have now about fourteen pieces to write, and then I shall have finished. [Footnote: He alludes to his Milan opera, "Lucio Silla."] Indeed, the trio and the duet may be considered as four. I cannot possibly write much, for I have no news, and in the next place I scarcely know what I am writing, as all my thoughts are absorbed in my opera, so there is some danger of my writing you a whole aria instead of a letter. I have learned a new game here, called mercanti in fiera. As soon as I come home we can play at it together. I have also learned a new language from Frau von Taste, which is easy to speak, though troublesome to write, but still useful. It is, I own, rather a little childish, but will do capitally for Salzburg. My kind regards to pretty Nandl and to the canary, for these two and yourself are the most innocent creatures in our house. Fischietti [the Archbishop's Capellmeister] will no doubt soon begin to work at his opera buffa (translated into German, his CRAZY opera!). Addio!

The following letter of Wolfgang's shows the sparkling state of his spirits, caused by the completion of his opera. At each line he turns the page, so that one line stands, as it were, on the head of the other. The father, too, in the joy of his heart that the arduous work was drawing to a close, and with it his long journey, writes four lines, one above another, round the edge of the page, so that the whole forms a framework for a sketch of a burning heart and four triangles (symbols of fidelity), and a bird on the wing from whose beak a distich is streaming:—

Oh! fly to seek my child so fair Here, and there, and everywhere!

Wolfgang adds:—

48. Milan, Dec. 18, 1772.

I HOPE, dear sister, that you are well, dear sister. When this letter reaches you, dear sister, my opera will be in scena, dear sister. Think of me, dear sister, and try, dear sister, to imagine with all your might that my dear sister sees and hears it also. In truth, it is hard to say, as it is now eleven o'clock at night, but I do believe, and don't at all doubt, that in the daytime it is brighter than at Easter. My dear sister, to-morrow we dine with Herr von Mayer; and do you know why? Guess! Because he invited us. The rehearsal to-morrow is to be in the theatre. The impresario, Signor Cassiglioni, has entreated me not to say a word of this to a soul, as all kinds of people would come crowding in, and that we don't wish. So, my child, I beg, my child, that you won't say one syllable to any one on the subject, or too many people would come crowding in, my child. Approposito, do you know the history that occurred here? Well, I will relate it to you. We were going home straight from Count Firmiani's, and when we came into our street we opened our door, and what do you think happened? We went in. Good-bye, my pet. Your unworthy brother (frater),

WOLFGANG.

On the 26th of December "an incomparable performance" of "Lucio Silla" took place; it was eminently successful, and continued to fill the house night after night in the most surprising way. The father writes home regularly, and Wolfgang subjoins the usual postscripts, which, however, at this time contain nothing worth quoting. We give only part of an Italian letter which he writes for practice:—

49.

.... Vi prego di dire al Sig. Giovanni Hagenauer da parte mia, che non dubiti, che andro a veder sicuramente in quella bottega delle armi, se ci sono quei nomi [?] che lui desidera, e che senza dubbio doppo averlo trovato le portero meco a Salisburgo. Mi dispiace che il Sig. Leitgeb e partito tanto tardi da Salisburgo [see No. 46] che non trovera piu in scena la mia opera e forte non ci trovera nemeno, se non in viaggio.

Hieri sera era la prima prova coi stromenti della seconda opera, ma ho sentito solamente il primo atto, perche a secondo mene andiedi essendo gia tardi. In quest' opera saranno sopra il balco 24 cavalli e . . . mondo di gente, che saro miracolo se non succede qualche disgrazia. La musica mi piace; se piace al replico non so, perche alle prime prove non e lecito l' andarci che alle personne che sono del Teatro. Io spero che domani il mio padre potra uscir di casa. Sta sera fa cativissimo tempo. La Signora Teyber e adesso a Bologna e il carnevale venturo recitera a Turino e l'anno sussiquente poi va a cantare a Napoli.

[Footnote: "Pray say from me to Johannes Hagenauer, that he may entirely rely on my going to the armorer's shop, to see if I can procure what he desires, and after getting it I will not fail to bring it with me to Salzburg. I regret that Herr Leitgeb delayed so long leaving Salzburg [see No. 46], for he will no longer find my opera in scena, nor will he find us either unless we meet on our travels. Yesterday evening was our first rehearsal of the second opera with instruments, but I only heard the first act, for I went away at the second, because it was so very late. In this opera there are to be twenty-four horses and a crowd of people on the stage at the same time, so it will be surprising if no accident happens. The music pleases me; whether it will please others I cannot tell, for no persons but those belonging to the theatre are permitted to attend the first rehearsals. I hope that papa will be able to leave the house to-morrow. The weather is detestable this evening. Madame Teyber is now at Bologna; she is to act at Turin in the ensuing Carnival, and the year following she is to sing at Naples."]

After enjoying some more of the amusements of the Carnival, they arrived again in Salzburg about the middle of March. This place, or rather their position at court there, was in the highest degree repugnant to both; so the father, in the course of his travels, applied to the Grand-Duke of Tuscany for an appointment for his son. As, however, nothing was to be got in that quarter, he directed his views to the Imperial capital itself; and thus, at the end of three months, we find him again with his son in Vienna. From thence Wolfgang often wrote to his loved ones at home.

50. Vienna, August 14, 1773.

I HOPE that your Majesty [Footnote 1: O. Jahn remarks that this epithet is a reminiscence of a fantastic game that often amused the boy on his journeys. He imagined a kingdom, the inhabitants of which were endowed with every gift that could make them good and happy.] enjoys the best state of health; and yet that now and then—or rather sometimes—or, better still, from time to time— or, still better, qualche volta, as the Italians say—your Majesty will impart to me some of your grave and important thoughts (emanating from that most admirable and solid judgment which, in addition to beauty, your Majesty so eminently possesses; and thus, although in such tender years, my Queen casts into the shade not only the generality of men but even the gray-haired).

P. S. This is a most sensible production.

51. Vienna, August 21, 1773.

When we contemplate the benefit of time, and yet are not entirely oblivious of the estimation in which we ought to hold the sun, then it is quite certain, Heaven be praised! that I am quite well. My second proposition is of a very different character. Instead of sun, let us put moon, and instead of benefit, science; then any one, gifted with a certain amount of reasoning powers, will at once draw the conclusion that—I am a fool because you are my sister. How is Miss Bimbles? [the dog.] I beg you will convey all sorts of amiable messages from me to her. I also send my kind remembrances to M. Kreibich [conductor of the Imperial chamber-music], whom we knew at Presburg and also at Vienna; and very best regards from Her Majesty the Empress, Frau Fischerin, and Prince Kaunitz. Oidda!

GNAGFLOW TRAZOM.

52. Vienna, Sept. 15, 1773.

WE are quite well, thank God; on this occasion we have contrived to make time to write to you, although we have so much business to do. We hope you also are well. Dr. Niderl's death grieved us very much. I assure you we cried a good deal, and moaned and groaned. Our kind regards to "Alle gute Geister loben Gott den Herrn" [to all good spirits who praise the Lord], and to all our friends. We graciously remain

Yours, WOLFGANG.

Given from our capital of Vienna.

The travellers returned home the end of September, for no situation was to be found in Vienna either; indeed, they did not even give a public concert there. Wolfgang remained in his native town during the whole of the ensuing year, writing instrumental and church music. At length he received a commission from the Elector of Bavaria, Maximilian III., to write an opera buffa for the Carnival of 1775,—"La finta Giardiniera."

53. Munich, Dec. 28, 1774.

My Dearest Sister,

I entreat you not to forget, before your journey, [FOOTNOTE: Nannerl had also the most eager desire to see the new opera, and the father at last succeeded in getting a lodging for her in the large market place, in the house of a widow, "a black-eyed brunette," Frau von Durst.] to perform your promise, that is, to make a certain visit. I have my reasons for this. Pray present my kind regards in that quarter, but in the most impressive and tender manner—the most tender; and, oh!——but I need not be in such anxiety on the subject, for I know my sister and her peculiarly loving nature, and I feel quite convinced that she will do all she can to give me pleasure—and from self-interest, too—rather a spiteful hit that! [Nannerl was considered a little selfish by her family.]

54. Munich, Dec. 30, 1774.

I BEG my compliments to Roxalana, who is to drink tea this evening with the Sultan, All sorts of pretty speeches to Madlle. Mizerl; she must not doubt my love. I have her constantly before my eyes in her fascinating neglige. I have seen many pretty girls here, but not one whose beauty can be compared with hers. Do not forget to bring the variations on Ekart's menuet d'exaude, and also those on Fischer's minuet. I was at the theatre last night. The play was "Der Mode nach der Haushaltung," which was admirably acted. My kind regards to all my friends. I trust that you will not fail to—Farewell! I hope to see you soon in Munich. Frau von Durst sends you her remembrances. Is it true that Hagenauer is become a professor of sculpture in Vienna? Kiss mamma's hand for me, and now I stop for to-day. Wrap yourself up warmly on your journey, I entreat, or else you may chance to pass the fourteen days of your visit in the house, stifling beside a stove, unable once to move. I see the vivid lightning flash, and fear there soon will be a crash!

Your brother.

55. Munich, Jan. 11, 1775.

To HIS MOTHER.
Munich, Jan. 11, 1775.

WE are all three well, Heaven be praised! I cannot possibly write much, for I must go forthwith to the rehearsal. Tomorrow the grand rehearsal takes place, and on the 13th my opera is to be in scena. I am much vexed that you should cast any slight on Count Seeau [Intendant of the Munich Theatre], for no one can be more kind or courteous, and he has more good breeding than many of his degree in Munich. Herr von Molk was in such a state of wonder and admiration at the opera seria when he heard it, that we felt quite ashamed of him, for it clearly showed every one that he had never in his life seen anything but Salzburg and Innspruck. Addio!

56. Munich, Jan. 14,1775.

To HIS MOTHER.
Munich, Jan. 14,1775.

GOD be praised! My opera was given yesterday, the 13th, and proved so successful that I cannot possibly describe all the tumult. In the first place, the whole theatre was so crammed that many people were obliged to go away. After each aria there was invariably a tremendous uproar and clapping of hands, and cries of Viva Maestro! Her Serene Highness the Electress and the Dowager (who were opposite me) also called out Bravo! When the opera was over, during the interval when all is usually quiet till the ballet begins, the applause and shouts of Bravo! were renewed; sometimes there was a lull, but only to recommence afresh, and so forth. I afterwards went with papa to a room through which the Elector and the whole court were to pass. I kissed the hands of the Elector and the Electress and the other royalties, who were all very gracious. At an early hour this morning the Prince Bishop of Chiemsee [who had most probably procured the scrittura for his young friend Wolfgang] sent to congratulate me that the opera had proved such a brilliant success in every respect. As to our return home, it is not likely to be soon, nor should mamma wish it, for she must know well what a good thing it is to have a little breathing time. We shall come quite soon enough to———. One most just and undeniable reason is, that my opera is to be given again on Friday next, and I am very necessary at the performance, or it might be difficult to recognize it again. There are very odd ways here. 1000 kisses to Miss Bimberl [the dog].

The Archbishop of Salzburg, who was very reluctant to admit the merits of his Concertmeister, was an involuntary witness of the universal approbation bestowed on Wolfgang's opera, although he would not go to hear it himself. On the 18th of January, 1775, Wolfgang added the following lines to his father's letter:—

57.

MY DEAB SISTER,

[FOOTNOTE: Nannerl had not yet gone home, but was enjoying the Carnival in various masks.]

How can I help the clock choosing at this moment to strike a quarter after seven o'clock? It is not papa's fault either. Mamma will hear all the rest from you. At present there is no fair sailing for me, as the Archbishop is staying here, though not for long. It is currently reported that he is to remain till he sets off again! I only regret that he is not to see the first masked ball.

Your faithful FRANZ v. NASENBLUT.

Milan, May 5,1756.

Immediately after Ash Wednesday the trio returned to Salzburg, where Mozart remained uninterruptedly for another year and a half, actively engaged in the duties of his situation. He wrote the following letter on the 4th of September, 1776, to the celebrated Pater Martini in Bologna:—

58.

MOLTO REVDO PADE MAESTRO, PADRONE MIO STIMATISSIMO,-

La venerazione, la stima e il rispetto, che porto verso la di lei degnissima persona mi spinse di incommodarla colle presente e di mandargli un debole pezzo di mia musica, rimmettendola alla di lei maestrale giudicatura. Scrissi l'anno scorso il Carnevale una opera buffa ("La finta Giardiniera") a Monaco in Baviera. Pochi giorni avanti la mia partenza di la desiderava S. A. Elletorale di sentire qualche mia musica in contrapunto: era adunque obligato di scriver questo Motetto in fretta per dar tempo a copiar lo spartito per Sua Altezza ed a cavar le parti per poter produrlo la prossima domenica sotto la Messa grande in tempo del Offertorio. Carissimo e stimatissimo Sigr. P. Maestro! Lei e ardentemente pregato di dirmi francamente e senza riserva il di lei parere. Viviamo in questo mondo per imparare sempre industriosamente, e per mezzo dei raggionamenti di illuminarsi l'un l'altro e d'affatigarsi di portar via sempre avanti le scienze e le belle arti. Oh quante e quante volte desidero d'esser piu vicino per poter parlar e raggionar con Vostra Paternita molto Revda. Vivo in una paese dove la musica fa pocchissimo fortuna, benche oltre di quelli che ci hanno abandonati, ne abbiamo ancora bravissimi professori e particolarmente compositori di gran fondo, sapere e gusto. Per il teatro stiamo male per mancanza dei recitanti. Non abbiamo Musici e non gli averemo si facilmente, giache vogliono esser ben pagati: e la generosita, non e il nostro difetto. Io mi diverto intanto a scrivere per la camera e per la chiesa: e ne son quivi altri due bravissimi contrapuntisti, cioe il Sgr. Haydn e Adlgasser. Il mio padre e maestro della chiesa Metropolitana, che mi da l'occasione di scrivere per la chiesa, quanto che ne voglio. Per altro il mio padre gia 36 anni in servizio di questa Corte e sapendo, che questo Arcivescovo non puo e non vuol vedere gente avanzata in eta, non lo se ne prende a core, si e messo alla letteratura per altro gia suo studio favorito. La nostra musica di chiesa e assai differente di quella d'Italia e sempre piu, che una Messa con tutto il Kyrie, Gloria, Credo, la Sonata all' Epistola, l'Offertorio osia Motetto, Sanctus ed Agnus Dei, ed anche la piu solenne, quando dice la Messa il Principe stesso, non ha da durare che al piu longo 3 quarti d'ora. Ci vuole un studio particolare per queste sorte di compositione, e che deve pero essere una Messa con tutti stromenti—Trombe di guerra, Tympani ecc. Ah! che siamo si lontani Carissmo Sgr. P. Maestro, quante cose che avrai a dirgli!—Reverisco devotamente tutti i Sgri. Filarmonici: mi raccommando via sempre nelle grazie di lei e non cesso d'affligermi nel vedermi lontano dalla persona del mondo che maggiormente amo, venero e stimo, e di cui inviolabilmente mi protesto di V. Pta molto Rda

    umilissmo e devotssmo servitore,
    WOLFGANGO AMADEO MOZART.
    Salisburgo, 4 Settembre, 1776.

[FOOTNOTE:

To Father Martini.
"Salzburg, Sept. 4,1776.

"MOST REVEREND AND ESTEEMED FATHER AND MAESTRO,—

"The veneration, the esteem, and the respect I feel for your illustrious person, induce me to intrude on you with this letter, and also to send you a small portion of my music, which I venture to submit to your masterly judgment. Last year, at Monaco, in Bavaria, I wrote an opera buffa ("La finta Giardiniera") for the Carnival. A few days previous to my departure from thence, his Electoral Highness wished to hear some of my contrapuntal music; I was therefore obliged to write this motett in haste, to allow time for the score to be copied for his Highness, and to arrange the parts so that it might be produced on the following Sunday at grand mass at the offertory. Most dear and highly esteemed Maestro, I do entreat you to give me unreservedly your candid opinion of the motett. We live in this world in order always to learn industriously, and to enlighten each other by means of discussion, and to strive vigorously to promote the progress of science and the fine arts. Oh, how many and many a time have I desired to be nearer you, that I might converse and discuss with your Reverence! I live in a country where music has very little success, though, exclusive of those who have forsaken us, we have still admirable professors, and more particularly composers of great solidity, knowledge, and taste. We are rather badly off at the theatre from the want of actors. We have no MUSICI, nor shall we find it very easy to get any, because they insist upon being well paid, and generosity is not a failing of ours. I amuse myself in the mean time by writing church and chamber music, and we have two excellent contrapuntists here, Haydn and Adlgasser. My father is maestro at the Metropolitan church, which gives me an opportunity to write for the church as much as I please. Moreover, my father has been thirty-six years in the service of this court, and knowing that our present Archbishop neither can nor will endure the sight of elderly people, he does not take it to heart, but devotes himself to literature, which was always his favorite pursuit Our church music is rather different from that of Italy, and the more so, as a mass including the Kyne, Gloria, Credo, the Sonata all Epistola, the Offertory or Motett, Sanctus, and Agnus Dei, and even a solemn mass, when the Prince himself officiates, must never last more than three-quarters of an hour. A particular course of study is required for this class of composition. And what must such a mass be, scored with all the instruments, war-drums, cymbals, Oh! why are we so far apart, dearest Signor Maestro? for how many things I have to say to you! I devoutly revere all the Signori Filarmonici. I venture to recommend myself to your good opinion, I shall never cease regretting being so distant from the person in the world whom I most love, venerate, and esteem. I beg to subscribe myself, reverend Father, always your most humble and devoted servant,

"WOLFGANG AMADEUS MOZART"

SECOND PART. MUNICH, AUGSBURG, MANNHEIM. SEPTEMBER 1771 TO MARCH 1778.

On the 22d of December, 1777, Mozart's father wrote as follows to Padre Martini in Bologna:—"My son has been now five years in the service of our Prince, at a mere nominal salary, hoping that by degrees his earnest endeavors and any talents he may possess, combined with the utmost industry and most unremitting study, would be rewarded; but in this hope we find ourselves deceived. I forbear all allusion to our Prince's mode of thinking and acting; but he was not ashamed to declare that my son knew nothing, and that he ought to go to the musical training school in Naples to learn music. And why did he say all this? In order to intimate that a young man should not be so absurd as to believe that he deserved a rather higher salary after such a decisive verdict had issued from the lips of a prince. This has induced me to sanction my son giving up his present situation. He therefore left Salzburg on the 23d of September" [with his mother].

59. Wasserburg, Sept. 23, 1777.

Mon Tres-Cher Pere,—

God be praised! we reached Waging, Stain, Ferbertshaim, and Wasserburg safely. Now for a brief report of our journey. When we arrived at the city gates, we were kept waiting for nearly a quarter of an hour till they could be thrown open for us, as they were under repair. Near Schinn we met a drove of cows, and one of these very remarkable, for each side was a different color, which we never before saw. When at last we got to Schinn, we met a carriage, which stopped, and ecce, our postilion called out we must change. "I don't care," said I. Mamma and I were parleying, when a portly gentleman came up, whose physiognomy I at once recognized; he was a Memmingen merchant. He stared at me for some time, and at last said, "You surely are Herr Mozart?" "At your service," said I; "I know you, too, by sight, but not your name. I saw you, a year ago, at Mirabell's [the palace garden in Salzburg] at a concert." He then told me his name, which, thank God! I have forgotten; but I retained one of probably more importance to me. When I saw this gentleman in Salzburg, he was accompanied by a young man whose brother was now with him, and who lives in Memmingen. His name is Herr Unhold, and he pressed me very much to come to Memmingen if possible. We sent a hundred thousand loves to papa by them, and to my sister, the madcap, which they promised to deliver without fail. This change of carriages was a great bore to me, for I wished to send a letter back from Waging by the postilion. We then (after a slight meal) had the honor of being conveyed as far as Stain, by the aforesaid post-horses, in an hour and a half. At Waging I was alone for a few minutes with the clergyman, who looked quite amazed, knowing nothing of our history. From Stain we were driven by a most tiresome phlegmatic postilion—N. B., in driving I mean; we thought we never were to arrive at the next stage. At last we did arrive, as you may see from my writing this letter. (Mamma is half asleep.) From Ferbertshaim to Wasserburg all went on well. Viviamo come i principi; we want nothing except you, dear papa. Well, this is the will of God; no doubt all will go on right. I hope to hear that papa is as well as I am and as happy. Nothing comes amiss to me; I am quite a second papa, and look after everything.[Footnote: The father had been very uneasy at the idea of allowing the inexperienced youth, whose unsuspicious good- nature exposed him still more to danger, to travel alone; for the mother also was not very expert in travelling.] I settled from the first to pay the postilions, for I can talk to such fellows better than mamma. At the Stern, in Wasserburg, we are capitally served; I am treated here like a prince. About half an hour ago (mamma being engaged at the time) the Boots knocked at the door to take my orders about various things, and I gave them to him with the same grave air that I have in my portrait. Mamma is just going to bed. We both beg that papa will be careful of his health, not go out too early, nor fret, [Footnote: The Father was strongly disposed to hypochondria.] but laugh and be merry and in good spirits. We think the Mufti H. C. [the Archbishop Hieronymus Colloredo] a MUFF, but we know God to be compassionate, merciful, and loving. I kiss papa's hands a thousand times, and embrace my SISTER MADCAP as often as I have to-day taken snuff. I think I have left my diplomas at home? [his appointment at court.] I beg you will send them to me soon. My pen is rude, and I am not refined.

60. Munich, Sept. 26, 1777.

WE arrived safely in Munich on the afternoon of the 24th, at half-past four o'clock. A complete novelty to me was being obliged to drive to the Custom House, escorted by a grenadier with a fixed bayonet. The first person we knew, who met us when driving, was Signer Consoli; he recognized me at once, and showed the utmost joy at seeing me again. Next day he called on us. I cannot attempt to describe the delight of Herr Albert [the "learned landlord" of the Black Eagle, on the Kaufinger Gasse, now Hotel Detzer]; he is indeed a truly honest man, and a very good friend of ours. On my arrival I went to the piano, and did not leave it till dinner-time. Herr Albert was not at home, but he soon came in, and we went down to dinner together. There I met M. Sfeer and a certain secretary, an intimate friend of his; both send their compliments to you. Though tired by our journey, we did not go to bed till late; we, however, rose next morning at seven o'clock. My hair was in such disorder that I could not go to Count Seeau's till half-past ten o'clock. When I got there I was told that he had driven out to the chasse. Patience! In the mean time I wished to call on Chorus-master Bernard, but he had gone to the country with Baron Schmid. I found Herr von Belvall deeply engaged in business; he sent you a thousand compliments. Rossi came to dinner, and at two o'clock Consoli, and at three arrived Becke [a friend of Mozart's and an admirable flute- player], and also Herr von Belvall. I paid a visit to Frau von Durst [with whom Nannerl had lived], who now lodges with the Franciscans. At six o'clock I took a short walk with Herr Becke. There is a Professor Huber here, whom you may perhaps remember better than I do; he says that the last time he either saw or heard me was at Vienna, at Herr von Mesmer's, junior. He is neither tall nor short, pale, with silvery-gray hair, and his physiognomy rather like that of Herr Unterbereiter. This gentleman is vice-intendant of the theatre; his occupation is to read through all the comedies to be acted, to improve or to spoil, to add to or to put them aside. He comes every evening to Albert's, and often talks to me. To-day, Friday, the 2eth, I called on Count Seeau at half-past eight o'clock. This was what passed. As I was going into the house I met Madame Niesser, the actress, just coming out, who said, "I suppose you wish to see the Count?" "Yes!" "He is still in his garden, and Heaven knows when he may come!" I asked her where the garden was. "As I must see him also," said she, "let us go together." We had scarcely left the house when we saw the Count coming towards us about twelve paces off; he recognized and instantly named me. He was very polite, and seemed already to know all that had taken place about me. We went up the steps together slowly and alone; I told him briefly the whole affair. He said that I ought at once to request an audience of his Highness the Elector, but that, if I failed in obtaining it, I must make a written statement. I entreated him to keep this all quite private, and he agreed to do so. When I remarked to him that there really was room for a genuine composer here, he said, "I know that well." I afterwards went to the Bishop of Chiemsee, and was with him for half an hour. I told him everything, and he promised to do all he could for me in the matter. At one o'clock he drove to Nymphenburg, and declared positively he would speak to the Electress. On Sunday the Count comes here. Herr Joannes Kronner has been appointed Vice-Concertmeister, which he owes to a blunt speech of his. He has produced two symphonies—Deo mene liberi [God preserve me from such]—of his own composition. The Elector asked him, "Did you really compose these?" "Yes, your Royal Highness!" "From whom did you learn?" "From a schoolmaster in Switzerland, where so much importance is attached to the study of composition. This schoolmaster taught me more than all your composers here, put together, could teach me." Count Schonborn and his Countess, a sister of the Archbishop [of Salzburg], passed through here to-day. I chanced to be at the play at the time. Herr Albert, in the course of conversation, told them that I was here, and that I had given up my situation. They were all astonishment, and positively refused to believe him when he said that my salary, of blessed memory, was only twelve florins thirty kreuzers! They merely changed horses, and would gladly have spoken with me, but I was too late to meet them. Now I must inquire what you are doing, and how you are. Mamma and I hope that you are quite well. I am still in my very happiest humor; my head feels as light as a feather since I got away from that chicanery. I have grown fatter already.

61. Munich, Sept. 29, 1777.

TRUE enough, a great many kind friends, but unluckily most of them have little or nothing in their power. I was with Count Seeau yesterday, at half-past ten o'clock, and found him graver and less natural than the first time; but it was only in appearance, for to-day I was at Prince Zeill's [Bishop of Chiemsee—No. 56], who, with all courtesy, said to me, "I don't think we shall effect much here. During dinner, at Nymphenburg, I spoke privately to the Elector, who replied: 'It is too soon at this moment; he must leave this and go to Italy and become famous. I do not actually reject him, but these are too early days as yet.'" There it is! Most of these grandees have such paroxysms of enthusiasm for Italy. Still, he advised me to go to the Elector, and to place my case before him as I had previously intended. I spoke confidentially at dinner to-day with Herr Woschitka [violoncellist in the Munich court orchestra, and a member of the Elector's private band], and he appointed me to come to-morrow at nine o'clock, when he will certainly procure me an audience. We are very good friends now. He insisted on knowing the name of my informant; but I said to him, "Rest assured that I am your friend and shall continue to be so; I am in turn equally convinced of your friendship, so you must be satisfied with this." But to return to my narrative. The Bishop of Chiemsee also spoke to the Electress when tete-a-tete with her. She shrugged her shoulders, and said she would do her best, but was very doubtful as to her success. I now return to Count Seeau, who asked Prince Zeill (after he had told him everything). "Do you know whether Mozart has not enough from his family to enable him to remain here with a little assistance? I should really like to keep him." Prince Zeill answered: "I don't know, but I doubt it much; all you have to do is to speak to himself on the subject. "This, then, was the cause of Count Seeau being so thoughtful on the following day. I like being here, and I am of the same opinion with many of my friends, that if I could only remain here for a year or two, I might acquire both money and fame by my works, and then more probably be sought by the court than be obliged to seek it myself. Since my return here Herr Albert has a project in his head, the fulfilment of which does not seem to me impossible. It is this: He wishes to form an association of ten kind friends, each of these to subscribe 1 ducat (50 gulden) monthly, 600 florins a year. If in addition to this I had even 200 florins per annum from Count Seeau, this would make 800 florins altogether. How does papa like this idea? Is it not friendly? Ought not I to accept it if they are in earnest? I am perfectly satisfied with it; for I should be near Salzburg, and if you, dearest papa, were seized with a fancy to leave Salzburg (which from my heart I wish you were) and to pass your life in Munich, how easy and pleasant would it be! For if we are obliged to live in Salzburg with 504 florins, surely we might live in Munich with 800.

To-day, the 30th, after a conversation with Herr Woschitka, I went to court by appointment. Every one was in hunting-costume. Baron Kern was the chamberlain on service. I might have gone there last night, but I could not offend M. Woschitka, who himself offered to find me an opportunity of speaking to the Elector. At 10 o'clock he took me into a narrow little room, through which his Royal Highness was to pass on his way to hear mass, before going to hunt. Count Seeau went by, and greeted me very kindly: "How are you, dear Mozart?" When the Elector came up to me, I said, "Will your Royal Highness permit me to pay my homage and to offer your Royal Highness my services?" "So you have finally left Salzburg?" "I have left it forever, your Royal Highness. I only asked leave to make a journey, and being refused, I was obliged to take this step, although I have long intended to leave Salzburg, which is no place for me, I feel sure." "Good heavens! you are quite a young man. But your father is still in Salzburg?" "Yes, your Royal Highness; he humbly lays his homage at your feet, I have already been three times in Italy. I have written three operas, and am a member of the Bologna Academy; I underwent a trial where several maestri toiled and labored for four or five hours, whereas I finished my work in one. This is a sufficient testimony that I have abilities to serve any court. My greatest wish is to be appointed by your Royal Highness, who is himself such a great "But, my good young friend, I regret that there is not a single vacancy. If there were only a vacancy!" "I can assure your Royal Highness that I would do credit to Munich." "Yes, but what does that avail when there is no vacancy?" This he said as he was moving on; so I bowed and took leave of his Royal Highness. Herr Woschitka advises me to place myself often in the way of the Elector. This afternoon I went to Count Salern's. His daughter is a maid of honor, and was one of the hunting-party. Ravani and I were in the street when the whole procession passed. The Elector and the Electress noticed me very kindly. Young Countess Salern recognized me at once, and waved her hand to me repeatedly. Baron Rumling, whom I had previously seen in the antechamber, never was so courteous to me as on this occasion. I will soon write to you what passed with Salern. He was very kind, polite, and straightforward.—P. S. Ma tres-chere soeur, next time I mean to write you a letter all for yourself. My remembrances to B. C. M. R. and various other letters of the alphabet. Adieu! A man built a house here and inscribed on it: "Building is beyond all doubt an immense pleasure, but I little thought that it would cost so much treasure." During the night some one wrote underneath, "You ought first to have counted the cost."

62. Munich, Oct. 2, 1777.

YESTERDAY, October 1st, I was again at Count Salern's, and to-day I even dined with him. I have played a great deal during the last three days, and with right good will too. Papa must not, however, imagine that I like to be at Count Salern's on account of the young lady; by no means, for she is unhappily in waiting, and therefore never at home, but I am to see her at court to-morrow morning, at ten o'clock, in company with Madame Hepp, formerly Madlle. Tosson. On Saturday the court leaves this, and does not return till the 20th. To-morrow I am to dine with Madame and Madlle. de Branca, the latter being a kind of half pupil of mine, for Sigl seldom comes, and Becke, who usually accompanies her on the flute, is not here. On the three days that I was at Count Salern's I played a great many things extempore—two Cassations [Divertimentos] for the Countess, and the finale and Rondo, and the latter by heart. You cannot imagine the delight this causes Count Salern. He understands music, for he was constantly saying Bravo! while other gentlemen were taking snuff, humming and hawing, and clearing their throats, or holding forth. I said to him, "How I do wish the Elector were only here, that he might hear me play! He knows nothing of me—he does not know what I can do. How sad it is that these great gentlemen should believe what any one tells them, and do not choose to judge for themselves! BUT IT IS ALWAYS SO. Let him put me to the test. He may assemble all the composers in Munich, and also send in quest of some from Italy and France, Germany, and England and Spain, and I will undertake to write against them all." I related to him all that had occurred to me in Italy, and begged him, if the conversation turned on me, to bring in these things.

He said, "I have very little influence, but the little that is in my power I will do with pleasure." He is also decidedly of opinion that if I could only remain here, the affair would come right of itself. It would not be impossible for me to contrive to live, were I alone here, for I should get at least 300 florins from Count Seeau. My board would cost little, for I should be often invited out; and even were it not so, Albert would always be charmed to see me at dinner in his house. I eat little, drink water, and for dessert take only a little fruit and a small glass of wine. Subject to the advice of my kind friends, I would make the following contract with Count Seeau:—I would engage to produce every year four German operas, partly buffe and partly serie; from each of these I should claim the profits of one performance, for such is the custom here. This alone would bring me in 500 florins, which along with my salary would make up 800 florins, but in all probability more; for Reiner, an actor and singer, cleared 200 florins by his benefit, and I am VERY MUCH BELOVED HERE, and how much more so should I be if I con-tributed to the elevation of the national theatre of Germany in music! And this would certainly be the case with me, for I was inspired with the most eager desire to write when I heard the German operettas. The name of the first singer here is Keiserin; her father is cook to a count here; she is a very pleasing girl, and pretty on the stage; I have not yet seen her near. She is a native of this place. When I heard her it was only her third appearance on the stage. She has a fine voice, not powerful, though by no means weak, very pure, and a good intonation. Her instructor is Valesi; and her style of singing shows that her master knows how to sing as well as how to teach. When she sustains her voice for a couple of bars, I am quite surprised at the beauty of her crescendo and decrescendo. She as yet takes her shakes slowly, and this I highly approve of, for it will be all the more pure and clear if she ever wishes to take it quicker; besides, it is easier when quick. She is a great favorite with the people here, and with me.

    Mamma was in the pit; she went as early as half-past four o'clock to get a place. I, however, did not go till half-past six o'clock, for I can go to any box I please, being pretty well known. I was in the Brancas' box; I looked at Keiserin with my opera-glass, and at times she drew tears from my eyes. I often called out bravo, bravissimo, for I always remembered that it was only her third appearance. The piece was Das Fischermadchen, a very good translation of Piccini's opera, with his music. As yet they have no original pieces, but are now anxious soon to

62. Munich, Oct. 2, 1777.

give a German opera seria, and a strong wish prevails that I should compose it. The aforesaid Professor Huber is one of those who wish this. I shall now go to bed, for I can sit up no longer. It is just ten o'clock. Baron Rumling lately paid me the following compliment: "The theatre is my delight—good actors and actresses, good singers, and a clever composer, such as yourself." This is indeed only talk, and words are not of much value, but he never before spoke to me in this way.

I write this on the 3d of October. To-morrow the court departs, and does not return till the 20th. If it had remained here, I would have taken the step I intended, and stayed on here for a time; but as it is, I hope to resume my journey with mamma next Tuesday. But meanwhile the project of the associated friends, which I lately wrote to you about, may be realized, so that when we no longer care to travel we shall have a resource to fall back upon. Herr von Krimmel was to-day with the Bishop of Chiemsee, with whom he has a good deal to do on the subject of salt. He is a strange man; here he is called "your Grace,"—that is, THE LACKEYS do so. Having a great desire that I should remain here, he spoke very zealously to the Prince in my favor. He said to me, "Only let me alone; I will speak to the Prince, and I have a right to do so, for I have done many things to oblige him." The Prince promised him that I should POSITIVELY be appointed, but the affair cannot be so quickly settled. On the return of the court he is to speak to the Elector with all possible earnestness and zeal. At eight o'clock this morning I called on Count Seeau. I was very brief, and merely said, "I have only come, your Excellency, to explain my case clearly. I have been told that I ought to go to Italy, which is casting a reproach on me. I was sixteen months in Italy, I have written three operas, and all this is notorious enough. What further occurred, your Excellency will see from these papers." And after showing him the diplomata, I added, "I only show these and say this to your Excellency that, in the event of my being spoken of, and any injustice done me, your Excellency may with good grounds take my part." He asked me if I was now going to France. I said I intended to remain in Germany; by this, however, he supposed I meant Munich, and said, with a merry laugh, "So you are to stay here after all? " I replied, "No! to tell you the truth, I should like to have stayed, if the Elector had favored me with a small sum, so that I might then have offered my compositions to your Excellency devoid of all interested motives. It would have been a pleasure to me to do this." At these words he half lifted his skull-cap.

At ten o'clock I went to court to call on Countess Salern. I dined afterwards with the Brancas. Herr Geheimrath von Branca, having been invited by the French Ambassador, was not at home. He is called "your Excellency." Countess Salern is a Frenchwoman, and scarcely knows a word of German; so I have always been in the habit of talking French to her. I do so quite boldly, and she says that I don't speak at all badly, and that I have the good habit of speaking slowly, which makes me more easily understood. She is a most excellent person, and very well-bred. The daughter plays nicely, but fails in time. I thought this arose from want of ear on her part, but I find I can blame no one but her teacher, who is too indulgent and too easily satisfied. I practised with her to-day, and I could pledge myself that if she were to learn from me for a couple of months, she would play both well and accurately.

At four o'clock I went to Frau von Tosson's, where I found mamma and also Frau von Hepp. I played there till eight o'clock, and after that we went home; and at half-past nine a small band of music arrived, consisting of five persons—two clarionet-players, two horns, and one bassoon. Herr Albert (whose name-day is to- morrow) arranged this music in honor of me and himself. They played rather well together, and were the same people whom we hear during dinner at Albert's, but it is well known that they are trained by Fiala. They played some of his pieces, and I must say they are very pretty: he has some excellent ideas. To-morrow we are to have a small musical party together, where I am to play. (Nota bene, on that miserable piano! oh, dear! oh, dear! oh, dear!) I beg you will excuse my horrid writing, but ink, haste, sleep, and dreams are all against me. I am now and forever amen, your dutiful son,

A. W. MOZART.

63. Munich, Oct. 6, 1777.

Mamma cannot write; in the first place, she is not inclined, and, secondly, she has a headache. So I must hold the pen for her and keep faith with her. I am just going with the Professor to call on Madlle. Keiserin. Yesterday we had in our house a clerical wedding, or altum tempus ecclesiasticum. There was dancing, but I only danced four minuets, and was in my own room again by eleven o'clock, for, out of

63. Munich, Oct. 6, 1777.

fifty young ladies, there was only one who danced in time—Madlle. Kaser, a sister of Count Perusa's secretary. The Professor thought fit to leave me in the lurch, so I did not go to Madlle. Keiserin, because I don't know where she lives. Last Saturday, the 4th, on the stately and solemn occasion of the name-day of his Royal Highness the Archduke Albert, we had a select music-party at home, which commenced at half-past three o'clock and finished at eight. M. Dubreil, whom papa no doubt remembers, was also present; he is a pupil of Tartini's. In the forenoon he gave a lesson on the violin to the youngest son, Carl, and I chanced to come in at the time, I never gave him credit for much talent, but I saw that he took great pains in giving his lesson; and when we entered into conversation about violin, concert, and orchestral playing, he reasoned very well, and was always of my opinion, so I retracted my former sentiments with regard to him, and was persuaded that I should find him play well in time, and a correct violinist in the orchestra. I, therefore, invited him to be so kind as to attend our little music rehearsal that afternoon. We played, first of all, the two quintets of Haydn, but to my dismay I could scarcely hear Dubreil, who could not play four continuous bars without a mistake. He could never find the positions, and he was no good friend to the sospirs [short pauses]. The only good thing was that he spoke politely and praised the quintets; otherwise—As it was, I said nothing to him, but he kept constantly saying himself, "I beg your pardon, but really I am out again! the thing is puzzling, but fine!" I invariably replied, "It does not in the least signify; we are only among ourselves." I then played the concertos in C, in B, and in E flat, and after that a trio of mine. This was finely accompanied, truly! In the adagio I was obliged to play six bars of his part. As a finale, I played my last divertimento in B; they all pricked up their ears. I played as if I had been the greatest violin-player in all Europe.

The Sunday after, at three o'clock, we were at a certain Herr von Hamm's. The Bishop of Chiemsee set off to-day for Salzburg. N. B.—I send my sister, by him, "6 duetti a clavicembalo e violino," by Schuster. I have often played them here; they are by no means bad. If I remain long enough, I intend to compose six in this style, for it is much liked here.

64. Munich, Oct. 11, 1777.

WHY have I not as yet written anything about Misliweczeck? [See No. 43.] Because I was only too glad not to think of him; for when he is spoken of I invariably hear how highly he praises me, and what a kind and true friend he is of mine; but then follow pity and lamentation. He was de-cribed to me, and deeply was I distressed. How could I bear that Misliweczeck, my intimate friend, should be in the same town, nay, even in the same corner of the world with me, and neither see him nor speak to him? Impossible! so I resolved to go to visit him. On the previous day, I called on the manager of the Duke's Hospital to ask if I might see my friend in the garden, which I thought best, though the doctors assured me there was no longer any risk of infection. The manager agreed to my proposal, and said I should find him in the garden between eleven and twelve o'clock, and, if he was not there when I came, to send for him. Next day I went with Herr von Hamm, secretary in the Crown Office, (of whom I shall speak presently,) and mamma to the Duke's Hospital. Mamma went into the Hospital church, and we into the garden. Misliweczeck was not there, so we sent him a message. I saw him coming across, and knew him at once from his manner of walking. I must tell you that he had already sent me his remembrances by Herr Heller, a violoncello-player, and begged me to visit him before I left Munich. When he came up to me, we shook hands cordially. "You see," said he, "how unfortunate I am." These words and his appearance, which papa is already aware of from description, so went to my heart that I could only say, with tears in my eyes, "I pity you from my heart, my dear friend." He saw how deeply I was affected, so rejoined quite cheerfully, "Now tell me what you are doing; when I heard that you were in Munich, I could scarcely believe it; how could Mozart be here and not long ago have come to see me?" "I hope you will forgive me, but I had such a number of visits to make, and I have so many kind friends here." "I feel quite sure that you have indeed many kind friends, but a truer friend than myself you cannot have." He asked me whether papa had told me anything of a letter he had received. I said, "Yes, he did write to me," (I was quite confused, and trembled so much in every limb that I could scarcely speak,) "but he gave me no details." He then told me that Signor Gaetano Santoro, the Neapolitan impresario, was obliged, owing to

64. Munich, Oct. 11, 1777.

impegni and protezione, to give the composition of the opera for this Carnival to a certain Maestro Valentini; but he added, "Next year he has three at liberty, one of which is to be at my service. But as I have already composed six times for Naples, I don't in the least mind undertaking the less promising one, and making over to you the best libretto, viz. the one for the Carnival. God knows whether I shall be able to travel by that time, but if not, I shall send back the scrittura. The company for next year is good, being all people whom I have recommended. You must know that I have such influence in Naples that, when I say engage such a one, they do so at once." Marquesi is the primo uomo, whom he, and indeed all Munich too, praises very highly; Marchiani is a good prima donna; and there is a tenor, whose name I cannot recall, but Misliweczeck says he is the best in all Italy. He also said, "I do beg of you to go to Italy; there one is esteemed and highly prized." And in truth he is right. When I come to reflect on the subject, in no country have I received such honors, or been so esteemed, as in Italy, and nothing contributes more to a man's fame than to have written Italian operas, and especially for Naples. He said he would write a letter for me to Santoro, which I was to copy out when I went to see him next day; but finding it impossible to return, he sent me a sketch of the letter to-day. I was told that when Misliweczeck heard people here speaking of Becke, or other performers on the piano, he invariably said, "Let no one deceive himself; none can play like Mozart; in Italy, where the greatest masters are, they speak of no one but Mozart; when his name is mentioned, not a word is said of others." I can now write the letter to Naples when I please; but, indeed, the sooner the better. I should, however, first like to have the opinion of that highly discreet Hofcapellmeister, Herr von Mozart. I have the most ardent desire to write another opera. The distance is certainly great, but the period is still a long way off when I am to write this opera, and there may be many changes before then. I think I might at all events undertake it. If, in the mean time, I get no situation, eh, bien! I shall then have a resource in Italy. I am at all events certain to receive 100 ducats in the Carnival; and when I have once written for Naples I shall be sought for everywhere. As papa well knows, there is an opera buffa in Naples in spring, summer, and autumn, for which I might write for the sake of practice, not to be quite idle. It is true that there is not much to be got by this, but still there is something, and it would be the means of gaining more honor and reputation than by giving a hundred concerts in Germany, and I am far happier when I have something to compose, which is my chief delight and passion; and if I get a situation anywhere, or have hopes of one, the scrittura would be a great recommendation to me, and excite a sensation, and cause me to be more thought of. This is mere talk, but still I say what is in my heart. If papa gives me any good grounds to show that I am wrong, then I will give it up, though, I own, reluctantly. Even when I hear an opera discussed, or am in a theatre myself and hear voices, oh! I really am beside myself!

To-morrow, mamma and I are to meet Misliweczeck in the Hospital garden to take leave of him; for he wished me last time to fetch mamma out of church, as he said he should like to see the mother of so great a virtuoso. My dear papa, do write to him as often as you have time to do so; you cannot confer a greater pleasure on him, for the man is quite forsaken. Sometimes he sees no one for a whole week, and he said to me, "I do assure you it does seem so strange to me to see so few people; in Italy I had company every day." He looks thin, of course, but is still full of fire and life and genius, and the same kind, animated person he always was. People talk much of his oratorio of "Abraham and Isaac," which he produced here. He has just completed (with the exception of a few arias) a Cantata, or Serenata, for Lent; and when he was at the worst he wrote an opera for Padua. Herr Heller is just come from him. When I wrote to him yesterday I sent him the Serenata that I wrote in Salzburg: for the Archduke Maximilian ["Il Re Pastore"].

Now to turn to something else. Yesterday I went with mamma immediately after dinner to take coffee with the two Fraulein von Freysinger. Mamma, however, took none, but drank two bottles of Tyrolese wine. At three o'clock she went home again to make preparations for our journey. I, however, went with the two ladies to Herr von Hamm's, whose three young ladies each played a concerto, and I one of Aichner's prima vista, and then went on extemporizing. The teacher of these little simpletons, the Demoiselles Hamm, is a certain clerical gentleman of the name of Schreier. He is a good organ-player, but no pianist. He kept staring at me with an eye-glass. He is a reserved kind of man who does not talk much; he patted me on the shoulder, sighed, and said, "Yes—you are—you understand—yes—it is true—you are an out-and-outer!" By the by, can you recall the name of Freysingen--the papa of the two pretty girls I mentioned? He says he knows you well, and that he studied with you. He particularly remembers Messenbrunn, where papa (this was quite new to me) played most incomparably on the organ. He said, "It was quite startling to see the pace at which both hands and feet went, but quite inimitable; a thorough master indeed; my father thought a great deal of him; and how he humbugged the priests about entering the Church! You are just what he was then, as like as possible; only he was a degree shorter when I knew him." A propos, a certain Hofrath Effeln sends you his kind regards; he is one of the best Hofraths here, and would long ago have been made chancellor but for one defect—TIPPLING. When we saw him for the first time at Albert's, both mamma and I thought, "What an odd-looking fish!" Just imagine a very tall man, stout and corpulent, and a ridiculous face. When he crosses the room to another table, he folds both hands on his stomach, stoops very low, and then draws himself up again, and makes little nods; and when this is over he draws back his right foot, and does this to each individual separately. He says that he knows papa intimately. I am now going for a little to the play. Next time I will write more fully, but I can't possibly go on to-day, for my fingers do ache uncommonly.

Munich, October 11th, at 1/4 to 12 at night, I write as follows:—I have been at the Drittl comedy, but only went in time for the ballet, or rather the pantomime, which I had not before seen. It is called "Das von der fur Girigaricanarimanarischaribari verfertigte Ei." It was very good and funny. We are going to-morrow to Augsburg on account of Prince Taxis not being at Ratisbon but at Teschingen. He is, in fact, at present at his country-seat, which is, however, only an hour from Teschingen. I send my sister, with this, four preludes; she will see and hear for herself the different keys into which they lead. My compliments to all my kind friends, particularly to young Count Arco, to Madlle. Sallerl, and to my best of all friends, Herr Bullinger; I do beg that next Sunday at the usual eleven-o'clock music he will be so good as to make an authoritative oration in my name, and present my regards to all the members of the orchestra and exhort them to industry, that I may not one day be accused of being a humbug, for I have everywhere extolled their orchestra, and I intend always to do so.

65. Augsburg, Oct. 14, 1777.

I HAVE made no mistake in my date, for I write before dinner, and I think that next Friday, the day after to-morrow, we shall be off again. Pray hear how generous the gentlemen of Augsburg are. In no place was I ever so overwhelmed with marks of distinction as here. My first visit was to the Stadtpfleger Longo Tabarro [Burgomaster Langenmantl]. My cousin, [Footnote: Leopold Mozart had a brother in Augsburg, a bookbinder, whose daughter, "das Basle" (the cousin), was two years younger than Mozart.] a good, kind, honest man and worthy citizen, went with me, and had the honor to wait in the hall like a footman till my interview with the high and mighty Stadtpfleger was over. I did not fail first of all to present papa's respectful compliments. He deigned graciously to remember you, and said, "And pray how have things gone with him?" "Vastly well, God be praised!" I instantly rejoined, "and I hope things have also gone well with you?" He then became more civil, and addressed me in the third person, so I called him "Sir"; though, indeed, I had done so from the first. He gave me no peace till I went up with him to see his son-in-law (on the second floor), my cousin meanwhile having the pleasure of waiting in the staircase-hall. I was obliged to control myself with all my might, or I must have given some polite hint about this. On going upstairs I had the satisfaction of playing for nearly three-quarters of an hour on a good clavichord of Stein's, in the presence of the stuck-up young son, and his prim condescending wife, and the simple old lady. I first extemporized, and then played all the music he had, prima, vista, and among others some very pretty pieces of Edlmann's. Nothing could be more polite than they all were, and I was equally so, for my rule is to behave to people just as they behave to me; I find this to be the best plan. I said that I meant to go to Stein's after dinner, so the young man offered to take me there himself. I thanked him for his kindness, and promised to return at two o'clock. I did so, and we went together in company with his brother-in-law, who looks a genuine student. Although I had begged that my name should not be mentioned, Herr von Langenmantl was so incautious as to say, with a simper, to Herr Stein, "I have the honor to present to you a virtuoso on the piano." I instantly protested against this, saying that I was only an indifferent pupil of Herr Sigl in Munich, who had charged me with a thousand compliments to him. Stein shook his head dubiously, and at length said, "Surely I have the honor of seeing M. Mozart?" "Oh, no," said I; "my name is Trazom, and I have a letter for you." He took the letter and was about to break the seal instantly, but I gave him no time for that, saying, "What is the use of reading the letter just now? Pray open the door of your saloon at once, for I am so very anxious to see your pianofortes." "With all my heart," said he, "just as you please; but for all that I believe I am not mistaken." He opened the door, and I ran straight up to one of the three pianos that stood in the room. I began to play, and he scarcely gave himself time to glance at the letter, so anxious was he to ascertain the truth; so he only read the signature. "Oh!" cried he, embracing me, and crossing himself and making all sorts of grimaces from intense delight. I will write to you another day about his pianos. He then took me to a coffee-house, but when we went in I really thought I must bolt, there was such a stench of tobacco- smoke, but for all that I was obliged to bear it for a good hour. I submitted to it all with a good grace, though I could have fancied that I was in Turkey. He made a great fuss to me about a certain Graf, a composer (of flute concertos only); and said, "He is something quite extraordinary," and every other possible exaggeration. I became first hot and then cold from nervousness. This Graf is a brother of the two who are in Harz and Zurich. He would not give up his intention, but took me straight to him—a dignified gentleman indeed; he wore a dressing-gown that I would not be ashamed to wear in the street. All his words are on stilts, and he has a habit of opening his mouth before knowing what he is going to say; so he often shuts it again without having said anything. After a great deal of ceremony he produced a concerto for two flutes; I was to play first violin. The concerto is confused, not natural, too abrupt in its modulations, and devoid of all genius. When it was over I praised it highly, for, indeed, he deserves this. The poor man must have had labor and study enough to write it. At last they brought a clavichord of Stein's out of the next room, a very good one, but inch-thick with dust. Herr Graf, who is director here, stood there looking like a man who had hitherto believed his own modulations to be something very clever, but all at once discovers that others may be still more so, and without grating on the ear. In a word, they all seemed lost in astonishment.

66. Augsburg, Oct. 17, 1777.

WITH regard to the daughter of Hamm, the Secretary of War, I can only say that there can be no doubt she has a decided talent for music, for she has only learned three years, and can play a number of pieces very well. I find it difficult, however, to explain distinctly the impression she makes on me while she is playing; she seems to me so curiously constrained, and she has such an odd way of stalking over the keys with her long bony fingers! To be sure, she has had no really good master, and if she remains in Munich she will never become what her father wishes and hopes, for he is eager beyond measure that she should one day be a distinguished pianiste. If she goes to papa at Salzburg, it will be a twofold benefit to her, both as to music and common sense, of which she certainly has no great share. She has often made me laugh very much, and you would have amusement enough for your trouble. She is too absent to think of eating much. You say I ought to have practised with her? I really could not for laughing, for when I occasionally played something with the right hand, she instantly said bravissimo, and that in the voice of a little mouse.

I will now relate to you as briefly as possible the Augsburg history to which I have already alluded. Herr von Fingerle, who sent his compliments to you, was also at Herr Grafs. The people were very civil, and discussed the concert I proposed to give, all saying, "It will be one of the most brilliant concerts ever given in Augsburg. You have a great advantage in having made the acquaintance of our Stadtpfleger Langenmantl; besides, the name of Mozart has much influence here." So we separated mutually pleased. I must now tell you that Herr von Langenmantl, junior, when at Herr Stein's, said that he would pledge himself to arrange a concert in the Stube, [Footnote: The Bauernstube, the Patrician Casino.] (as something very select, and complimentary to me,) for the nobility alone. You can't think with what zeal he spoke, and promised to undertake it. We agreed that I should call on him the next morning for the answer; accordingly I went; this was on the 13th. He was very polite, but said that as yet he could not say anything decided. I played there again for an hour, and he invited me next day, the 14th, to dinner. In the forenoon he sent to beg that I would come to him at eleven o'clock, and bring some pieces with me, as he had asked some of the professional musicians, and they intended to have some music. I immediately sent some music, and went myself at eleven, when, with many lame excuses, he coolly said, "By the by, I could do nothing about the concert; oh, I was in such a rage yesterday on your account. The patrician members of the Casino said that their cashbox was at a very low ebb, and that you were not the kind of virtuoso who could expect a souverain d'or." I merely smiled, and said, "I quite agree with them." N. B.—He is Intendant of Music in the Casino, and the old father a magistrate! but I cared very little about it. We sat down to dinner; the old gentleman also dined up-stairs with us, and was very civil, but did not say a word about the concert. After dinner I played two concertos,

66. Augsburg, Oct. 17, 1777.

something out of my head, and then a trio of Hafeneder's on the violin. I would gladly have played more, but I was so badly accompanied that it gave me the colic. He said to me, good-naturedly, "Don't let us part company to-day; go to the play with us, and return here to supper." We were all very merry. When we came back from the theatre, I played again till we went to supper. Young Langenmantl had already questioned me in the forenoon about my cross, [Footnote: Mozart, by his father's desire, wore the "Order of the Golden Spur," conferred on him by the Pope.] and I told him exactly how I got it, and what it was. He and his brother-in-law said over and over again, "Let us order a cross, too, that we may be on a par with Herr Mozart." I took no notice of this. They also repeatedly said, "Hallo! you sir! Knight of the Spur!" I said not a word; but during supper it became really too bad. "What may it have cost? three ducats? must you have permission to wear it? Do you pay extra for leave to do so? We really must get one just like it." An officer there of the name of Bach, said, "For shame! what would you do with the cross?" That young ass, Kurzen Mantl, winked at him, but I saw him, and he knew that I did. A pause ensued, and then he offered me snuff, saying, "There, show that you don't care a pinch of snuff for it." I still said nothing. At length he began once more in a sneering tone: "I may then send to you to-morrow, and you will be so good as to lend me the cross for a few minutes, and I will return it immediately after I have spoken to the goldsmith about it. I know that when I ask him its value (for he is a queer kind of man) he will say a Bavarian thaler; it can't be worth more, for it is not gold, only copper, ha! ha!" I said, "By no means—it is lead, ha! ha!" I was burning with anger and rage. "I say," rejoined he, "I suppose I may, if need be, leave out the spur?" "Oh, yes," said I, "for you have one already in your head; I, too, have one in mine, but of a very different kind, and I should be sorry to exchange mine for yours; so there, take a pinch of snuff on that!" and I offered him snuff. He became pale with rage, but began again: "Just now that order looked so well on that grand waistcoat of yours." I made no reply, so he called the servant and said "Hallo! you must have greater respect for my brother-in-law and myself when we wear the same cross as Herr Mozart; take a pinch of snuff on that!" I started up; all did the same, and showed great embarrassment. I took my hat and my sword, and said, "I hope to have the pleasure of seeing you to-morrow." "To-morrow I shall not be here." "Well, then, the next morning, when I shall still be here." "Ho, ho! you surely don't mean to"— "I mean nothing; you are a set of boors, so goodnight," and off I went.

Next day I told the whole story to Herr Stein, Herr Geniaulx, and to Herr Director Graf—I don't mean about the cross, but how highly disgusted I was at their having bragged so much about a concert, and now it had come to nothing. "I call this making a fool of a person and leaving him in the lurch. I am very sorry that I ever came here. I could not possibly have believed that in Augsburg, my papa's native town, such an insult could have been offered to his son." You cannot imagine, dear papa, how angry and indignant these three gentlemen were, saying, "Oh, you must positively give a concert here; we don't stand in need of the patricians." I, however, adhered to my resolution and said, "I am willing to give a small farewell concert at Herr Stein's, for my few kind friends here who are connoisseurs." The Director was quite distressed, and exclaimed, "It is abominable—shameful; who could have believed such a thing of Langenmantl! Par Dieu! if he really wished it, no doubt it would have been carried through." We then separated. The Director went downstairs with me in his dressing-gown as far as the door, and Herr Stein and Geniaulx walked home with me. They urged us to make up our mind to stay here for a time, but we remained firm. I must not forget to say that, when young Langenmantl lisped out to me, in his usual cool indifferent way, the pleasant news as to my concert, he added, that the patricians invited me to their concert next Thursday. I said, "I will come as one of the audience." "Oh, we hope you will give us the pleasure of hearing you play also." "Well, perhaps I may; why not?" But having received so grievous an insult the next evening, I resolved not to go near him again, to steer clear of the whole set of patricians, and to leave Augsburg. During dinner, on the 16th, I was called out by a servant-maid of Langenmantl's, who wished to know whether he might expect me to go with him to the concert? and he begged I would come to him immediately after dinner. I sent my compliments in return, that I had no intention of going to the concert; nor could I come to him, as I was already engaged (which was quite true); but that I would call next morning to take leave of him, as on Saturday next, at furthest, I was to leave Augsburg. In the meantime Herr Stein had been to see the other patricians of the Evangelical party, and spoke so strongly to them that these gentlemen were quite excited. "What!" said they, "shall we permit a man who does us so much honor to leave this without even hearing

66. Augsburg, Oct. 17, 1777.

him? Herr von Langenmantl, having already heard him, thinks that is enough."

At last they became so excited that Herr Kurzenmantl, the excellent youth, was obliged to go to Herr Stein himself to entreat him, in the name of the patricians, to do all in his power to persuade me to attend the concert, but to say that I must not expect great things. At last I went with him, though with considerable reluctance. The principal gentlemen were very polite, particularly Baron Belling, who is a director or some such animal; he opened my music-portfolio himself. I brought a symphony with me, which they played, and I took a violin part. The orchestra is enough to throw any one into fits. That young puppy Langenmantl was all courtesy, but his face looked as impertinent as ever; he said to me, "I was rather afraid you might have escaped us, or been offended by our jokes the other evening." "By no means," said I coolly; "you are still very young; but I advise you to be more cautious in future, for I am not accustomed to such jokes. The subject on which you were so facetious did you no credit, nor did it answer your purpose, for you see I still wear the order; you had better have chosen some other topic for your wit." "I assure you," said he, "it was only my brother-in-law who"—"Let us say no more about it," said I. "We had nearly been deprived of the pleasure of seeing you altogether," he rejoined. "Yes; had it not been for Herr Stein, I certainly should not have come; and, to tell you the truth, I am only here now to prevent you Augsburg gentlemen being the laughing-stock of other countries, which would have been the case if I had told them that I was eight days in the city where my father was born, without any one there taking the trouble to hear me!" I played a concerto, and all went off well except the accompaniment; and as a finale I played a sonata. At the close, Baron Belling thanked me in the warmest manner in the name of all the company; and, begging me to consider only their good will, presented me with two ducats.

They give me no peace here till I agree to give a public concert next Saturday. Perhaps—but I own I am heartily sick of it all. I shall be indeed glad when I arrive at a place where there is a court. I may with truth say that, were it not for my kind cousins, my regrets would be as numberless as the hairs on my head for ever having come to Augsburg. I must write you some account of my fair cousin, but you must excuse my deferring this till to-morrow, for one ought to be quite fresh to praise her as highly as she deserves.

The 17th.—I now write early in the morning to say that my cousin is pretty, intelligent, lovable, clever, and gay, probably because she has lived so much in society; she was also some time at Munich. We do, indeed, exactly suit each other, for she too is rather inclined to be satirical, so we banter our friends most merrily together. [The Mozart family were both well known and dreaded for their somewhat sharp tongues.]

67. Augsburg, Oct. 17, 1777.

I must now tell you about the Stein pianos. Before seeing these, Spath's pianos were my favorites; but I must own that I give the preference to those of Stein, for they damp much better than those in Ratisbon. If I strike hard, whether I let my fingers rest on the notes or lift them, the tone dies away at the same instant that it is heard. Strike the keys as I choose, the tone always remains even, never either jarring or failing to sound. It is true that a piano of this kind is not to be had for less than three hundred florins, but the pains and skill which Stein bestows on them cannot be sufficiently repaid. His instruments have a feature of their own; they are supplied with a peculiar escapement. Not one in a hundred makers attends to this; but, without it, it is impossible that a piano should not buzz and jar. His hammers fall as soon as they touch the strings, whether the keys be held down by the fingers or not. When he has completed an instrument of this class, (which he told me himself,) he tries all kinds of passages and runs on it, and works away at it, testing its powers till it is capable of doing anything, for he labors not for his own benefit alone, (or he might be saved much trouble,) but for that of music. He often says, "If I were not such a passionate lover of music, playing also myself a little on the piano, I should long ago have lost patience with my work, but I like my instruments to respond to the player, and to be durable." His pianos do really last well. He warrants the sounding-board neither breaking nor cracking; when he has finished one, he exposes it in the air to rain, snow, sun, and every kind of devilry, that it may give way, and then inserts slips of wood which he glues in, making it quite strong and solid. He is very glad when it does crack, for then he is pretty sure nothing further can happen to it. He frequently makes cuts into them himself, and then glues them up, thus making them doubly

67. Augsburg, Oct. 17, 1777.

strong. He has three of these pianos at this moment finished, and I played on them again to-day.

We dined to-day with young Herr Gassner, who is the handsome widower of a lovely young wife; they were only married two years. He is an excellent and kind young man; he gave us a capital dinner. A colleague of the Abbe Henri Bullinger, and Wishofer also dined there, and an ex-Jesuit, who is at present Capellmeister in the cathedral here. He knows Herr Schachtner well [court-trumpeter at Salzburg], and was leader of his band in Ingolstadt; he is called Father Gerbl. Herr Gassner, and one of his wife's unmarried sisters, mamma, our cousin, and I went after dinner to Herr Stein's. At four o'clock came the Capellmeister and Herr Schmittbauer, the organist of St. Ulrich, a worthy good old man. I played at sight a sonata of Becke's, which was rather difficult, but very poor, al solito. The astonishment of the Capellmeister and the organist was indescribable. I have played my six sonatas by heart repeatedly, both here and in Munich. The fifth in G, I played at the distinguished Casino concert, and the last in D, which has an incomparable effect on Stein's pianos. The pedals, pressed by the knees, are also better made by him than by any one else; you scarcely require to touch them to make them act, and as soon as the pressure is removed not the slightest vibration is perceptible.

To-morrow perhaps I shall come to his organs, that is, write to you about them, and I reserve for the last the subject of his little daughter. When I said to Herr Stein that I should like to play on one of his organs, as the organ was my passion, he seemed surprised, and said, "What! such a man as you, so great a pianist, like to play on an instrument devoid of sweetness and expression, with no gradations from piano to forte, but always going on the same?" "That does not signify; the organ always was, both in my eyes and ears, the king of all instruments." "Well, just as you please." So we went together. I could readily perceive from his conversation that he did not expect me to do great things on his organ, evidently thinking that I should handle it in the style of a piano. He told me that by Schobert's own desire he had taken him also to the organ, "and very nervous it made me," said he, "for Schobert had told everybody, and the church was nearly full. I did not doubt the man's spirit, fire, and execution; still, this does not much suit the organ. But the moment he began my opinion was entirely changed." I only said in reply, "Do you then think, Herr Stein, that I am likely to run wild on the organ?" "Oh! you!"—When we came to the organ-loft, I began a prelude, when he laughed. A fugue followed. "I can now quite understand why you like to play the organ," said he, "when you can play in this manner." At first the pedal was a little awkward for me, as it was without the breaks, beginning with C, then D E in one row, whereas with us D and E are above, just where E flat and F sharp are here; but I quickly mastered it.

I went also to try the old organ at St. Ulrich's. The stair that leads to it is really dreadful. I requested that some other person might play the organ for me, that I might go down and listen to it, for above the organ has no effect; but I profited very little by this, for the young leader of the choir, a priest, made such reckless runs on the organ that it was impossible to understand them, and when he attempted harmonies they proved only discords, being always false. Afterwards they would insist on our going to a coffee-room, for mamma and my cousin were with us. A certain Father Emilian, a conceited jackass and a sorry witling, was very sweet on my cousin, and wished to have his jest with her, but she made a jest of him. At last, when rather tipsy, (which soon occurred,) he began to talk about music, and sang a canon, saying, "I never in my life heard anything finer." I said, "I regret that I can't sing it with you, for nature has not given me the power of intoning." "No matter," said he. So he began. I made the third, but I sang different words—thus: "Pater Emilian, oh! thou numskull"—sotto voce to my cousin; then we laughed on for at least half an hour. The Pater said to me, "If we only could be longer together, we could discuss the art of musical composition." "In that case," said I, "our discussion would soon come to an end." A famous rap on the knuckles for him!

TO BE CONTINUED.

68. Augsburg, Oct. 23, 1777.

MY concert took place yesterday. Count Wolfeck interested himself much in it, and brought some chanoinesses with him. I went to his lodgings the very day I arrived, but he was not here at that time. A few days ago he returned, and on hearing that I was still in Augsburg, he did not wait for a visit from me, but at the very moment when I was taking my hat and sword to go to call on him he walked in. I must now give you a description of the last few days before my concert. Last Saturday I was

68. Augsburg, Oct. 23, 1777.

at St. Ulrich's, as I already told you. Some days before my cousin took me with him to present me to the Prelate of the Holy Cross, a kind excellent old man. Previous to going to St. Ulrich's last Saturday, I went with my cousin to the Monastery of the Holy Cross, as the first time I was there neither the Deacon nor the Procurator was at home, and my cousin told me that the Procurator was very jolly. [Here mamma inserts a few lines—which frequently occurs in the letters. She says at the close:] "I am quite surprised that Schuster's duets [see No. 63] are still"— Wolfgang: "Oh, he has got them." Mamma: "No, indeed; he always writes that he has not got them." Wolfgang: "I hate arguing; I am sure he has got them, so there's an end of it." Mamma: "You are mistaken." Wolfgang: "No; I am right. I will show it to mamma in his own writing." Mamma: "Well, where is it?" Wolfgang: "Here; read it." She is reading it at this moment.

Last Sunday I attended service at the Holy Cross, and at ten o'clock we went to Herr Stein's, where we tried over a couple of symphonies for the concert. Afterwards I dined with my cousin at the Holy Cross, where a band played during dinner. Badly as they play in the monastery, I prefer it to the Augsburg orchestra. I played a symphony, and a concerto in B of Vanhall's, on the violin, with unanimous applause. The Dean is a kind, jovial man, a cousin of Eberlin [deceased Capellmeister of Salzburg]. His name is Zeschinger. He knows papa well. At night, after supper, I played the Strassburg concerto; it went as smooth as oil; every one praised the fine pure tone. A small clavichord was then brought in, on which I preluded, and played a sonata and the Fischer variations. Some of those present whispered to the Dean that he ought to hear me play in the organ style. I asked him to give me a theme, which he declined, but one of the monks did so. I handled it quite leisurely, and all at once (the fugue being in G minor) I brought in a lively movement in the major key, but in the same tempo, and then at the end the original subject, only reversed. At last it occurred to me to employ the lively movement for the subject of the fugue also, I did not hesitate long, but did so at once, and it went as accurately as if Daser [a Salzburg tailor] had taken its measure. The Dean was in a state of great excitement. "It is over," said he, "and it's no use talking about it, but I could scarcely have believed what I have just heard; you are indeed an able man. My prelate told me beforehand that in his life he never heard any one play the organ in a more finished and solid style" (he having heard me some days previously when the Dean was not here). At last some one brought me a fugued sonata, and asked me to play it. But I said, "Gentlemen, I really must say this is asking rather too much, for it is not likely I shall be able to play such a sonata at sight." "Indeed, I think so too; it is too much; no one could do it," said the Dean eagerly, being all in my favor. "At all events," said I, "I can but try." I heard the Dean muttering all the time behind me, "Oh, you rogue! oh, you knave!" I played till 11 o'clock, bombarded and besieged, as it were, by fugue themes.

Lately, at Stein's, he brought me a sonata of Becke's, but I think I already told you this. A propos, as to his little girl, [Footnote: Nanette, at that time eight years old; afterwards the admirable wife of Andreas Streicher, the friend of Schiller's youth, and one of Beethoven's best friends in Vienna.] any one who can see and hear her play without laughing must be Stein [stone] like her father. She perches herself exactly opposite the treble, avoiding the centre, that she may have more room to throw herself about and make grimaces. She rolls her eyes and smirks; when a passage comes twice she always plays it slower the second time, and if three times, slower still. She raises her arms in playing a passage, and if it is to be played with emphasis she seems to give it with her elbows and not her fingers, as awkwardly and heavily as possible. The finest thing is, that if a passage occurs (which ought to flow like oil) where the fingers must necessarily be changed, she does not pay much heed to that, but lifts her hands, and quite coolly goes on again. This, moreover, puts her in a fair way to get hold of a wrong note, which often produces a curious effect. I only write this in order to give you some idea of pianoforte-playing and teaching here, so that you may in turn derive some benefit from it. Herr Stein is quite infatuated about his daughter. She is eight years old, and learns everything by heart. She may one day be clever, for she has genius, but on this system she will never improve, nor will she ever acquire much velocity of finger, for her present method is sure to make her hand heavy. She will never master what is the most difficult and necessary, and in fact the principal thing in music, namely, time; because from her infancy she has never been in the habit of playing in correct time. Herr Stein and I discussed this point together for at least two hours. I have, however, in some degree converted him; he asks my advice now on every subject. He was quite devoted to Becke, and now he sees and hears that I can do more than Becke, that I make no grimaces, and yet play with so much expression that he himself acknowledges none of his acquaintances have ever handled his pianos as I do. My keeping so accurately in time causes them all much surprise. The left hand being quite independent in the tempo rubato of an adagio, they cannot at all comprehend. With them the left hand always yields to the right. Count Wolfeck and others, who have a passionate admiration for Becke, said lately publicly in a concert that I beat Becke hollow. Count Wolfeck went round the room saying, "In my life I never heard anything like this." He said to me, "I must tell you that I never heard you play as you did to-day, and I mean to say so to your father as soon as I go to Salzburg." What do you think was the first piece after the symphony? The concerto for three pianos. Herr Demmler took the first part, I the second, and Herr Stein the third. I then played a solo, my last sonata in D, for Durnitz, and afterwards my concerto in B; then again a solo in the organ style, namely, a fugue in C minor, then all of a sudden a splendid sonata in C major, finishing with a rondo, all extempore. What a noise and commotion there was! Herr Stein did nothing but make faces and grimaces of astonishment. Herr Demmler was seized with fits of laughter, for he is a queer creature, and when anything pleases him exceedingly, he can't help laughing heartily; indeed, on this occasion he actually began to swear! Addio!

69. Augsburg, Oct. 25, 1777.

The receipts of the concert were 90 florins, without deducting the expenses. Including, therefore, the two ducats we took in the Casino concert, we had 100 florins. The expenses of the concert did not exceed 16 florins 30 kreutzers; the room I had gratis. I believe most of the musicians will make no charge. We have now ALTOGETHER lost about 26 or 27 florins. This is not of much moment. I am writing this on Saturday the 25th. This morning early I received the letter with the sad news of Frau Oberbereiterin's death. Madlle. Tonerl can now purse up her mouth, or perhaps open it wide, and shut it again as empty as ever. As to the baker's daughter, I have no objection to make; I foresaw all this long ago. This was the cause of my reluctance to leave home, and finding it so difficult to go. I hope the affair is not by this time known all over Salzburg? I beg you, dear papa, most urgently to keep the matter quiet as long as possible, and in the mean time to pay her father on my account any expenses he may have incurred by her entrance into the convent, which I will repay gladly when I return to Salzburg.

I thank you most truly, dear papa, for your good wishes on my name-day. Do not be uneasy on my account, for I have always God before my eyes, I acknowledge His omnipotence, I dread His wrath; but I also know His love, His compassion and mercy towards His creatures, and that He will never forsake His servants. When His will is done I am resigned; so I never can fail to be happy and contented. I shall certainly also strive to live as strictly as possible in accordance with your injunctions and advice. Thank Herr Bullinger a thousand times for his congratulations. I mean to write to him soon and thank him myself, but I may in the mean time assure him that I neither know nor have any better, more sincere, or truer friend than himself. I beg also humbly to thank Madlle. Sallerl; pray tell her I mean to enclose some verses to show my gratitude to her in my letter to Herr Bullinger. Thank my sister also; she is to keep the Schuster duets, and give herself no further trouble on the subject.

In your first letter, dear papa, you write that I lowered myself by my conduct to that lad Langenmantl. Anything but that! I was only straightforward, no more. I see you think he is still a boy; he is one or two and twenty, and a married man. Can any one be considered a boy who is married? I have never gone near him since. I left two cards for him to-day, and excused myself for not going in, having so many indispensable calls to make. I must now conclude, for mamma insists absolument on going to dinner, and then to pack. To-morrow we go straight to Wallerstein. My dear little cousin, who sends you her regards, is anything but a prude. She dressed a la Francaise to please me yesterday. She looked at least 5 per cent, prettier in consequence. Now, Addio!

On the 26th of October the mother and son set off to Mannheim. The mother writes that Wolfgang intended to write to Augsburg, "but he will scarcely be able to do so to-day, for he is now at the rehearsal of the oratorio; so I must beg you to accept my humble self instead." Wolfgang then adds:—

70. Mannheim, Oct. 30, 1777.

I must beg you also to accept my insignificancy. I went to-day with Herr Danner to M. Cannabich's [Director of the Elector's orchestra]. He was uncommonly polite, and I played something for him on his piano,

71. Mannheim, Nov. 4, 1777.

which is a very good one. We went together to the rehearsal. I could scarcely help laughing when I was presented to the musicians, because, though some who knew me by renomme were very civil and courteous, the rest, who knew nothing whatever about me, stared in such a ludicrous way, evidently thinking that because I am little and young nothing great or mature is to be found in me; but they shall soon find it out. Herr Cannabich is to take me himself to-morrow to Count Savioli, the Intendant of Music. One good thing is that the Elector's name-day is close at hand. The oratorio they are rehearsing is Handel's, but I did not stay to hear it, for they first rehearsed a Psalm Magnificat of the Vice-Capellmeister here, [Abbe] Vogler, which lasted a good hour. I must now conclude, for I have still to write to my cousin.

71. Mannheim, Nov. 4, 1777.

I am at Cannabich's every day, and mamma went with me there to-day. He is a very different man from what he formerly was, [FOOTNOTE: Mozart had been at his house, when a boy, with his father.] and the whole orchestra say the same. He is very fond of me. He has a daughter who plays the piano very nicely, and in order to make him still more friendly towards me I am working just now at a sonata for her, which is finished all but the Rondo. When I had completed the first allegro and andante, I took it to him myself and played it over; you can't think what applause this sonata receives. There chanced to be some of the musicians there at the moment—young Danner, Lang, who plays the French horn, and the hautboy-player, whose name I forget, but who plays remarkably well, and has a pleasing delicate tone [Ramm]. I made him a present of a concerto for the hautboy; it is being copied in Cannabich's room. The man is wild with delight. I played him the concerto to-day at Cannabich's, and THOUGH KNOWN TO BE MINE it pleased very much. No one said that it was NOT WELL COMPOSED, because people here don't understand these things. They ought to apply to the Archbishop; he would soon put them on the right scent. [FOOTNOTE: The Archbishop never was satisfied with any of the compositions that Mozart wrote for his concerts, but invariably had some fault to find with them.] I played all my six sonatas to-day at Cannabich's. Herr Kapellmeister Holzbauer went with me to-day to Count Savioli's. Cannabich was there at the time. Herr Holzbauer said to the Count in

Italian that I wished to have the honor of playing before his Serene Highness the Elector. "I was here fifteen years ago," said I, "but now I am older and more advanced, and I may say in music also"—"Oh!" said the Count, "you are"—I have no idea whom he took me for, as Cannabich interrupted him, but I affected not to hear, and entered into conversation with the others. Still I observed that he was speaking of me very earnestly. The Count then said to me, "I hear that you play the piano very tolerably?" I bowed.

I must now tell you about the music here. On Saturday, All-Saints' day, I attended high mass. The orchestra is very good and numerous. On each side ten or eleven violins, four tenors, two hautboys, two flutes, and two clarionets, two corni, four violoncellos, four bassoons, and four double basses, besides trumpets and kettle-drums. This should give fine music, but I would not venture to produce one of my masses here. Why? From their being short? No, everything is liked short. From their church style? By no means; but solely because NOW in Mannheim, under present circumstances, it is necessary to write chiefly for the instruments, for nothing can possibly be conceived worse than the voices here. Six soprani, six alti, six tenori, and six bassi, to twenty violins and twelve bassi, are in the same proportion as 0 to 1. Is it not so, Herr Bullinger? It proceeds from this:—The Italians are miserably represented: they have only two musici here, and they are already old. This race is dying out. These soprano singers, too, would prefer singing counter-tenor; for they can no longer take the high notes. The few boys they have are wretched. The tenor and bass just like our singers at funerals. Vogler, who lately conducted the mass, is barren and frivolous—a man who imagines he can do a great deal, and does very little. The whole orchestra dislike him. To-day, Sunday, I heard a mass of Holzbauer's, which is now twenty-six years old, but excellent. He writes very well, and has a good church style, arranges the vocal parts as well as the instrumental, and writes good fugues. They have two organists here; it would be worth while to come to Mannheim on purpose to hear them—which I had a famous opportunity of doing, as it is the custom here for the organist to play during the whole of the Benedictus. I heard the second organist first, and then the other. In my opinion the second is preferable to the first; for when I heard the former, I asked, "Who is that playing on the organ?" "Our second organist." "He plays miserably." When the other began, I said, "Who may that be?" "Our first organist." "Why, he plays more miserably still." I believe if they were pounded together, something even worse would be the result. It is enough to kill one with laughing to look at these gentlemen. The second at the organ is like a child trying to lift a millstone. You can see his anguish in his face. The first wears spectacles. I stood beside him at the organ and watched him with the intention of learning something from him; at each note he lifts his hands entirely off the keys. What he believes to be his forte is to play in six parts, but he mostly makes fifths and octaves. He often chooses to dispense altogether with his right hand when there is not the slightest need to do so, and plays with the left alone; in short, he fancies that he can do as he will, and that he is a thorough master of his organ.

Mamma sends her love to you all; she cannot possibly write, for she has still to say her officium. We came home very late from the grand opera rehearsal. I must go to-morrow after high mass to the illustrious Electress; she is resolved absolument to teach me to knit filee. I am very eager about this, as she and the Elector wish that I should knit in public next Thursday at the great gala concert. The young Princess here, who is a child compared with the Electress, knits very prettily. The Zweenbruck and his Zwobrucken (Deux Ponts) arrived here at eight o'clock. A propos, mamma and I earnestly beg you, dear papa, to send our charming cousin a souvenir; we both regretted so much having nothing with us, but we promised to write to you to send her something. We wish two things to be sent—a double neckerchief in mamma's name, like the one she wears, and in mine some ornament; a box, or etui, or anything you like, only it must be pretty, for she deserves it. [FOOTNOTE: The father was still in possession of many of the ornaments and jewels presented to these children during their artistic tours.] She and her father took a great deal of trouble on our account, and wasted much time on us. My cousin took the receipts for me at my concert. Addio!

72. Mannheim, Nov. 5, 1777.

My dear Coz—Buzz,—

I have safely received your precious epistle—thistle, and from it I perceive—achieve, that my aunt—gaunt, and you—shoe, are quite well—bell. I have to-day a letter—setter, from my papa— ah-ha, safe in my hands—sands. I hope you also got—trot, my Mannheim letter—

setter. Now for a little sense—pence. The prelate's seizure—leisure, grieves me much—touch, but he will, I hope, get well—sell. You write—blight, you will keep—cheap, your promise to write to me—he-he, to Augsburg soon—spoon. Well, I shall be very glad—mad. You further write, indeed you declare, you pretend, you hint, you vow, you explain, you distinctly say, you long, you wish, you desire, you choose, command, and point out, you let me know and inform me that I must send you my portrait soon—moon. Eh, bien! you shall have it before long—song. Now I wish you good night—tight.

The 5th.—Yesterday I conversed with the illustrious Electress; and to-morrow, the 6th, I am to play in the gala concert, and afterwards, by desire of the Princess, in their private apartments. Now for something rational! I beg of you—why not?—I beg of you, my very dear cousin—why not?—when you write to Madame Tavernier in Munich, to convey a message from me to the two Demoiselles Freysinger—why not? odd enough! but why not?— and I humbly ask pardon of Madlle. Josepha—I mean the youngest, and pray why not? why should I not ask her pardon? strange! but I don't know why I should not, so I do ask her pardon very humbly— for not having yet sent the sonata I promised her, but I mean to do so as soon as possible. Why not? I don't know why not. I can now write no more—which makes my heart sore. To all my kind friends much love—dove. Addio! Your old young, till death— breath,

WOLFGANG AMADE ROSENCRANZ.
Miennham, eht ht5 rebotoc, 7771.

73. Mannheim, Nov. 8, 1777.

This forenoon, at Herr Cannabich's, I wrote the Rondo of the sonata for his daughter; so they would not let me leave them all day. The Elector and the Electress, and the whole court, are very much pleased with me. Both times I played at the concert, the Elector and she stood close beside me at the piano. After the music was at an end, Cannabich managed that I should be noticed by the court. I kissed the Elector's hand, who said, "I think it is now fifteen years since you were here?" "Yes, your Highness, it is fifteen years since I had that honor." "You play

73. Mannheim, Nov. 8, 1777.

inimitably." The Princess, when I kissed her hand, said, "Monsieur, je vous assure, on ne peut pas jouer mieux."

Yesterday I went with Cannabich to pay the visit mamma already wrote to you about [to Duke Carl Theodor's children], and there I conversed with the Elector as if he had been some kind friend. He is a most gracious and good Prince. He said to me, "I hear you wrote an opera at Munich" ["La finta Giardiniera"]? "Yes, your Highness, and, with your gracious permission, my most anxious wish is to write an opera here; I entreat you will not quite forget me. I could also write a German one, God be praised!" said I, smiling. "That may easily be arranged." He has one son and three daughters, the eldest of whom and the young Count play the piano. The Elector questioned me confidentially about his children. I spoke quite honestly, but without detracting from their master. Cannabich was entirely of my opinion. The Elector, on going away, took leave of me with much courtesy.

After dinner to-day I went, at two o'clock, with Cannabich to Wendling's, the flute-player, where they were all complaisance. The daughter, who was formerly the Elector's favorite, plays the piano very prettily; afterwards I played. I cannot describe to you the happy mood I was in. I played extempore, and then three duets with the violin, which I had never in my life seen, nor do I now know the name of the author. They were all so delighted that I—was desired to embrace the ladies. No hard task with the daughter, for she is very pretty.

We then went again to the Elector's children; I played three times, and from my heart too,—the Elector himself each time asking me to play. He seated himself each time close to me and never stirred. I also asked a certain Professor there to give me a theme for a fugue, and worked it out.

Now for my congratulations!

My very dearest papa,—I cannot write poetically, for I am no poet. I cannot make fine artistic phrases that cast light and shadow, for I am no painter; I can neither by signs nor by pantomime express my thoughts and feelings, for I am no dancer; but I can by tones, for I am a musician. So to-morrow, at Cannabich's, I intend to play my congratulations both for your name-day and birthday. Mon tres-cher pere, I can only on this day wish for you, what from my whole heart I wish for you every day and every night—health, long life, and a cheerful spirit. I would fain hope, too, that you have now less annoyance than when I was in Salzburg; for I must admit that I was the chief cause of this. They treated me badly, which I did not deserve, and you naturally took my part, only too lovingly. I can tell you this was indeed one of the principal and most urgent reasons for my leaving Salzburg in such haste. I hope, therefore, that my wish is fulfilled. I must now close by a musical congratulation. I wish that you may live as many years as must elapse before no more new music can be composed. Farewell! I earnestly beg you to go on loving me a little, and, in the mean time, to excuse these very poor congratulations till I open new shelves in my small and confined knowledge-box, where I can stow away the good sense which I have every intention to acquire.

74. Mannheim, Nov. 13, 1777.

We received your last two letters, and now I must answer them in detail. Your letter desiring me to inquire about Becke's parents [in Wallerstein, No. 68] I did not get till I had gone to Mannheim, so too late to comply with your wish; but it never would have occurred to me to do so, for, in truth, I care very little about him. Would you like to know how I was received by him? Well and civilly; tbat is, he asked where I was going. I said, most probably to Paris. He then gave me a vast deal of advice, saying he had recently been there, and adding, "You will make a great deal by giving lessons, for the piano is highly prized in Paris." He also arranged that I should dine at the officers' table, and promised to put me in the way of speaking to the Prince. He regretted very much having at that moment a sore throat, (which was indeed quite true,) so that he could not go out with me himself to procure me some amusement. He was also sorry that he could have no music in honor of me, because most of the musical people had gone that very day on some pedestrian excursion to—Heaven knows where! At his request I tried his piano, which is very good. He often said Bravo! I extemporized, and also played the sonatas in B and D. In short, he was very polite, and I was also polite, but grave. We conversed on a variety of topics—among others, about Vienna, and more particularly that the Emperor [Joseph II.] was no great lover of music. He said, "It is true he has some knowledge of composition, but of nothing else. I can still recall (and he rubbed his forehead) that when I was to play before him I had no idea what to play; so I began with some fugues and trifles of that kind, which in my own

74. Mannheim, Nov. 13, 1777.

mind I only laughed at." I could scarcely resist saying, "I can quite fancy your laughing, but scarcely so loud as I must have done had I heard you!" He further said (what is the fact) that the music in the Emperor's private apartments is enough to frighten the crows. I replied, that whenever I heard such music, if I did not quickly leave the room it gave me a headache. "Oh! no; it has no such effect on me; bad music does not affect my nerves, but fine music never fails to give me a headache." I thought to myself again, such a shallow head as yours is sure to suffer when listening to what is beyond its comprehension.

Now for some of our news here. I was desired to go yesterday with Cannabich to the Intendant, Count Savioli, to receive my present. It was just what I had anticipated—a handsome gold watch. Ten Carolins would have pleased me better just now, though the watch and chain, with its appendages, are valued at twenty Carolins. Money is what is most needed on a journey; and, by your leave, I have now five watches. Indeed, I have serious thoughts of having a second watch-pocket made, and, when I visit a grandee, to wear two watches, (which is indeed the fashion here,) that no one may ever again think of giving me another. I see from your letter that you have not yet read Vogler's book. [FOOTNOTE: Ton Wissenschaft und Ton Kunst.] I have just finished it, having borrowed it from Cannabich. His history is very short. He came here in a miserable condition, performed on the piano, and composed a ballet. This excited the Elector's compassion, who sent him to Italy. When the Elector was in Bologna, he questioned Father Valoti about Vogler. "Oh! your Highness, he is a great man," He then asked Father Martini the same question. "Your Highness, he has talent; and by degrees, when he is older and more solid, he will no doubt improve, though he must first change considerably." When Vogler came back he entered the Church, was immediately appointed Court Chaplain, and composed a Miserere which all the world declares to be detestable, being full of false harmony. Hearing; that it was not much commended, he went to the Elector and complained that the orchestra played badly on purpose to vex and annoy him; in short, he knew so well how to make his game (entering into so many petty intrigues with women) that he became Vice-Capellmeister. He is a fool, who fancies that no one can be better or more perfect than himself. The whole orchestra, from the first to the last, detest him. He has been the cause of much annoyance to Holzbauer. His book is more fit to teach arithmetic than composition. He says that he can make a composer in three weeks, and a singer in six months; but we have not yet seen any proof of this. He despises the greatest masters. To myself he spoke with contempt of Bach [Johann Christian, J. Sebastian's youngest son, called the London Bach], who wrote two operas here, the first of which pleased more than the second, Lucio Silla. As I had composed the same opera in Milan, I was anxious to see it, and hearing from Holzbauer that Vogler had it, I asked him to lend it to me. "With all my heart," said he; "I will send it to you to-morrow without fail, but you won't find much talent in it. Some days after, when he saw me, he said with a sneer, "Well, did you discover anything very fine— did you learn anything from it? One air is rather good. What are the words?" asked he of some person standing near. "What air do you mean?" "Why, that odious air of Bach's, that vile—oh! yes, pupille amate. He must have written it after a carouse of punch." I really thought I must have laid hold of his pigtail; I affected, however, not to hear him, said nothing, and went away. He has now served out his time with the Elector.

The sonata for Madlle. Rosa Cannabich is finished. Last Sunday I played the organ in the chapel for my amusement. I came in while the Kyrie was going on, played the last part, and when the priest intoned the Gloria I made a cadence, so different, however, from what is usually heard here, that every one looked round in surprise, and above all Holzbauer. He said to me, "If I had known you were coming, I would have put out another mass for you." "Oh!" said I, "to puzzle me, I suppose?" Old Toeschi and Wendling stood all the time close beside me. I gave them enough to laugh at. Every now and then came a pizzicato, when I rattled the keys well; I was in my best humor. Instead of the Benedictus here, there is always a voluntary, so I took the ideas of the Sanctus and worked them out in a fugue. There they all stood making faces. At the close, after Ita missa est, I played a fugue. Their pedal is different from ours, which at first rather puzzled me, but I soon got used to it. I must now conclude. Pray write to us still at Mannheim. I know all about Misliweczeck's sonatas [see No. 64], and played them lately at Munich; they are very easy and agreeable to listen to. My advice is that my sister, to whom I humbly commend myself, should play them with much expression, taste, and fire, and learn them by heart. For these are sonatas which cannot fail to please every one, are not difficult to commit to memory, and produce a good effect when played with precision.

75. Mannheim, Nov. 13, 1777.

Potz Himmel! Croatians, demons, witches, hags, and cross batteries! Potz Element! air, earth, fire, and water! Europe, Asia, Africa, and America! Jesuits, Augustines, Benedictines, Capucins, Minorites, Franciscans, Dominicans, Carthusians, and Knights of the Cross! privateers, canons regular and irregular, sluggards, rascals, scoundrels, imps, and villains all! donkeys, buffaloes, oxen, fools, blockheads, numskulls, and foxes! What means this? Four soldiers and three shoulder-belts! Such a thick packet and no portrait! [FOOTNOTE: The "Basle" (his cousin) had promised him her portrait. She sent it subsequently to Salzburg, where it still hangs in the Mozarteum.] I was so anxious about it—indeed, I felt sure of getting it, having yourself written long ago to say that I should have it soon, very soon. Perhaps you doubt my keeping my promise [about the ornaments—see No. 71], but I cannot think this either. So pray let me have the likeness as quickly as you can; and I trust it is taken as I entreated—in French costume.

How do I like Mannheim? As well as I can any place where my cousin is not. I hope, on the other hand, that you have at all events received my two letters—one from Hohenaltheim, and one from Mannheim—this, such as it is, being the third from here, but making the fourth in all. I must conclude, for we are just going to dinner, and I am not yet dressed. Love me as I love you, and then we shall never cease loving each other. Adieu! J'espere que vous aurez deja pris quelque lection dans la langue francaise, et je ne doute point que—ecoutez!—que vous aurez bientot le francais mieux que moi; car il y a certainement deux ans que je n'ai pas ecrit un mot de cette langue. Encore adieu! Je vous baise les mains.

76. Mannheim, Nov. 14-16, 1777.

I, Johannes, Chrysostomus, Amadeus, Wolfgangus, Sigismundus, Mozart, plead guilty to having both yesterday and the day before (and very often besides) stayed away from home till twelve o'clock at night, from ten o'clock till the aforesaid hour, I being in the presence and company of M. Cannabich, his wife and daughter, the Herrn Schatzmeister, Ramm, and Lang, making doggerel rhymes with the utmost facility, in thought and word, but not in deed. I should not, however, have conducted myself in so reckless a manner if our ringleader, namely, the so-called Lisel (Elisabeth Cannabich), had not inveigled and instigated me to mischief, and I am bound to admit that I took great pleasure in it myself. I confess all these my sins and shortcomings from the depths of my heart; and in the hope of often having similar ones to confess, I firmly resolve to amend my present sinful life. I therefore beg for a dispensation if it can be granted; but, if not, it is a matter of indifference to me, for the game will go on all the same. Lusus enim suum habet ambitum, says the pious singer Meissner, (chap. 9, p. 24,) and also the pious Ascenditor, patron of singed coffee, musty lemonade, milk of almonds with no almonds in it, and, above all, strawberry ice full of lumps of ice, being himself a great connoisseur and artist in these delicacies.

The sonata I composed for Madlle. Cannabich I intend to write out as soon as possible on small paper, and to send it to my sister. I began to teach it to Madlle. Rose three days ago, and she has learned the allegro. The andante will give us most trouble, for it is full of expression, and must be played with accuracy and taste, and the fortes and pianos given just as they are marked. She is very clever, and learns with facility. Her right hand is very good, but the left is unhappily quite ruined. I must say that I do really feel very sorry for her, when I see her laboring away till she is actually panting for breath; and this not from natural awkwardness on her part, but because, being so accustomed to this method, she cannot play in any other way, never having been shown the right one. I said, both to her mother and herself, that if I were her regular master I would lock up all her music, cover the keys of the piano with a handkerchief, and make her exercise her right and left hand, at first quite slowly in nothing but passages and shakes, until her hands were thoroughly trained; and after that I should feel confident of making her a genuine pianiste. They both acknowledged that I was right. It is a sad pity; for she has so much genius, reads very tolerably, has great natural aptitude, and plays with great feeling.

Now about the opera briefly. Holzbauer's music [for the first great German operetta, "Gunther von Schwarzburg"] is very beautiful, but the poetry is not worthy of such music. What surprises me most is, that so old a man as Holzbauer should still have so much spirit, for the opera is

76. Mannheim, Nov. 14-16, 1777.

incredibly full of fire. The prima donna was Madame Elisabeth Wendling, not the wife of the flute-player, but of the violinist. She is in very delicate health; and, besides, this opera was not written for her, but for a certain Madame Danzi, who is now in England; so it does not suit her voice, and is too high for her. Herr Raaff, in four arias of somewhere about 450 bars, sang in a manner which gave rise to the remark that his want of voice was the principal cause of his singing so badly. When he begins an air, unless at the same moment it recurs to your mind that this is Raaff, the old but once so renowned tenor, I defy any one not to burst out laughing. It is a fact, that in my own case I thought, if I did not know that this is the celebrated Raaff, I should be bent double from laughing, but as it is—I only take out my handkerchief to hide a smile. They tell me here that he never was a good actor; that people went to hear, but not to see him. He has by no means a pleasing exterior. In this opera he was to die, singing in a long, long, slow air; and he died laughing! and towards the end of the aria his voice failed him so entirely that it was impossible to stand it! I was in the orchestra next Wendling the flute-player, and as he had previously criticized the song, saying it was unnatural to sing so long before dying, adding, "I do think he will never die!" I said in return, "Have a little patience; it will soon be all over with him, for I can hear he is at the last gasp!" "And I too," said he, laughing. The second singer, Madlle. Strasserin, sang very well, and is an admirable actress.

There is a national stage here, which is permanent like that at Munich; German operettas are sometimes given, but the singers in them are wretched. Yesterday I dined with the Baron and Baroness von Hagen, Oberstjagermeister here. Three days ago I called on Herr Schmalz, a banker, to whom Herr Herzog, or rather Nocker and Schidl, had given me a letter. I expected to have found a very civil good sort of man. When I gave him the letter he read it through, made me a slight bow, and said nothing. At last, after many apologies for not having sooner waited on him, I told him that I had played before the Elector. "Really!" Altum silentium. I said nothing, he said nothing. At last I began again: "I will no longer intrude on you. I have the honor to"—Here he interrupted me. "If I can be of any service to you, I beg"— "Before I leave this I must take the liberty to ask you"—"Not for money?" "Yes, if you will be so good as to"—"Oh! that I can't do; there is nothing in the letter about money. I cannot give you any money, but anything else"—"There is nothing else in which you can serve me—nothing whatever. I have the honor to take my leave." I wrote the whole history yesterday to Herr Herzog in Augsburg. We must now wait here for the answer, so you may still write to us at Mannheim. I kiss your hand, and am your young brother and father, as in your last letter you say "I am the old man and son." To-day is the 16th when I finish this, or else you will not know when it was sent off. "Is the letter ready?" "Yes, mamma, here it is!"

77. Mannheim, Nov. 20, 1777.

The gala began again yesterday [in honor of the Elector's name-day]. I went to hear the mass, which was a spick-and-span new composition of Vogler's. Two days ago I was present at the rehearsal in the afternoon, but came away immediately after the Kyrie. I never in my life heard anything like it; there is often false harmony, and he rambles into the different keys as if he wished to drag you into them by the hair of your head; but it neither repays the trouble, nor does it possess any originality, but is only quite abrupt. I shall say nothing of the way in which he carries out his ideas. I only say that no mass of Vogler's can possibly please any composer (who deserves the name). For example, I suddenly hear an idea which is NOT BAD. Well, instead of remaining NOT BAD, no doubt it soon becomes good? Not at all! it becomes not only BAD, but VERY BAD, and this in two or three different ways: namely, scarcely has the thought arisen when something else interferes to destroy it; or he does not finish it naturally, so that it may remain good; or it is not introduced in the right place; or it is finally ruined by bad instrumentation. Such is Vogler's music.

Cannabich composes far better than when we knew him in Paris, but what both mamma and I remarked here at once in the symphonies is, that one begins just like another, always slow and unisono. I must now, dear papa, write you something about the Holy Cross in Augsburg, which I have always forgotten to do. I met with a great many civilities there, and the Prelate is the most good-natured man in the world—a kind, worthy old simpleton, who may be carried off at any moment, for his breath fails sadly. He recently—in fact, the very day we left—had an attack of paralysis. He, and the Dean and Procurator, begged us when we came back to Augsburg to drive straight to the Holy Cross. The Procurator is as jolly as Father Leopold at Seeon.

78. Mannheim, Nov. 22, 1777.

[FOOTNOTE: A cloister in Lower Bavaria, that Wolfgang often visited with his father, as they had a dear friend there, Father Johannes.] My cousin told me beforehand what kind of man he was, so we soon became as well acquainted as if we had known each other for twenty years. I lent him the mass in F, and the first of the short masses in C, and the offertorium in counterpoint in D minor. My fair cousin has undertaken to be custodian of these. I got back the offertorium punctually, having desired that it should be returned first. They all, and even the Prelate, plagued me to give them a litany, De venerabili. I said I had not got it with me. I really was by no means sure; so I searched, but did not find it. They gave me no peace, evidently thinking that I only wished to evade their request; so I said, "I really have not the litany with me; it is at Salzburg. Write to my father; it is his affair. If he chooses to give it to you, well and good; if not, I have nothing to do with it." A letter from the Deacon to you will therefore probably soon make its appearance. Do just as you please, but if you do send him one, let it be the last in E flat; they have voices enough for anything, and a great many people will be assembled at that time; they even write for them to come from a distance, for it is their greatest festival. Adieu!

78. Mannheim, Nov. 22, 1777.

THE first piece of information that I have to give you is, that my truthful letter to Herr Herzog in Augsburg, puncto Schmalzii, has had a capital effect. He wrote me a very polite letter in return, expressing his annoyance that I should have been received so uncourteously by detto Schmalz [melted butter]; so he herewith sent me a sealed letter to detto Herr Milk, with a bill of exchange for 150 florins on detto Herr Cheese. You must know that, though I only saw Herr Herzog once, I could not resist asking him to send me a draft on Herr Schmalz, or to Herrn Butter, Milk, and Cheese, or whom he would—a ca! This joke has succeeded; it is no good making a poor mouth!

We received this forenoon (the 21st) your letter of the 17th. I was not at home, but at Cannabich's, where Wendling was rehearsing a concerto for which I have written the orchestral accompaniments. To-day at six o'clock the gala concert took place. I had the pleasure of hearing Herr Franzl (who married a sister of Madame Cannabich's) play a concerto on the violin; he pleased me very much. You know that I am no lover of mere difficulties. He plays difficult music, but it does not appear to be so; indeed, it seems as if one could easily do the same, and this is real talent. He has a very fine round tone, not a note wanting, and everything distinct and well accentuated. He has also a beautiful staccato in bowing, both up and down, and I never heard such a double shake as his. In short, though in my opinion no WIZARD, he is a very solid violin-player.—I do wish I could conquer my confounded habit of writing crooked.

I am sorry I was not at Salzburg when that unhappy occurrence took place about Madame Adlgasserin, so that I might have comforted her; and that I would have done—particularly being so handsome a woman. [Footnote: Adlgasser was the organist of the cathedral. His wife was thought very stupid. See the letter of August 26, 1781.] I know already all that you write to me about Mannheim, but I never wish to say anything prematurely; all in good time. Perhaps in my next letter I may tell you of something VERY GOOD in your eyes, but only GOOD in mine; or something you will think VERY BAD, but I TOLERABLE; possibly, too, something only TOLERABLE for you, but VERY GOOD, PRECIOUS, and DELIGHTFUL for me! This sounds rather oracular, does it not? It is ambiguous, but still may be divined.

My regards to Herr Bullinger; every time that I get a letter from you, usually containing a few lines from him, I feel ashamed, as it reminds me that I have never once written to my best and truest friend, from whom I have received so much kindness and civility. But I cannot try to excuse myself. I only beg of him to do so for me as far as possible, and to believe that, as soon as I have a little leisure, I will write to him—as yet I have had none; for from the moment I know that it is even possible or probable that I may leave a place, I have no longer a single hour I can call my own, and though I have now a glimmer of hope, still I shall not be at rest till I know how things are. One of the oracle's sayings must come to pass. I think it will be the middle one or the last—I care not which, for at all events it will be something settled.

I no doubt wrote to you that Holzbauer's grand opera is in German. If not, I write it now. The title is "Gunther von Schwarzburg," but not our worshipful Herr Gunther, barber and councillor at Salzburg! "Rosamunde" is to be given during the ensuing Carnival, the libretto being a recent composition of Wieland's, and the music also a new composition of Herr Schweitzer. Both are to come here. I have already seen some parts of the opera and tried it over on the piano, but I say nothing about it as yet. The target you have had painted for me, to be given in my name to the shooting-match, is first-rate, and the verses inimitable. [Footnote: For cross-bow practice, attended weekly by a circle of his Salzburg friends. On the target was represented "the melancholy farewell of two persons dissolved in tears, Wolfgang and the 'Basle.'"] I have now no more to write, except that I wish you all a good night's rest, and that you may all sleep soundly till this letter comes to wake you. Adieu! I embrace from my heart—cart, my dear sister—blister, and am your dutiful and attached son,

WOLFGANG AMADE MOZART,

Knight of the Golden Spur, Member of the great Verona Academy, Bologna—oui, mon ami!

79. Mannheim, Nov. 26, 1777.

—MOREOVER, every one acquainted with Mannheim, even the nobility, advised me to come here. The reason why we are still in this place is that I have some thoughts of remaining the winter here, and I am only waiting for an answer from the Elector to decide my plans. The Intendant, Count Savioli, is a very worthy gentleman, and I told him to inform the Elector that, this being such severe weather for travelling, I am willing to remain here to teach the young Count [Carl Theodor's son]. He promised me to do his best for me, but said that I must have patience till the gala days were over. All this took place with the consent and at the SUGGESTION of Cannabich. When I told him that I had spoken to Savioli and what I had said, he replied he really thought it was more likely to be brought about than not. Indeed, Cannabich spoke to the Elector on the subject before the Count did so; and now I must wait to hear the result. I am going to call on Herr Schmalz to draw my 150 florins, for my landlord would no doubt prefer the sound of gold to that of music. I little thought that I should have the gift of a watch here, [see No. 74,] but such is again the case. I would have been off long ago, but every one says to me, "Where do you intend to go for the winter? Travelling is detestable in such weather; stay here." Cannabich also wishes it very much; so now I have taken steps to do so, and as such an affair cannot be hurried, I must wait with patience, and I hope soon to be able to send you good news. I have already two pupils certain, besides the ARCH ones, who certainly won't give me less than a louis each monthly. Without these I could not indeed manage to remain. Now let the matter rest as it is, or as it may be, what avail useless speculations? What is to occur we do not know; still in so far we do! what God wills!

Now for a cheerful allegro—non siete si pegro. [Footnote: "Don't be so desponding."] If we do leave this, we shall go straight to- -where? To Weilburg, or whatever the name of the place may be, to the Princess, sister of the Prince of Orange, whom we knew so well at the Hague. There we shall stay—N. B., so long as we like the officers' table, and no doubt receive at least six louis- d'or.

A few days ago Herr Sterkel came here from Wurzburg. The day before yesterday, the 24th, I dined with Cannabich's, and again at Oberstjager von Hagen's, and spent the evening al solito with Cannabich, where Sterkel joined us, [Footnote: Abbe Sterkel, a favorite composer and virtuoso on the piano, whom Beethoven, along with Simrock, Ries, and the two Rombergs, visited in the autumn of 1791, in Aschaffenberg.] and played five duets [sonatas with violin], but so quick that it was difficult to follow the music, and neither distinctly nor in time. Every one said the same. Madlle. Cannabich played my six sonatas, and in fact better than Sterkel. I must now conclude, for I cannot write in bed, and I am too sleepy to sit up any longer.

80. Mannheim, Nov. 29, 1777.

I RECEIVED this morning your letter of the 24th, and perceive that you cannot reconcile yourself to the chances of good or bad fortune, if, indeed, the latter is to befall us. Hitherto, we four have neither been very lucky nor very unlucky, for which I thank God. You make us many reproaches which we do not deserve. We spend nothing but what is absolutely necessary, and as to what is required on a journey, you know that as well or better than we do. No one BUT MYSELF has been the cause of our remaining so long in Munich; and had I been alone I should have stayed there altogether. Why were we fourteen days in Augsburg? Surely you cannot have got my letters from there? I wished to give a concert. They played me false, so I thus lost eight days. I was absolument determined to go away, but was not allowed, so strong was the wish that I should give a concert. I wished to be urged to do so, and I was urged. I gave the concert; this accounts for the fourteen days. Why did we go

80. Mannheim, Nov. 29, 1777.

direct to Mannheim? This I answered in my last letter. Why are we still here? How can you suppose that I would stay here without good cause? But my father, at all events, should—Well! you shall hear my reasons and the whole course of the affair; but I had quite resolved not to write to you on the subject until I could say something decided, (which even yet I cannot do,) on purpose to avoid causing you care and anxiety, which I always strive to do, for I knew that uncertain intelligence would only fret you. But when you ascribe this to my negligence, thoughtlessness, and indolence, I can only regret your having such an opinion of me, and from my heart grieve that you so little know your son. I am not careless, I am only prepared for the worst; so I can wait and bear everything patiently, so long as my honor and my good name of Mozart remain uninjured. But if it must be so, so let it be. I only beg that you will neither rejoice nor lament prematurely; for whatever may happen, all will be well if we only have health; for happiness exists—merely in the imagination.

Last Thursday week I went in the forenoon to wait on Count Savioli, and asked him if it were possible to induce the Elector to keep me here this winter, as I was anxious to give lessons to his children. His answer was, "I will suggest it to the Elector, and if it depends on me, the thing will certainly be done." In the afternoon I went to Cannabich's, and as I had gone to Savioli by his advice, he immediately asked me if I had been there. I told him everything, on which he said, "I should like you very much to spend the winter with us, but still more to see you in some permanent situation." I replied, "I could wish nothing better than to be settled near you, but I don't see how it is possible. You have already two Capellmeisters, so I don't know what I could have, for I would not be subordinate to Vogler." "That you would never be," said he. "Here not one of the orchestra is under the Capellmeister, nor even under the Intendant. The Elector might appoint you Chamber Court composer; only wait a little, and I will speak to Count Savioli on the subject." On the Thursday after there was a grand concert. When the Count saw me, he apologized for not having yet spoken to the Elector, these being still gala days; but as soon as they were over (next Monday) he would certainly speak to his Royal Highness. I let three days pass, and, still hearing nothing whatever, I went to him to make inquiries. He said, "My good M. Mozart, (this was yesterday, Friday,) today there was a chasse, so it was impossible for me to ask the Elector, but to-morrow at this hour I will certainly give you an answer." I begged him not to forget it. To tell you the truth, when I left him I felt rather indignant, so I resolved to take with me the easiest of my six variations of the Fischer minuet, (which I wrote here for this express purpose,) to present to the young Count, in order to have an opportunity to speak to the Elector myself. When I went there, you cannot conceive the delight of the governess, by whom I was most politely received. When I produced the variations, and said that they were intended for the young Count, she said, "Oh! that is charming, but I hope you have something for the Countess also." "Nothing as yet," said I, "but if I stay here long enough to have time to write something I will do so." "A propos," said she, "I am so glad that you stay the winter here." "I? I have not heard a word of it." "That does surprise me; how very odd! for the Elector told me so himself lately; he said, 'By the by, Mozart remains here all winter.'" "Well, when he said so, he was the only man who could say so, for without the Elector I of course cannot remain here;" and then I told her the whole story. We agreed that I should come the next day (that is, to-day) at four o'clock, and bring some piece of music for the Countess. She was to speak to the Elector before I came; and I should be certain to meet him. I went today, but he had not been there at all; but I shall go again to-morrow. I have written a Rondo for the Countess. Have I not then sufficient cause to stay here and await the result? As this important step is finally taken, ought I at this moment to set off? I have now an opportunity of speaking to the Elector myself. I shall most probably spend the winter here, for I am a favorite with his Royal Highness, who thinks highly of me, and knows what I can do. I hope to be able to give you good news in my next letter. I entreat you once more neither to rejoice nor to be uneasy too soon, and not to confide the affair to any one except Herr Bullinger and my sister. I send my sister the allegro and the andante of the sonata I wrote for Madlle. Cannabich. The Rondo will follow shortly; the packet would have been too heavy had I sent it with the others. You must be satisfied with the original, for you can more easily get it copied for six kreutzers a sheet than I for twenty-four. Is not that dear? Adieu! Possibly you have heard some stray bits of this sonata; for at Cannabich's it is sung three times a day at least, played on the piano and violin, or whistled—only sotto voce, to be sure.

81. Mannheim, Dec. 3, 1777.

I CAN still write nothing certain about my fate here. Last Monday, after going three days in succession to my ARCH pupils, morning and afternoon, I had the good fortune at last to meet the Elector. We all, indeed, thought that I had again come in vain, as it was so late in the day, but at length we saw him coming. The governess made the Countess seat herself at the piano, and I placed myself beside her to give her a lesson, and it was thus the Elector found us on entering. We rose, but he desired us to continue the lesson. When she had finished playing, the governess addressed him, saying that I had written a beautiful Rondo. I played it, and it pleased him exceedingly. At last he said, "Do you think that she will be able to learn it?" "Oh! yes," said I; "I only wish I had the good fortune to teach it to her myself." He smiled, and said, "I should also like it; but would it not be prejudicial to her to have two masters?" "Oh, no! your Highness," said I; "it all depends on whether she has a good or a bad one. I hope your Highness will place trust and confidence in me." "Oh, assuredly," said he. The governess then said, "M. Mozart has also written these variations on the Fischer minuet for the young Count." I played them, and he seemed to like them much. He now began to jest with the Countess. I thanked him for his present of a watch. He said, "I must reflect on your wish; how long do you intend to remain here?" My answer was, "As long as your Highness commands me to do so;" and then the interview was at an end. I went there again this morning, and was told that the Elector had repeated yesterday, "Mozart stays here this winter." Now I am fairly in for it; so you see I must wait.

I dined to-day (for the fourth time) with Wendling. Before dinner, Count Savioli came in with Capellmeister Schweitzer, who arrived yesterday evening. Savioli said to me, "I spoke again yesterday to the Elector, but he has not yet made up his mind." I answered, "I wish to say a few words to you privately;" so we went to the window. I told him the doubt the Elector had expressed, and complained of the affair dragging on so long, and said how much I had already spent here, entreating him to persuade the Elector to engage me permanently; for I fear that he will give me so little during the winter that it will be impossible for me to remain. "Let him give me work; for I like work." He said he would certainly suggest it to him, but this evening it was out of the question, as he was not to go to court; to-morrow, however, he promised me a decided answer. Now, let what will happen. If he does not engage me, I shall, at all events, apply for a sum of money for my travelling expenses, as I have no intention to make him a present of the Rondo and the variations. I assure you I am very easy on the subject, because I feel quite certain that, come what may, all will go right. I am entirely submissive to the will of God.

Your letter of the 27th arrived yesterday, and I hope you received the allegro and andante of the sonata. I now enclose the Rondo. Schweitzer is a good, worthy, upright man, dry and candid like our Haydn; only his mode of speaking is more polished. There are some very beautiful things in his new opera, and I don't doubt that it will prove a great success. "Alceste" is much liked, and yet it is not half so fine as "Rosamunde." Being the first German operetta no doubt contributed very much to its popularity; but now—N. B., on minds chiefly attracted by novelty—it scarcely makes the same impression. Herr Wieland, whose poetry it is, is also to come here this winter. That is a man I should indeed like to see. Who knows? Perhaps I may. When you read this, dear papa, please God, all will be settled.

If I do stay here, I am going to Paris during Lent with Herr Wendling, Herr Ramm, the hautboy-player, who plays admirably, and Ballet-master Cauchery. Wendling assures me I shall never regret it; he has been twice in Paris, and has only just returned from there. He says, "It is, in fact, the only place where either real fame or money is to be acquired. You are a man of genius; I will put you on the right path. You must write an opera seria and comique, an oratorio, and every kind of thing. Any one who composes a couple of operas in Paris receives a certain sum yearly. There is also the Concert Spirituel and the Academie des Amateurs, where you get five louis-d'or for a symphony. If you teach, the custom is three louis-d'or for twelve lessons; and then you get your sonatas, trios, and quartets published by subscription. Cannabich and Toeschi send a great part of their music to Paris." Wendling is a man who understands travelling. Write me your opinion of this scheme, I beg; it seems to me both wise and profitable. I shall travel with a man who knows all the ins and outs of Paris (as it now is) by heart, for it is very much changed. I should spend very little—indeed, I believe not one half of what I do at present, for I should only have to pay for myself, as mamma would stay here, and probably with the Wendlings.

82. Mannheim, Dec. 6, 1777.

On the 12th of this month, Herr Ritter, who plays the bassoon beautifully, sets off for Paris. If I had been alone, this would have been a famous opportunity for me; indeed, he spoke to me himself about it. Ramm (hautboy-player) is a good, jolly, worthy man, about thirty-five, who has travelled a great deal, so has much experience. The first and best musicians here like me very much, and respect me too. They always call me Herr Capellmeister. I cannot say how much I regret not having at least the copy of a mass with me, for I should certainly have had it performed, having lately heard one of Holzbauer's, which is also in our style. If I had only a copy of the Misericordias! But so it is, and it can't be helped now. I would have had one transcribed here, but copying does cost so much. Perhaps I should not have got as much for the mass itself as I must have paid for the copy. People here are by no means so very liberal.

82. Mannheim, Dec. 6, 1777.

I CAN tell you nothing certain yet. I begin to be rather tired of this joke; I am only curious to know the result. Count Savioli has spoken three times to the Elector, and the answer was invariably a shrug of the shoulders, and "I will give you an answer presently, but—I have not yet made up my mind." My kind friends here quite agree with me in thinking that this hesitation and reserve are rather a favorable omen than the reverse. For if the Elector was resolved not to engage me, he would have said so at once; so I attribute the delay to Denari siamo un poco scrocconi [we are a little stingy of our money]. Besides, I know for certain that the Prince likes me; a buon canto, so we must wait. I may now say that it will be very welcome to me if the affair turns out well; if not, I shall much regret having lingered here so long and spent so much money. At all events, whatever the issue may be, it cannot be an evil one if it be the will of God; and my daily prayer is that the result may be in accordance with it. You have indeed, dear papa, rightly guessed the chief cause of Herr Cannabich's friendship for me. There is, however, another small matter in which he can make use of me— namely, he is obliged to publish a collection of all his ballets arranged for the piano. Now, he cannot possibly write these out himself in such a manner that the work may be correct and yet easy. For this purpose I am very welcome to him; (this was the case already with one of his contredanses.) He has been out shooting for the last week, and is not to return till next Tuesday. Such things contribute, indeed, very much to our good friendship; but, independent of this, he would at least never be inimical to me, for he is very much changed. When a man comes to a certain age, and sees his children grown up, he then no doubt thinks a little differently. His daughter, who is fifteen, and his eldest child, is a very pretty, pleasing girl. She has great good sense for her age, and an engaging demeanor; she is rather grave and does not talk much, but what she does say is always amiable and good-natured. She caused me most indescribable pleasure yesterday, by playing my sonata in the most admirable manner. The andante (which must not be played QUICK) she executed with the greatest possible feeling; and she likes to play it. You know that I finished the first allegro when I had been only two days here, and that I had then only seen Madlle. Cannabich once. Young Danner asked me how I intended to compose the andante. "Entirely in accordance with Madlle. Rose's character," said I. When I played it, it seemed to please much. Danner mentioned afterwards what I had said. And it is really so; she is just what the andante is. To-day I dined for the sixth time with Wendling, and for the second time in the company of Herr Schweitzer. To-morrow, by way of a change, I dine there again; I actually have my board there. I must now go to bed, so I wish you good-night.

I have this moment returned from Wendling's, and as soon as I have posted this letter I am going back there, for the opera is to be rehearsed in camera caritatis, as it were. I am going to Cannabich's afterwards, at half-past six o'clock, to give my usual daily music-lesson. A propos, I must correct a statement of mine. I said yesterday that Madlle. Cannabich was fifteen; it seems, however, that she is only just thirteen. Our kind regards to all our friends, especially to Herr Bullinger.

83. Mannheim, Dec. 10, 1777.

ALL is at an end, for the present, with the Elector. I went to the court concert the day before yesterday, in the hope of getting an answer. Count Savioli evidently wished to avoid me; but I went up to him. When he saw me he shrugged his shoulders. "What!" said I, "still no answer?" "Pardon me!" said he, "but I grieve to say nothing can be done." "Eh, bien!" said I, "the Elector might have told me so sooner!" "True," said

83. Mannheim, Dec. 10, 1777.

he, "but he would not even now have made up his mind, if I had not driven him to it by saying that you had already stayed here too long, spending your money in a hotel." "Truly, that is what vexes me most of all," I replied; "it is very far from pleasant. But, at all events, I am very much indebted to you, Count, (for he is not called "your Excellency,") for having taken my part so zealously, and I beg you will thank the Elector from me for his gracious, though somewhat tardy information; and I can assure him that, had he accepted my services, he never would have had cause to regret it." "Oh!" said he, "I feel more convinced of that than perhaps you think." When I told Herr Wendling of the final decision, he colored and said, quite indignantly, "Then we must find the means; you must, at least, remain here for the next two months, and after that we can go together to Paris. To-morrow Cannabich returns from shooting, and then we can talk further on the subject." I left the concert immediately, and went straight to Madame Cannabich. On my way thither, Herr Schatzmeister having come away from the concert with me, I told him all about it, as he is a good worthy man and a kind friend of mine. You cannot conceive how angry he was. When we went into Madame Cannabich's house, he spoke first, saying, "I bring you a man who shares the usual happy fate of those who have to do with courts." "What!" said Madame, "so it has all come to nothing?" I told her the whole, and in return they related to me numbers of similar things which had occurred here. When Madlle. Rose (who was in the third room from us, busy with the linen) had finished, she came in and said to me, "Do you wish me to begin now?" as it was the hour for her lesson. "I am at your orders," said I. "Do you know," said she, "that I mean to be very attentive to-day?" "I am sure you will," answered I, "for the lessons will not continue much longer." "How so? What do you mean?—Why?" She turned to her mamma, who told her. "What!" said she, "is this quite certain? I cannot believe it." "Yes—yes; quite certain," said I. She then played my sonata, but looked very grave. Do you know, I really could not suppress my tears; and at last they had all tears in their eyes—mother, daughter, and Schatzmeister, for she was playing the sonata at the moment, which is the favorite of the whole family. "Indeed," said Schatzmeister, "if the Herr Capellmeister (I am never called anything else here) leaves us, it will make us all weep." I must say that I have very kind friends here, for it is under such circumstances that we learn to know them; for they are so, not only in words but in deeds. Listen to this! The other day I went, as usual, to dine with Wendling, when he said to me, "Our Indian friend (a Dutchman, who lives on his own means, and is an amateur of all the fine arts, and a great friend and admirer of mine) is certainly an excellent fellow. He will give you twenty florins to write for him three little easy short concertos, and a couple of quattros for a leading flute. Cannabich can get you at least two pupils, who will play well; and you could write duets for the piano and violin, and publish them by subscription. Dinner and supper you will always have with us, and lodgings you have at the Herr Hofkammerrath's; so all this will cost you nothing. As for your mother, we can easily find her a cheap lodging for these two months, till you have had time to write about the matter to your father, when she will leave this for Salzburg and we for Paris." Mamma is quite satisfied; so all that is yet wanting is your consent, of which I feel so sure that, if the time for our journey were now come, I would set off for Paris without waiting for your reply; for I could expect nothing else from a sensible father, hitherto so anxious for the welfare of his children. Herr Wendling, who sends you his compliments, is very intimate with our dear friend Grimm, who, when he was here, spoke a great deal about me to Wendling; this was when he had just come from us at Salzburg. As soon as I receive your answer to this letter, I mean to write to him, for a stranger whom I met at dinner to-day told me that Grimm was now in Paris. As we don't leave this till the 8th of March, I beg you, if possible, to try to procure for me, either through Herr Mesmer at Vienna, or some one else, a letter to the Queen of France, if it can be done without much difficulty; if not, it does not much matter. It would be better if I could have one—of that there is no doubt; this is also the advice of Herr Wendling. I suppose what I am now writing must appear very strange to you, because you are in a city where there are only stupid enemies, and weak and simple friends, whose dreary daily bread at Salzburg is so essential to them, that they become flatterers, and are not to be depended on from day to day. Indeed, this was why I wrote you nothing but childish nonsense, and jokes, and folly; I wished to await the event here, to save you from vexation, and my good friends from blame; for you very unwarrantably accuse them of working against me in an underhand way, which they certainly never did. Your letters obliged me to relate the whole affair to you. I entreat you most earnestly not to distress yourself on the subject; God has willed it so. Reflect also on this most undoubted truth, that we cannot do all we wish. We often think that such and such a thing would be very good, and another equally bad and evil, and yet if these things came to pass, we should sometimes learn that the very reverse was the case.

I must now go to bed. I shall have plenty of work to do during the two months of my stay,—three concertos, two quartets, five or six duets for the piano, and I also have thoughts of composing a new grand mass, and dedicating it to the Elector. Adieu! I will write to Prince Zeill next post-day to press forward matters in Munich; if you would also write to him, I should be very glad. But short and to the point—no cringing! for that I cannot bear. It is quite certain that he can do it if he likes, for all Munich told me so [see Nos. 56 and 60].

84. Mannheim, Dec. 14, 1777.

I CAN only write a few words, as I did not get home till four o'clock, when I had a lesson to give to the young lady of the house. It is now nearly half-past five, so time to close my letter. I will ask mamma to write a few days beforehand, so that all our news may not be of the same date, for I can't easily do this. The little time that I have for writing must be devoted to composition, for I have a great deal of work before me. I entreat you to answer me very soon as to my journey to Paris. I played over my concertone on the piano to Herr Wendling, who said it was just the thing for Paris; if I were to play that to Baron Bach, he would be in ecstasies. Adieu!

85. Mannheim, Dec. 18, 1777.

[A P.S. TO A LETTER FROM HIS MOTHER.]
Mannheim, Dec. 18, 1777.

IN the greatest haste and hurry! The organ that was tried to-day in the Lutheran church is very good, not only in certain registers, but in its whole compass. [Footnote: The mother writes: "A Lutheran of degree called on us to-day, and invited Wolfgang, with all due politeness, to try their new organ."] Vogler played on it. He is only a juggler, so to speak; as soon as he wishes to play in a majestic style, he becomes dull. Happily this seems equally tedious to himself, so it does not last long; but then, what follows? only an incomprehensible scramble. I listened to him from a distance. He began a fugue, in chords of six notes, and presto. I then went up to him, for I would far rather see than hear him. There were a great many people present, and among the musicians Holzbauer, Cannabich, Toeschi,

A quartet for the Indian Dutchman, that true benefactor of man, will soon be finished. A propos, Herr told me that he had written to you by the last post. Addio! I was lately obliged to direct the opera with some violins at Wendling's, Schweitzer being unwell.

86. Mannheim, Dec. 20, 1777.

I WISH you, dearest papa, a very happy new-year, and that your health, so precious in my eyes, may daily improve, for the benefit and happiness of your wife and children, the satisfaction of your true friends, and for the annoyance and vexation of your enemies. I hope also that in the coming year you will love me with the same fatherly tenderness you have hitherto shown me. I on my part will strive, and honestly strive, to deserve still more the love of such an admirable father. I was cordially delighted with your last letter of the 15th of December, for, thank God! I could gather from it that you are very well indeed. We, too, are in perfect health, God be praised! Mine is not likely to fail if constant work can preserve it. I am writing this at eleven at night, because I have no other leisure time. We cannot very well rise before eight o'clock, for in our rooms (on the ground-floor) it is not light till half-past eight. I then dress quickly; at ten o'clock I sit down to compose till twelve or half-past twelve, when I go to Wendling's, where I generally write till half-past one; we then dine. At three o'clock I go to the Mainzer Hof (an hotel) to a Dutch officer, to give him lessons in galanterie playing and thorough bass, for which, if I mistake not, he gives me four ducats for twelve lessons. At four o'clock I go home to teach the daughter of the house. We never begin till half past four, as we wait for lights. At six o'clock I go to Cannabich's to instruct Madlle. Rose. I stay to supper there, when we converse and sometimes play; I then invariably take a book out of my pocket and read, as I used to do at Salzburg. I have already written to you the pleasure your last letter caused me, which is quite true; only one thing rather vexed me, the inquiry whether I had not perchance forgotten to go to confession. I shall not say anything further on this. Only allow me to make you one request, which is, not to think so badly of me. I like to be merry, but rest assured that I can be as serious as any one. Since I quitted Salzburg (and even in Salzburg) I have met with people who spoke and acted in a way that I should have felt ashamed to do, though they were ten, twenty, and thirty years older than myself. I implore of you therefore once more, and most earnestly, to have a better opinion of me.

87. Mannheim, Dec. 27, 1777.

A PRETTY sort of paper this! I only wish I could make it better; but it is now too late to send for any other. You know, from our previous letters, that mamma and I have a capital lodging. It never was my intention that she should live apart from me; in fact, when the Hofkammerrath Serrarius so kindly offered me his house, I only expressed my thanks, which is by no means saying yes. The next day I went to see him with Herr Wendling and M. de Jean (our worthy Dutchman), and only waited till he should himself begin the subject. At length he renewed his offer, and I thanked him in these words: "I feel that it is a true proof of friendship on your part to do me the honor to invite me to live in your house; but I regret that unfortunately I cannot accept your most kind proposal. I am sure you will not take it amiss when I say that I am unwilling to allow my mother to leave me without sufficient cause; and I certainly know no reason why mamma should live in one part of the town and I in another. When I go to Paris, her not going with me would be a considerable pecuniary advantage to me, but here for a couple of months a few gulden more or less do not signify."

By this speech my wish was entirely fulfilled,—that is, that our board and lodging do not at all events make us poorer. I must go upstairs to supper, for we have now chatted till half-past ten o'clock. I lately went with my scholar, the Dutch officer, M. de la Pottrie, into the Reformed church, where I played for an hour and a half on the organ. It came right from my heart too. We— that is, the Cannabichs, Wendlings, Serrariuses, and Mozarts—are going to the Lutheran Church, where I shall amuse myself gloriously on the organ. I tried its tone at the same rehearsal that I wrote to you about, but played very little, only a prelude and a fugue.

I have made acquaintance with Herr Wieland. He does not, however, know me as I know him, for he has heard nothing of me as yet. I had not at all imagined him to be what I find him. He speaks in rather a constrained way, and has a childish voice, his eyes very watery, and a certain pedantic uncouthness, and yet at times provokingly condescending. I am not, however, surprised that he should choose to behave in this way at Mannheim, though no doubt very differently at Weimar and elsewhere, for here he is stared at as if he had fallen from the skies. People seem to be so ceremonious in his presence, no one speaks, all are as still as possible, striving to catch every word he utters. It is unlucky that they are kept so long in expectation, for he has some impediment in his speech which causes him to speak very slowly, and he cannot say six words without pausing. Otherwise he is, as we all know, a man of excellent parts. His face is downright ugly and seamed with the small-pox, and he has a long nose. His height is rather beyond that of papa.

You need have no misgivings as to the Dutchman's 200 florins. I must now conclude, as I should like to compose for a little time. One thing more: I suppose I had better not write to Prince Zeill at present. The reason you no doubt already know, (Munich being nearer to Salzburg than to Mannheim,) that the Elector is at the point of death from small-pox. This is certain, so there will be a struggle there. Farewell! As for mamma's journey home, I think it could be managed best during Lent, by her joining some merchants. This is only my own idea; but what I do feel quite sure of is, that whatever you think right will be best, for you are not only the Herr Hofcapellmeister, but the most rational of all rational beings. If you know such a person as papa, tell him I kiss his hands 1000 times, and embrace my sister from my heart, and in spite of all this scribbling I am your dutiful son and affectionate brother.

88. Mannheim, Jan. 7, 1778.

I HOPE you are both well. I am, thank God! in good health and spirits. You may easily conceive my sorrow at the death of the Elector of Bavaria. My sole wish is that our Elector here may have the whole of Bavaria, and transfer himself to Munich. I think you also would like this. This forenoon at twelve o'clock, Carl Theodor was proclaimed at court Duke of Bavaria. At Munich, Count Daun, Oberststallmeister, immediately on the death of the Prince, received homage in the name of the Elector, and sent the dragoons to ride all round the environs of the city with trumpets and kettledrums, and to shout "Long live our Elector, Carl Theodor!" If all goes well, as I hope it may, Count Daun will receive a very handsome present. His aid-de-camp, whom he dispatched here with the tidings, (his name is Lilienau,) got 3000 florins from the Elector.

89. Mannheim, Jan 10, 1778

YES, indeed! I also wish that from my heart. [Footnote: In the mother's letter, she had written, "May God grant us the blessing of peace"' for there was much talk about the invasion of Bavaria by the Prussians and Austrians, on account of the succession.] You have already learned my true desire from my last letter. It is really high time that we should think of mamma's journey home, for though we have had various rehearsals of the opera, still its being performed is by no means certain, and if it is not given, we shall probably leave this on the 15th of February, When that time arrives, (after receiving your advice on the subject,) I mean to follow the opinions and habits of my fellow-travellers, and, like them, order a suit of black clothes, reserving the laced suit for Germany, as it is no longer the fashion in Paris. In the first place, it is an economy, (which is my chief object in my Paris journey,) and, secondly, it wears well and suits both country and town. You can go anywhere with a black coat. To-day the tailor brought Herr Wendling his suit. The clothes I think of taking with me are my puce-brown spagnolet coat, and the two waistcoats.

Now for something else. Herr Wieland, after meeting me twice, seems quite enchanted with me. The last time, after every sort of eulogium, he said, "It is really fortunate for me having met you here," and pressed my hand. To-day "Rosamunde" has been rehearsed in the theatre; it is well enough, but nothing more, for if it were positively bad it could not be performed, I suppose,—just as some people cannot sleep without lying in a bed! But there is no rule without an exception, and I have seen an instance of this; so good night! Now for something more to the purpose. I know for certain that the Emperor intends to establish a German opera in Vienna, and is eagerly looking out for a young Capellmeister who understands the German language, and has genius, and is capable of bringing something new into the world. Benda at Gotha has applied, but Schweitzer is determined to succeed. I think it would be just the thing for me, but well paid of course. If the Emperor gives me 1000 gulden, I will write a German opera for him, and if he does not choose to give me a permanent engagement, it is all the same to me. Pray write to every kind friend you can think of in Vienna, that I am capable of doing credit to the Emperor. If he will do nothing else, he may at least try me with an opera, and as to what may occur hereafter I care not. Adieu! I hope you will put the thing in train at once, or some one may forestall me.

90. Mannheim, Jan. 17, 1778.

NEXT Wednesday I am going for some days to Kirchheim-Boland, the residence of the Princess of Orange. I have heard so much praise of her here, that at last I have resolved to go. A Dutch officer, a particular friend of mine, [M. de la Pottrie,] was much upbraided by her for not bringing me with him when he went to offer his new-year's congratulations. I expect to receive at least eight louis-d'or, for as she has a passionate admiration of singing, I have had four arias copied out for her. I will also present her with a symphony, for she has a very nice orchestra and gives a concert every day. Besides, the copying of the airs will not cost me much, for a M. Weber who is going there with me has copied them. He has a daughter who sings admirably, and has a lovely pure voice; she is only fifteen. [Footnote: Aloysia, second daughter of the prompter and theatrical copyist, Weber, a brother of Carl Maria von Weber's father.] She fails in nothing but in stage action; were it not for that, she might be the prima donna of any theatre. Her father is a downright honest German who brings up his children well, for which very reason the girl is persecuted here. He has six children,—five girls and a son. He and his wife and children have been obliged to live for the last fourteen years on an income of 200 florins, but as he has always done his duty well, and has lately provided a very accomplished singer for the Elector, he has now actually 400 florins. My aria for De' Amicis she sings to perfection with all its tremendous passages: she is to sing it at Kirchheim-Boland.

Now for another subject. Last Wednesday there was a great feast in our house, [at Hofkammerrath Serrarius's,] to which I was also invited.

90. Mannheim, Jan. 17, 1778.

There were fifteen guests, and the young lady of the house [Pierron, the "House Nymph"] was to play in the evening the concerto I had taught her at eleven o'clock in the forenoon. The Herr Kammerrath and Herr Vogler called on me. Herr Vogler seems quite determined to become acquainted with me, as he often importuned me to go to see him, but he has overcome his pride and paid me the first visit. Besides, people tell me that he is now very different, being no longer so much admired; for at first he was made quite an idol of here. We went up-stairs together, when by degrees the guests assembled, and there was no end to talking. After dinner, Vogler sent for two pianos of his, which were tuned alike, and also his wearisome engraved sonatas. I had to play them, while he accompanied me on the other piano. At his urgent request I sent for my sonatas also. N. B.—Before dinner he had scrambled through my sonata at sight, (the Litzau one which the young lady of the house plays.) He took the first part prestissimo—the Andante allegro—and the Rondo more prestissimo still. He played great part of the bass very differently from the way in which it is written, inventing at times quite another harmony and melody. It is impossible to do otherwise in playing at such a pace, for the eyes cannot see the notes, nor the hands get hold of them. What merit is there in this? The listeners (I mean those worthy of the name) can only say that they have SEEN music and piano-playing. All this makes them hear, and think, and feel as little—as he does. You may easily believe that this was beyond all endurance, because I could not venture to say to him MUCH TOO QUICK! besides, it is far easier to play a thing quickly than slowly; some notes may then be dropped without being observed. But is this genuine music? In rapid playing the right and left hands may be changed, and no one either see or hear it; but is this good? and in what does the art of reading prima vista consist? In this—to play the piece in the time in which it ought to be played, and to express all the notes and apoggiaturas, with proper taste and feeling as written, so that it should give the impression of being composed by the person who plays it. His fingering also is miserable; his left thumb is just like that of the late Adlgasser, all the runs downwards with the right hand he makes with the first finger and thumb!

91. Mannheim, Feb.2 1778.

I COULD no delay writing to you till the usual Saturday arrived, because it was so long since I had the pleasure of conversing with you by means of my pen. The first thing I mean to write about is how my worthy friends and I got on at Kirchheim-Boland. It was simply a holiday excursion, and nothing more. On Friday morning at eight o'clock we drove away from here, after I had breakfasted with Herr Weber. We had a capital covered coach which held four; at four o'clock we arrived at Kirchheim-Boland. We immediately sent a list of our names to the palace. Next morning early, Herr Concertmeister Rothfischer called on us. He had been already described to me at Mannheim as a most honorable man, and such I find him to be. In the evening we went to court, (this was on Saturday,) where Madlle. Weber sang three airs. I say nothing of her singing, but it is indeed admirable. I wrote to you lately with regard to her merits; but I cannot finish this letter without writing further about her, as I have only recently known her well, so now first discover her great powers. We dined afterwards at the officers' table. Next day we went some distance to church, for the Catholic one is rather far away. This was on Sunday. In the forenoon we dined again with the officers. In the evening there was no music, because it was Sunday. Thus they have music only 300 times during the year. In the evening we might have supped at court, but we preferred being all together at the inn. We would gladly have made them a present also of the dinners at the officers' table, for wre were never so pleased as when by ourselves; but economy rather entered our thoughts, since we were obliged to pay heavily enough at the inn.

The following day, Monday, we had music again, and also on Tuesday and Wednesday. Madlle. Weber sang in all thirteen times, and played twice on the piano, for she plays by no means badly. What surprises me most is, that she reads music so well. Only think of her playing my difficult sonatas at sight, SLOWLY, but without missing a single note. I give you my honor I would rather hear my sonatas played by her than by Vogler. I played twelve times, and once, by desire, on the organ of the Lutheran church. I presented the Princess with four symphonies, and received only seven louis-d'or in silver, and our poor dear Madlle. Weber only five. This I certainly did not anticipate! I never

91. Mannheim, Feb. 2 1778.

expected great things, but at all events I hoped that each of us would at least receive eight louis-d'or. Basta! We were not, however, losers, for I have a profit of forty-two florins, and the inexpressible pleasure of becoming better acquainted with worthy upright Christian people, and good Catholics, I regret much not having known them long ago.

The 4th.—Now comes something urgent, about which I request an answer. Mamma and I have discussed the matter, and we agree that we do not like the sort of life the Wendlings lead. Wendling is a very honorable and kind man, but unhappily devoid of all religion, and the whole family are the same. I say enough when I tell you that his daughter was a most disreputable character. Ramm is a good fellow, but a libertine. I know myself, and I have such a sense of religion that I shall never do anything which I would not do before the whole world; but I am alarmed even at the very thoughts of being in the society of people, during my journey, whose mode of thinking is so entirely different from mine (and from that of all good people). But of course they must do as they please. I have no heart to travel with them, nor could I enjoy one pleasant hour, nor know what to talk about; for, in short, I have no great confidence in them. Friends who have no religion cannot he long our friends. I have already given them a hint of this by saying that during my absence three letters had arrived, of which I could for the present divulge nothing further than that it was unlikely I should be able to go with them to Paris, but that perhaps I might come later, or possibly go elsewhere; so they must not depend on me. I shall be able to finish my music now quite at my ease for De Jean, who is to give me 200 florins for it. I can remain here as long as I please, and neither board nor lodging cost me anything. In the meantime Herr Weber will endeavor to make various engagements for concerts with me, and then we shall travel together. If I am with him, it is just as if I were with you. This is the reason that I like him so much; except in personal appearance, he resembles you in all respects, and has exactly your character and mode of thinking. If my mother were not, as you know, too COMFORTABLY LAZY to write, she would say precisely what I do. I must confess that I much enjoyed my excursion with them. We were pleased and merry; I heard a man converse just like you; I had no occasion to trouble myself about anything; what was torn I found repaired. In short, I was treated like a prince. I am so attached to this oppressed family that my greatest wish is to make them happy, and perhaps I may be able to do so. My advice is that they should go to Italy, so I am all anxiety for you to write to our good friend Lugiati [impresario], and the sooner the better, to inquire what are the highest terms given to a prima donna in Verona—the more the better, for it is always easy to accept lower terms. Perhaps it would be possible to obtain the Ascensa in Venice. I will be answerable with my life for her singing, and her doing credit to my recommendation. She has, even during this short period, derived much profit from me, and how much further progress she will have made by that time! I have no fears either with regard to her acting. If this plan be realized, M. Weber, his two daughters, and I, will have the happiness of visiting my dear papa and dear sister for a fortnight, on our way through Salzburg. My sister will find a friend and companion in Madlle. Weber, for, like my sister in Salzburg, she enjoys the best reputation here, owing to the careful way in which she has been brought up; the father resembles you, and the whole family that of Mozart. They have indeed detractors, as with us, but when it comes to the point they must confess the truth; and truth lasts longest. I should be glad to go with them to Salzburg, that you might hear her. My air that De' Amicis used to sing, and the bravura aria "Parto m' affretto," and "Dalla sponda tenebrosa," she sings splendidly. Pray do all you can to insure our going to Italy together. You know my greatest desire is—to write operas.

I will gladly write an opera for Verona for thirty zecchini, solely that Madlle. Weber may acquire fame by it; for, if I do not, I fear she may be sacrificed. Before then I hope to make so much money by visiting different places that I shall be no loser. I think we shall go to Switzerland, perhaps also to Holland; pray write to me soon about this. Should we stay long anywhere, the eldest daughter [Josepha, afterwards Madaine Hofer, for whom the part of the Queen of the Night in the "Flauto magico" was written] would be of the greatest use to us; for we could have our own menage, as she understands cooking.

Send me an answer soon, I beg. Don't forget my wish to write an opera; I envy every person who writes one; I could almost weep from vexation when I hear or see an aria. But Italian, not German—seria, not buffa! I have now written you all that is in my heart; my mother is satisfied with my plan.

The mother, however, adds the following postscript:—

"No doubt you perceive by the accompanying letter that when Wolfgang makes new friends he would give his life for them. It is true that she does sing incomparably; still, we ought not to lose sight of our own interests. I never liked his being in the society of Wendling and

Ramm, but I did not venture to object to it, nor would he have listened to me; but no sooner did he know these Webers than he instantly changed his mind. In short, he prefers other people to me, for I remonstrate with him sometimes, and that he does not like. I write this quite secretly while he is at dinner, for I don't wish him to know it."

A few days later Wolfgang urges his father still more strongly.

92. Mannheim, Feb. 7, 1778.

HERR SCHIEDENHOFEN might have let me know long ago through you that his wedding was soon to take place [see Nos. 7, 10, 19], and I would have composed a new minuet for the occasion. I cordially wish him joy; but his is, after all, only one of those money matches, and nothing else! I hope never to marry in this way; I wish to make my wife happy, but not to become rich by her means; so I will let things alone, and enjoy my golden freedom till I am so well off that I can support both wife and children. Herr Schiedenhofen was forced to choose a rich wife; his title imposed this on him. The nobility must not marry for love or from inclination, but from interest, and all kinds of other considerations. It would not at all suit a grandee to love his wife after she had done her duty, and brought into the world an heir to the property. But we poor humble people are privileged not only to choose a wife who loves us, and whom we love, but we may, can, and do take such a one, because we are neither noble, nor highborn, nor rich, but, on the contrary, lowly, humble, and poor; we therefore need no wealthy wife, for our riches being in our heads, die with us, and these no man can deprive us of unless he cut them off, in which case we need nothing more.

I lately wrote to you my chief reason for not going to Paris with these people, but another is that I have reflected well on what I have to do in Paris. I could not get on passably without pupils, which is a kind of work that does not suit me—of this I have a strong example here. I might have had two pupils: I went three times to each, but finding one of them not at home, I never went back. I am willing to give lessons out of complaisance, especially when I see genius, and inclination and anxiety to learn; but to be obliged to go to a house at a certain hour, or else to wait at home, is what I cannot submit to, if I were to gain twice what I do. I find it impossible, so must leave it to those who can do nothing but play the piano. I am a composer, and born to become a Kapellmeister, and I neither can nor ought thus to bury the talent for composition with which God has so richly endowed me (I may say this without arrogance, for I feel it now more than ever); and this I should do were I to take many pupils, for it is a most unsettled metier; and I would rather, SO TO SPEAK, neglect the piano than composition, for I look on the piano to be only a secondary consideration, though, thank God! a very strong one too. My third reason is, that I am by no means sure our friend Grimm is in Paris. If he is, I can go there at any time with the post-carriage, for a capital one travels from here to Paris by Strassburg. We intended at all events to have gone by it. They travel also in this way. Herr Wendling is inconsolable at my not going with them, but I believe this proceeds more from self-interest than from friendship. Besides the reason I gave him (about the three letters that had come during my absence), I also told him about the pupils, and begged him to procure something certain for me, in which case I would be only too glad to follow him to Paris, (for I can easily do so,)— above all, if I am to write an opera, which is always in my thoughts; but French rather than German, and Italian rather than French or German. The Wendlings, one and all, are of opinion that my compositions would please much in Paris. I have no fears on the subject, for, as you know, I can pretty well adapt or conform myself to any style of composition. Shortly after my arrival I composed a French song for Madlle. Gustel (the daughter), who gave me the words, and she sings it inimitably. I have the pleasure to enclose it for you. It is sung every day at Wendling's, for they are quite infatuated with it.

93. Mannheim, Feb. 14, 1778.

I PERCEIVE by your letter of the 9th of February that you have not yet received my last two letters. Wendling and Kamm leave this early tomorrow morning. If I thought that you would be really displeased with me for not going to Paris with them, I should repent having stayed here; but I hope it is not so. The road to Paris is still open to me. Wendling has promised to inquire immediately about Herr Grimm, and to send me information at once. With such a friend in Paris, I certainly shall go there, for no donbt he will bring something to bear for me. The main cause of my not going with them is, that we have not been able to

93. Mannheim, Feb. 14, 1778.

arrange about mamma returning to Augsburg. The journey will not cost much, for there are vetturini here who can be engaged at a cheap rate. By that time, however, I hope to have made enough to pay mamma's journey home. Just now I don't really see that it is possible. Herr de Jean sets off to-morrow for Paris, and as I have only finished two concertos and three quartets for him, he sent me 96 florins (having made a mistake of four florins, thinking this sum the half of the 200); he must, however, pay me in full, for such was the agreement I made with Wendling, and I can send him the other pieces. It is not surprising that I have been unable to finish them, for I never have a single quiet hour here. I can only write at night, so I cannot rise early; besides, one is not always disposed to work. I could, to be sure, scrawl away all day, but a thing of this kind goes forth to the world, and I am resolved not to have cause to be ashamed of my name on the title-page. Moreover, you know that I become quite obtuse when obliged to write perpetually for an instrument that I cannot bear; so from time to time I do something else, such as duets for the piano and violin, and I also worked at the mass. Now I have begun the pianoforte duets in good earnest, in order to publish them. If the Elector were only here, I would very quickly finish the mass; but what must be must be!

I am very grateful to you, dear papa, for your fatherly letter; I will preserve it as a treasure, and always refer to it. Pray do not forget about my mother's journey from Augsburg to Salzburg, and let me know the precise day; and I beg you will also remember the arias I mentioned in my last letter. If I recollect rightly, there are also some cadenzas which I once jotted down, and at all events an aria cantabile with coloraturas? I wish to have these first, for they will serve as exercises for Madlle. Weber. I have just taught her an andantino cantabile of Bach's. Yesterday there was a concert at Cannabich's, where from first to last all the music was of my composition, except the first symphony, which was Cannabich's. Madlle. Rose played my concerto in B, then Herr Ramm (by way of a change) played for the fifth time the hautboy concerto dedicated to Ferlendi, which makes a great sensation here. It is now quite Ramm's cheval de bataille. Madlle. Weber sang De' Amicis's aria di bravura quite charmingly. Then I played my old concerto in D, because it is such a favorite here, and likewise extemporized for half an hour, after which Madlle. Weber sang De' Amicis's air, "Parto m' affretto;" and, as a finale, my symphony "Il Re Pastore" was given. I do entreat you urgently to interest yourself in Madlle. Weber; it would make me so happy if good-fortune were to attend her. Husband and wife, five children, and a salary of 450 florins! Don't forget about Italy, and my desire to go there; you know my strong wish and passion. I hope all may go right. I place my trust in God, who will never forsake us. Now farewell, and don't forget all my requests and recommendations.

These letters alarmed the father exceedingly, so he wrote a long and very earnest letter to his son as follows:—"The object of your journey was to assist your parents, and to contribute to your dear sister's welfare, but, above all, that you might acquire honor and fame in the world, which you in some degree did in your boyhood; and now it rests entirely with you to raise yourself by degrees to one of the highest positions ever attained by any musician. This is a duty you owe to a kind Providence in return for the remarkable talents with which He has gifted you; and it depends wholly on your own good sense and good conduct, whether you become a commonplace artist whom the world will forget, or a celebrated Capellmeister, of whom posterity will read hereafter in books,—whether, infatuated with some pretty face, you one day breathe your last on a straw sack, your wife and children in a state of starvation, or, after a well-spent Christian life, die peacefully in honor and independence, and your family well provided for." He goes on to represent to him how little he has hitherto fulfilled the object of his journey, and, above all, the folly of wishing to place so young a girl on the Italian stage as a prima donna, both time and great training being previously required. Moreover, it would be quite unworthy of him to wander about the world with strangers, and to compose at random merely for money. "Get off to Paris without delay. Take your place by the side of really great people. Aut Caesar aut nihil. The very idea of Paris should have guarded you from all passing fancies."

To this Wolfgang replies:—

94. Mannheim, Feb. 19, 1778.

I ALWAYS thought that you would disapprove of my journey with the Webers, but I never had any such intention—I mean, UNDER PRESENT CIRCUMSTANCES. I gave them my word of honor to write to you to that effect. Herr Weber does not know how we stand, and I certainly shall tell it to no one. I wish my position had been such that I

94. Mannheim, Feb. 19, 1778.

had no cause to consider any one else, and that we were all independent; but in the intoxication of the moment I forgot the present impossibility of the affair, and also to tell you what I had done. The reasons of my not being now in Paris must be evident to you from my last two letters. If my mother had not first begun on the subject, I certainly would have gone with my friends; but when I saw that she did not like it, I began to dislike it also. When people lose confidence in me, I am apt to lose confidence in myself. The days when, standing on a stool, I sang Oragna fiaguta fa, [Footnote: Words sounding like Italian, but devoid of meaning, for which he had invented a melody. Nissen gives it in his Life of Mozart, p. 35.] and at the end kissed the tip of your nose, are indeed gone by; but still, have my reverence, love, and obedience towards yourself ever failed on that account? I say no more. As for your reproach about the little singer in Munich [see No. 62], I must confess that I was an ass to write such a complete falsehood. She does not as yet know even what singing means. It was true that, for a person who had only learned music for three months, she sang surprisingly; and, besides, she has a pleasing pure voice. The reason why I praised her so much was probably my hearing people say, from morning to night, "There is no better singer in all Europe; those who have not heard her have heard nothing." I did not venture to disagree with them, partly because I wished to acquire friends, and partly because I had come direct from Salzburg, where we are not in the habit of contradicting any one; but as soon as I was alone I never could help laughing. Why, then, did I not laugh at her in my letter to you? I really cannot tell.

The bitter way in which you write about my merry and innocent intercourse with your brother's daughter, makes me justly indignant; but as it is not as you think, I require to give you no answer on the subject. I don't know what to say about Wallerstein; I was very grave and reserved with Becke, and at the officers' table also I had a very serious demeanor, not saying one word to anybody. But let this all pass; you only wrote it in a moment of irritation [see No. 74]. Your remarks about Madlle. Weber are just; but at the time I wrote to you I knew quite as well as you that she is still too young, and must be first taught how to act, and must rehearse frequently on the stage. But with some people one must proceed step by step. These good people are as tired of being here as—you know WHO and WHERE, [meaning the Mozarts, father and son, in Salzburg,] and they think everything feasible. I promised them to write everything to my father; but when the letter was sent off to Salzburg, I constantly told her that she must have a little patience, for she was still rather too young, They take in all I say in good part, for they have a high opinion of me. By my advice, Herr Weber has engaged Madlle. Toscani (an actress) to give his daughter lessons in acting. All you write of Madlle. Weber is true, except, that she sings like a Gabrielli, [see Nos. 10, 37,] for I should not at all like her to sing in that style. Those who have heard Gabrielli say, and must say, that she was only an adept in runs and roulades; but as she adopted so uncommon a reading, she gained admiration, which, however, did not last longer than hearing her four times. She could not please in the long run, for roulades soon become very tiresome, and she had the misfortune of not being able to sing. She was not capable of sustaining a breve properly, and having no messa di voce, she could not dwell on her notes; in short, she sang with skill, but devoid of intelligence. Madlle. Weber's singing, on the contrary, goes to the heart, and she prefers a cantabile. I have lately made her practise the passages in the Grand Aria, because, if she goes to Italy, it is necessary that she should sing bravuras. The cantabile she certainly will never forget, being her natural bent. Raaff (who is no flatterer), when asked to give his sincere opinion, said, "She does not sing like a scholar, but like a professor."

So now you know everything. I do still recommend her to you with my whole heart, and I beg you will not forget about the arias, cadenzas, I can scarcely write from actual hunger. My mother will display the contents of our large money-box. I embrace my sister lovingly. She is not to lament about every trifle, or I will never come back to her.

95. Mannheim, Feb. 22, 1778.

I HAVE been now two days confined to the house, and taking antispasmodics, black powders, and elderflower tea as a sudorific, because I have had a catarrh, a cold in my head, sore throat, headache, pains in my eyes, and earache; but, thank God, I am now better, and hope to be able to go out tomorrow, being Sunday. I got your letter of the 16th and the two unsealed letters of introduction for Paris. I rejoice that my French song pleases you [see No. 92]. You must forgive my not writing much this time, but I really cannot—I am so afraid of bringing back my headache, and, besides, I feel no inclination to write to-day. It is impossible to write all we think—at least, I find it to be so. I would rather say it than write it. My last letter told you the whole thing just as it stands. Believe what you please of me, only nothing bad. There are people who think no one can love a poor girl without evil designs. But I am no Brunetti [a violinist in Salzburg], no Misliweczeck. I am a Mozart; and, though young, still a high-principled Mozart. Pardon me if, in my eagerness, I become somewhat excited—which is, I suppose, the term, though I might rather say, if I write as I feel. I might have said a great deal on this subject, but I cannot—I feel it to be impossible. Among my many faults I have also that of believing that those friends who know me, do so thoroughly. Then many words are not necessary; and if they do not know me, oh! how could I find words sufficient? It is painful enough to employ words and letters for such a purpose. This, however, is not at all meant to apply to you, dearest papa. No! You understand me too well, and you are too kind to try to deprive any one of his good name. I only meant it for—you can guess to whom I allude—to people who can believe such a thing.

I have resolved to stay in the house to-day, although Sunday, as it is snowing heavily. To-morrow I must go out, for our "house-nymph," Madlle. Pierron, my highly esteemed pupil, who has usually a French concert every Monday, intends to scramble through my hochgrafliche Litzau concerto. I also mean, for my sins, to let them give me something to hack away at, and show that I can do something too prima fista; for I am a regular greenhorn, and all I can do is to strum a little on the piano! I must now conclude, being more disposed to-day to write music than letters. Don't forget the cadenzas and the cantabile. Many thanks for having had the arias written out so quickly, for it shows that you place confidence in me when I beg a favor of you.

96. Mannheim, Feb. 28, 1778.

I HOPE to receive the arias next Friday or Saturday, although in your last letter you made no further mention of them, so I don't know whether you sent them off on the 22d by the post-carriage. I hope so, for I should like to play and sing them to Madlle. Weber. I was yesterday at Raafl's to take him an aria that I lately wrote for him [Kochel, No. 295]. The words are—"Se al labbro mio non credi, nemica mia." I don't think they are by Metastasio, The aria pleased him beyond all measure. It is necessary to be very particular with a man of this kind. I chose these words expressly, because he had already composed an aria for them, so of course he can sing it with greater facility, and more agreeably to himself. I told him to say honestly if it did not suit his voice or please him, for I would alter it if he wished, or write another. "Heaven forbid!" said he; "it must remain just as it is, for nothing can be more beautiful. I only wish you to curtail it a little, for I am no longer able to sustain my voice through so long a piece." "Most gladly," I answered, "as much as ever you please; I made it purposely rather long, for it is always easy to shorten, but not so easy to lengthen." After he had sung the second part, he took off his spectacles, and, looking at me deliberately, said, "Beautiful! beautiful! This second part is quite charming;" and he sang it three times. When I went away he cordially thanked me, while I assured him that I would so arrange the aria that he would certainly like to sing it. I think an aria should fit a singer as accurately as a well-made coat. I have also, for practice, arranged the air "Non so d' onde viene" which has been so charmingly composed by Bach. Just because I know that of Bach so well, and it pleases me and haunts my ear, I wished to try if, in spite of all this, I could succeed in writing an aria totally unlike the other. And, indeed, it does not in the very least resemble it. I at first intended this aria for Raaff; but the beginning seemed to me too high for Raaff's voice, but it pleased me so much that I would not alter it; and from the orchestral accompaniment, too, I thought it better suited to a soprano. I therefore resolved to write it for Madlle. Weber. I laid it aside, and took the words "Se al labbro" for Raaff. But all in vain, for I could write nothing else, as the first air always came back into my head; so I returned to it, with the intention of making it exactly in accordance with Madlle. Weber's voice. It is andante sostenuto, (preceded by a short recitative,) then follows the other part, Nel seno destarmi, and after this the sostenuto again. When it was finished, I said to Madlle. Weber, "Learn the air by yourself, sing it according to your own taste, then let me hear it, and I will afterwards tell you candidly what pleases and what displeases me."

In the course of a couple of days I went to see her, when she sang it for me and accompanied herself, and I was obliged to confess that she had sung it precisely as I could have wished, and as I would have taught it to her myself. This is now the best aria that she has, and will insure her success wherever she goes. [Footnote: This wonderfully beautiful aria is appended to my Life of Mozart.—Stuttgart, Bruckmaun, 1863.] Yesterday at Wendling's I sketched the aria I promised his wife [Madame Wendling was a fine singer], with a short recitative. The words were

96. Mannheim, Feb. 28, 1778.

chosen by himself from "Didone": "Ah non lasciarmi no." She and her daughter quite rave about this air. I promised the daughter also some French ariettes, one of which I began to-day. I think with delight of the Concert Spirituel in Paris, for probably I shall be desired to compose something for it. The orchestra is said to be good and numerous, so my favorite style of composition can be well given there—I mean choruses, and I am very glad to hear that the French place so much value on this class of music. The only fault found with Piccini's [Gluck's well-known rival] new opera "Roland" is that the choruses are too meagre and weak, and the music also a little monotonous; otherwise it was universally liked. In Paris they are accustomed to hear nothing but Gluck's choruses. Only place confidence in me; I shall strive with all my might to do honor to the name of Mozart. I have no fears at all on the subject.

My last letters must have shown you HOW THINGS ARE, and WHAT I REALLY MEANT. I do entreat of you never to allow the thought to cross your mind that I can ever forget you, for I cannot bear such an idea. My chief aim is, and always will be, to endeavor that we may meet soon and happily, but we must have patience. You know even better than I do that things often take a perverse turn, but they will one day go straight—only patience! Let us place our trust in God, who will never forsake us. I shall not be found wanting; how can you possibly doubt me? Surely it concerns me also to work with all my strength, that I may have the pleasure and the happiness (the sooner the better, too) of embracing from my heart my dearest and kindest father. But, lo and behold! nothing in this world is wholly free from interested motives. If war should break out in Bavaria, I do hope you will come and join me at once. I place faith in three friends—and they are powerful and invincible ones—namely, God, and your head and mine. Our heads are, indeed, very different, but each in its own way is good, serviceable, and useful; and in time I hope mine may by degrees equal yours in that class of knowledge in which you at present surpass me. Farewell! Be merry and of good cheer! Remember that you have a son who never intentionally failed in his filial duty towards you, and who will strive to become daily more worthy of so good a father.

After these frank confessions, which would, he knew, restore the previous good understanding between him and his father, Mozart's genuine good heart was so relieved and lightened, that the natural balance of his mind, which had for some weeks past been entirely destroyed, was speedily restored, and his usual lively humor soon began to revive. Indeed, his old delight in doggerel rhymes and all kinds of silly puns seems to return. He indulges fully in these in a letter to his Basle (cousin), which is undoubtedly written just after the previous one.

97. Mannheim, Feb. 28, 1778.

MADEMOISELLE, MA TRES-CHERE COUSINE,—

You perhaps think or believe that I must be dead? Not at all! I beg you will not think so, for how could I write so beautifully if I were dead? Could such a thing be possible? I do not attempt to make any excuses for my long silence, for you would not believe me if I did. But truth is truth; I have had so much to do that though I have had time to think of my cousin, I have had no time to write to her, so I was obliged to let it alone. But at last I have the honor to inquire how you are, and how you fare? If we soon shall have a talk? If you write with a lump of chalk? If I am sometimes in your mind? If to hang yourself you're inclined? If you're angry with me, poor fool? If your wrath begins to cool?—Oh! you are laughing! VICTORIA! I knew you could not long resist me, and in your favor would enlist me. Yes! yes! I know well how this is, though I'm in ten days off to Paris. If you write to me from pity, do so soon from Augsburg city, so that I may get your letter, which to me would be far better.

Now let us talk of other things. Were you very merry during the Carnival? They are much gayer at Augsburg at that time than here. I only wish I had been there that I might have frolicked about with you. Mamma and I send our love to your father and mother, and to our cousin, and hope they are well and happy; better so, so better! A propos, how goes on your French? May I soon write you a French letter? from Paris, I suppose?

Now, before I conclude, which I must soon do because I am in haste, (having just at this moment nothing to do,) and also have no more room, as you see my paper is done, and I am very tired, and my fingers tingling from writing so much, and lastly, even if I had room, I don't know what I could say, except, indeed, a story which I have a great mind to tell you. So listen! It is not long since it happened, and in this very country too, where it made a great sensation, for really it seemed almost incredible, and, indeed, between ourselves, no one yet knows the result

97. Mannheim, Feb. 28, 1778.

of the affair. So, to be brief, about four miles from here—I can't remember the name of the place, but it was either a village or a hamlet, or something of that kind. Well, after all, it don't much signify whether it was called Triebetrill or Burmsquick; there is no doubt that it was some place or other. There a shepherd or herdsman lived, who was pretty well advanced in years, but still looked strong and robust; he was unmarried and well-to-do, and lived happily. But before telling you the story, I must not forget to say that this man had a most astounding voice when he spoke; he terrified people when he spoke! Well! to make my tale as short as possible, you must know that he had a dog called Bellot, a very handsome large dog, white with black spots. Well! this shepherd was going along with his sheep, for he had a flock of eleven thousand under his care, and he had a staff in his hand, with a pretty rose-colored topknot of ribbons, for he never went out without his staff; such was his invariable custom. Now to proceed; being tired, after having gone a couple of miles, he sat down on a bank beside a river to rest. At last he fell asleep, when he dreamt that he had lost all his sheep, and this fear awoke him, but to his great joy he saw his flock close beside him. At length he got up again and went on, but not for long; indeed, half an hour could scarcely have elapsed, when he came to a bridge which was very long, but with a parapet on both sides to prevent any one falling into the river. Well; he looked at his flock, and as he was obliged to cross the bridge, he began to drive over his eleven thousand sheep. Now be so obliging as to wait till the eleven thousand sheep are all safely across, and then I will finish the story. I already told you that the result is not yet known; I hope, however, that by the time I next write to you, all the sheep will have crossed the bridge; but if not, why should I care? So far as I am concerned, they might all have stayed on this side. In the meantime you must accept the story so far as it goes; what I really know to be true I have written, and it is better to stop now than to tell you what is false, for in that case you would probably have discredited the whole, whereas now you will only disbelieve one half.

    I must conclude, but don't think me rude; he who begins must cease, or the world would have no peace. My compliments to every friend, welcome to kiss me without end, forever and a day, till good sense comes my way; and a fine kissing that will be, which frightens you as well as me. Adieu, ma chere cousine! I am, I was, I have been, oh! that I were, would to heavens I were! I will or shall be, would, could, or should be—what?—A blockhead! W. A. M.

98. Mannheim, March 7, 1778.

I have received your letter on the 26th February, and am much obliged to you for all the trouble you have taken about the arias, which are quite accurate in every respect. "Next to God comes papa" was my axiom when a child, and I still think the same. You are right when you say that "knowledge is power"; besides, except your trouble and fatigue, you will have no cause for regret, as Madlle. Weber certainly deserves your kindness. I only wish that you could hear her sing my new aria which I lately mentioned to you,—I say, hear her sing it, because it seems made expressly for her; a man like you who really understands what portamento in singing means, would certainly feel the most intense pleasure in hearing her. When I am happily settled in Paris, and our circumstances, please God, improved, and we are all more cheerful and in better humor, I will write you my thoughts more fully, and ask you to do me a great kindness. I must now tell you I was so shocked that tears came to my eyes, on reading in your last letter that you are obliged to go about so shabbily dressed. My very dearest papa, this is certainly not my fault; you know it is not. We economize in every possible way here; food and lodging, wood and light, cost us nothing, which is all we could hope for. As for dress, you are well aware that, in places where you are not known, it is out of the question to be badly dressed, for appearances must be kept up.

My whole hopes are now centred in Paris, for German princes are all niggards. I mean to work with all my strength, that I may soon have the happiness of extricating you from your present distressing circumstances.

99. Mannheim, March. 11, 1778.

I HAVE duly received your letter of the 26th February, and learn from it with great joy that our best and kindest of all friends, Baron Grimm [the well-known Encyclopedist, with whom Mozart had become acquainted during his last visit to France], is now in Paris. The vetturino has offered to convey us to Paris by Metz (which, as you probably know, is the shortest route) for eleven louis-d'or. If to-morrow he agrees to do it for ten, I shall certainly engage him, and perhaps at eleven, for even then it will be the cheapest way for us, which is the main point, and more

99. Mannheim, March. 11, 1778.

convenient too, for he will take our carriage—that is, he will place the body on wheels of his own. The convenience is great, as we have so many small packages that we can stow away quite comfortably in our own carriage, which we cannot do in the DILIGENCE, and besides we shall be alone and able to talk as we like. But I do assure you that if, after all, we go in the DILIGENCE, my sole annoyance is the bore of not being able to say what we choose and wish, though, as it is very necessary that we should take the cheapest conveyance, I am still rather disposed to do so.

THIRD PART. PARIS. MARCH 1778 TO JANUARY 1779.

100. Paris, March 24, 1778.

YESTERDAY (Monday, the 23d), at four o'clock in the afternoon, we arrived here, thank God! safely, having been nine days and a half on our journey. We thought we really could not have gone through with it; in my life I never was so wearied. You may easily imagine what it was to leave Mannheim and so many dear kind friends, and then to travel for ten days, not only without these friends, but without any human being—without a single soul whom we could associate with or even speak to. Now, thank Heaven! we are at our destination, and I trust that, with the help of God, all will go well. To-day we are to take a fiacre and go in quest of Grimm and Wendling. Early to-morrow I intend to call on the Minister of the Palatinate, Herr von Sickingen, (a great connoisseur and passionate lover of music, and for whom I have two letters from Herr von Gemmingen and M. Cannabich.) Before leaving Mannheim I had the quartet transcribed that I wrote at Lodi one evening in the inn there, and also the quintet and the Fischer variations for Herr von Gemmingen [author of the "Deutsche Hausvater"], on which he wrote me a most polite note, expressing his pleasure at the souvenir I had left him, and sending me a letter to his intimate friend Herr von Sickingen, adding, "I feel sure that you will be a greater recommendation to the letter than the letter can possibly be to you;" and, to repay the expense of writing out the music, he sent me three louis- d'or; he also assured me of his friendship, and requested mine in return. I must say that all those who knew me, Hofrathe, Kammerrathe, and other high-class people, as well as all the court musicians, were very grieved and reluctant to see me go; and really and truly so.

We left on Saturday, the 14th, and on the previous Thursday there was an afternoon concert at Cannabich's, where my concerto for three pianos was given. Madlle. Rose Cannabich played the first, Madlle. Weber the second, and Madlle. Pierron Serrarius (our "house-nymph")

100. Paris, March 24, 1778.

the third. We had three rehearsals of the concerto, and it went off well. Madlle. Weber sang three arias of mine, the "Aer tranquillo" from the "Re Pastore," [Footnote: A festal opera that Mozart had composed in 1775, in honor of the visit of the Archduke Maximilian Francis to Salzburg.] and the new "Non so d' onde viene." With this last air my dear Madlle. Weber gained very great honor both for herself and for me. All present said that no aria had ever affected them like this one; and, indeed, she sang it as it ought to be sung. The moment it was finished, Cannabich exclaimed, "Bravo! bravissimo maestro! veramente scritta da maestro! It was given for the first time on this occasion with instruments. I should like you to have heard it also, exactly as it was executed and sung there, with such precision in time and taste, and in the pianos and fortes. Who knows? you may perhaps still hear her. I earnestly hope so. The members of the orchestra never ceased praising the aria and talking about it.

I have many kind friends at Mannheim (both highly esteemed and rich) who wished very much to keep me there. Well! where I am properly paid, I am content to be. Who can tell? it may still come to pass. I wish it may; and thus it ever is with me—I live always in hope. Herr Cannabich is an honorable, worthy man, and a kind friend of mine. He has only one fault, which is, that although no longer very young, he is rather careless and absent,- -if you are not constantly before his eyes, he is very apt to forget all about you. But where the interests of a real friend are in question, he works like a horse, and takes the deepest interest in the matter; and this is of great use, for he has influence. I cannot, however, say much in favor of his courtesy or gratitude; the Webers (for whom I have not done half so much), in spite of their poverty and obscurity, have shown themselves far more grateful. Madame Cannabich and her daughter never thanked me by one single word, much less thought of offering me some little remembrance, however trifling, merely as a proof of kindly feeling; but nothing of the sort, not even thanks, though I lost so much time in teaching the daughter, and took such pains with her. She can now perfectly well perform before any one; as a girl only fourteen, and an amateur, she plays remarkably well, and for this they have to thank me, which indeed is very well known to all in Mannheim. She has now neatness, time, and good fingering, as well as even shakes, which she had not formerly. They will find that they miss me much three months hence, for I fear she will again be spoiled, and spoil herself; unless she has a master constantly beside her, and one who thoroughly understands what he is about, she will do no good, for she is still too childish and giddy to practise steadily and carefully alone. [Footnote: Rosa Cannabich became, indeed, a remarkable virtuoso. C L. Junker mentions her, even in his musical almanac of 1783, among the most eminent living artists.]

Madlle. Weber paid me the compliment kindly to knit two pairs of mits for me, as a remembrance and slight acknowledgment. M. Weber wrote out whatever I required gratis, gave me the music-paper, and also made me a present of Moliere's Comedies (as he knew that I had never read them), with this inscription:—"Ricevi, amico, le opere di Moliere, in segno di gratitudine, e qualche volta ricordati di me." [Footnote: "Accept, my dear friend, Moliere's works as a token of my gratitude; and sometimes think of me."] And when alone with mamma he said, "Our best friend, our benefactor, is about to leave us. There can be no doubt that your son has done a great deal for my daughter, and interested himself much about her, and she cannot be too thankful to him." [Footnote: Aloysia Weber became afterwards Madame Lange. She had great fame as a singer. We shall hear more of her in the Vienna letters.] The day before I set off, they would insist on my supping with them, but I managed to give them two hours before supper instead. They never ceased thanking me, and saying they only wished they were in a position to testify their gratitude, and when I went away they all wept. Pray forgive me, but really tears come to my eyes when I think of it. Weber came down-stairs with me, and remained standing at the door till I turned the corner and called out Adieu!

In Paris he at once plunged into work, so that his love-affair was for a time driven into the background. Compositions for the Concert Spirituel, for the theatre, and for dilettanti, as well as teaching and visits to great people, occupied him. His mother writes: "I cannot describe to you how much Wolfgang is beloved and praised here. Herr Wendling had said much in his favor before he came, and has presented him to all his friends. He can dine daily, if he chooses, with Noverre [the famed ballet-master], and also with Madame d'Epinay" [Grimm's celebrated friend]. The mother herself scarcely saw him all day, for on account of their small close apartment, he was obliged to compose at Director Le Gros's house. She had (womanlike) written to the father about the composition of a Miserere. Wolfgang continues the letter, more fully explaining the matter.

101. Paris, April 5, 1778.

I MUST now explain more, clearly what mamma alludes to, as she has written rather obscurely. Capellmeister Holzbauer has sent a Miserere here, but as the choruses at Mannheim are weak and poor, whereas here they are strong and good, his choruses would make no effect. M. Le Gros (Director of the Concert Spirituel) requested me therefore to compose others; Holzbauer's introductory chorus being retained. "Quoniam iniquitatem meam," an allegro, is the first air by me. The second an adagio, "Ecce enim in iniquitatibus." Then an allegro, "Ecce enim veritatem dilexisti" to the "ossa humiliata." Then an andante for soprano, tenor, and bass Soli; "Cor mundum," and "Redde mihi," allegro to "ad se convertentur." I also composed a recitative for a bass air, "Libera me de sanguinibus," because a bass air of Holzbauer's follows. The "sacrificium Deo spiritus" being an aria andante for Raaff, with a hautboy and a bassoon solo obligato. I have added a short recitative with hautboy and bassoon, for here recitative is much liked. "Benigne fac" to "muri Jerusalem" andante moderate. Chorus. Then "Tunc acceptabis" to "super altare," allegro and tenor solo (Le Gros) and chorus. Finis. [None of this music is known.]

I must say that I am right glad to have done with this task, for it is really detestable not to be able to write at home, and to be hurried into the bargain; but now, God be praised! it is finished, and I hope it will make some effect. M. Gussec, whom you no doubt know, when he saw my first chorus, said to Le Gros (I was not present) that it was charming, and could not fail to bo successful, that the words were so well arranged, and, above all, admirably set to music. He is a kind friend of mine, but very reserved. I am not merely to write an act for an opera, but an entire one in two acts. The poet has already completed the first act. Noverre [ballet-master], with whom I dine as often as I please, managed this, and indeed suggested the idea. I think it is to be called "Alexander and Roxana." Madame Jenome is also here. I am about to compose a sinfonie concertante,—flute, Wendling; oboe, Ramm; French horn, Punto; and bassoon, Ritter. Punto plays splendidly. I have this moment returned from the Concert Spirituel. Baron Grimm and I often give vent to our wrath at the music here; N.B.—when tete-a-tete, for in public we call out "Bravo! bravissimo!" and clap our hands till our fingers tingle.

102. Paris, May 1, 1778.

THE little violoncellist Zygmatofsky and his unprincipled father are here. Perhaps I may already have written you this; I only mention it cursorily, because I just remember that I met him at a house which I must now tell you about. I mean that of the Duchesse de Chabot. M. Grimm gave me a letter to her, so I drove there, the purport of the letter being chiefly to recommend me to the Duchesse de Bourbon, who when I was last here [during Mozart's first visit to Paris] was in a convent, and to introduce me afresh to her and recall me to her memory. A week elapsed without the slightest notice of my visit, but as eight days previously she had appointed me to call on her, I kept my engagement and went. I waited half an hour in a large room without any fire, and as cold as ice. At last the Duchess came in, and was very polite, begging me to make allowances for her piano, as none of her instruments were in good order, but I might at least try it. I said that I would most gladly play something, but at this moment it was impossible, as my fingers were quite benumbed from the cold, so I asked her at all events to take me to a room where there was a fire. "Oh! oui, Monsieur, vous avez raison"—was her answer. She then seated herself, and drew for a whole hour in company with several gentlemen, all sitting in a circle round a large table, and during this time I had the honor to wait. The windows and doors were open, so that not only my hands, but my body and my feet were cold, and my head also began to ache. Moreover, there was altum silentium, and I really did not know what to do from cold, headache, and weariness. I again and again thought to myself, that if it were not on M. Grimm's account I would leave the house at once. At last, to cut matters short, I played on the wretched, miserable piano. What however vexed me most of all was, that the Duchess and all the gentlemen did not cease drawing for a single moment, but coolly continued their occupation; so I was left to play to the chairs and tables, and the walls. My patience gave way under such unpropitious circumstances. I therefore began the Fischer variations, and after playing one half of them I rose. Then came eulogiums without end. I, however, said all that could be said—which was, that I could do myself no justice on such a piano, but I should be very glad to fix some other day to play, when a better instrument might

102. Paris, May 1, 1778.

be found. But the Duchess would not hear of my going away; so I was obliged to wait till her husband came in, who placed himself beside me and listened to me with great attention, while, as for me, I became unconscious of all cold and all headache, and, in spite of the wretched piano, played as I CAN play when I am in the right mood. Give me the best piano in Europe, and listeners who understand nothing, or don't wish to understand, and who do not sympathize with me in what I am playing, I no longer feel any pleasure. I afterwards told all this to M. Grimm.

You write to me that I ought to pay a good many visits in order to make new acquaintances, and to renew former ones. This is, however, impossible, from the distances being so great, and it is too muddy to go on foot, for really the mud in Paris is beyond all description. To go in a carriage entails spending four or five livres a day, and all for nothing; it is true the people say all kinds of civil things, but there it ends, as they appoint me to come on such and such a day, when I play, and hear them exclaim, "Oh! c'est un prodige, c'est inconcevable, c'est etonnant!" and then, Adieu! At first I spent money enough in driving about, and to no purpose, from not finding the people at home. Unless you lived here, you could not believe what an annoyance this is. Besides, Paris is much changed; the French are far from being as polite as they were fifteen years ago; their manner now borders on rudeness, and they are odiously self-sufficient.

I must proceed to give you an account of the Concert Spirituel. By the by, I must first briefly tell you that my chorus-labors were in a manner useless, for Holzbauer's Miserere was too long in itself, and did not please, so they gave only two of my choruses instead of four, and chose to leave out the best; but this was of no great consequence, for many there were not aware that any of the music was by me, and many knew nothing at all about me. Still, at the rehearsal great approbation was expressed, and I myself (for I place no great reliance on Parisian praise) was very much satisfied with my choruses. With regard to the sinfonie concertante there appears to be a hitch, and I believe that some unseen mischief is at work. It seems that I have enemies here also; where have I not had them? But this is a good sign. I was obliged to write the symphony very hurriedly, and worked very hard at it. The four performers were and are perfectly enchanted with the piece. Le Gros had it for the last four days to be copied, but I invariably saw it lying in the same place. Two days ago I could not find it, though I searched carefully among the music; and at last I discovered it hidden away. I took no notice, but said to Le Gros, "A propos, have you given my sinfonie to be copied?" "No; I forgot all about it." As, of course, I have no power to compel him to have it transcribed and performed, I said nothing; but I went to the concert on the two days when the sinfonie was to have been performed, when Ramm and Punto came to me in the greatest rage to ask me why my sinfonie concertante was not to be given. "I don't know. This is the first I hear of it. I cannot tell." Ramm was frantic, and abused Le Gros in the music-room in French, saying how very unhandsome it was on his part, ject. I alone was to be kept in the dark! If he had even made an excuse—that the time was too short, or something of the kind!—but he never said a syllable. I believe the real cause to be Cambini, an Italian maestro; for at our first meeting at Le Gros's, I unwittingly took the wind out of his sails. He composes quintets, one of which I heard at Mannheim; it was very pretty, so I praised it, and played the beginning to him. Ritter, Ramm, and Punto were all present, and gave me no peace till I agreed to continue, and to supply from my own head what I could not remember. I therefore did so, and Cambini was quite excited, and could not help saying, "Questa e una gran testa!" Well, I suppose after all he did not quite relish this, [The symphony in question has also entirely disappeared.]

If this were a place where people had ears to hear or hearts to feel, and understood just a little of music, and had some degree of taste, these things would only make me laugh heartily, but as it is (so far as music is concerned) I am surrounded by mere brute beasts. But how can it be otherwise? for in all their actions, inclinations, and passions, they are just the same. There is no place in the world like Paris. You must not think that I exaggerate when I speak in this way of the music here; refer to whom you will, except to a Frenchman born, and (if trustworthy) you will hear the same. But I am now here, and must endure it for your sake. I shall be grateful to Providence if I get away with my natural taste uninjured. I pray to God every day to grant me grace to be firm and steadfast here, that I may do honor to the whole German nation, which will all redound to His greater honor and glory, and to enable me to prosper and make plenty of money, that I may extricate you from your present emergencies, and also to permit us to meet soon, and to live together happily and contentedly; but "His will be done in earth as it is in heaven." I entreat you, dearest father, in the meantime, to take measures that I may see Italy, in order to bring me to life again. Bestow this great happiness upon me, I implore you! I do hope you will keep up your spirits; I shall cut my way through here as I best can, and trust I shall get off safely. Adieu!

103. Paris, May 14, 1778.

I HAVE already so much to do that I don't know how I am to manage when winter comes. I think I wrote to you in my last letter that the Duc de Guines, whose daughter is my pupil in composition, plays the flute inimitably, and she the harp magnificently; she has a great deal of talent and genius, and, above all, a wonderful memory, for she plays all her pieces, about 200 in number, by heart. She, however, doubts much whether she has any genius for composition, especially as regards ideas or invention; but her father (who, entre nous, is rather too infatuated about her) declares that she certainly has ideas, and that she is only diffident and has too little self-reliance. Well, we shall see. If she acquires no thoughts or ideas, (for hitherto she really has none whatever,) it is all in vain, for God knows I can't give her any! It is not the father's intention to make her a great composer. He says, "I don't wish her to write operas, or arias, or concertos, or symphonies, but grand sonatas for her instrument and for mine." I gave her to-day her fourth lesson on the rules of composition and harmony, and am pretty well satisfied with her. She made a very good bass for the first minuet, of which I had given her the melody, and she has already begun to write in three parts; she can do it, but she quickly tires, and I cannot get her on, for it is impossible to proceed further as yet; it is too soon, even if she really had genius, but, alas! there appears to be none; all must be done by rule; she has no ideas, and none seem likely to come, for I have tried her in every possible way. Among other things it occurred to me to write out a very simple minuet, and to see if she could not make a variation on it. Well, that utterly failed. Now, thought I, she has not a notion how or what to do first. So I began to vary the first bar, and told her to continue in the same manner, and to keep to the idea. At length this went tolerably well. When it was finished, I told her she must try to originate something herself—only the treble of a melody. So she thought it over for a whole quarter of an hour, AND NOTHING CAME. Then I wrote four bars of a minuet, saying to her, "See what an ass I am! I have begun a minuet, and can't even complete the first part; be so very good as to finish it for me." She declared this was impossible. At last, with great difficulty,

SOMETHING CAME, and I was only too glad that ANYTHING AT ALL CAME. I told her then to complete the minuet—that is, the treble only. The task I set her for the next lesson was to change my four bars, and replace them by something of her own, and to find out another beginning, even if it were the same harmony, only changing the melody. I shall see to-morrow what she has done.

I shall soon now, I think, receive the poetry for my two-act opera, when I must first present it to the Director, M. de Vismes, to see if he will accept it; but of this there can be no doubt, as it is recommended by Noverre, to whom De Vismes is indebted for his situation. Noverre, too, is soon to arrange a new ballet, for which I am to write the music. Rudolf (who plays the French horn) is in the royal service here, and a very kind friend of mine; he understands composition thoroughly, and writes well. He has offered me the place of organist at Versailles if I choose to accept it: the salary is 2000 livres a year, but I must live six months at Versailles and the remaining six in Paris, or where I please. I don't, however, think that I shall close with the offer; I must take the advice of good friends on the subject. 2000 livres is no such very great sum; in German money it may be so, but not here. It amounts to 83 louis-d'or 8 livres a year— that is, 915 florins 45 kreutzers of our money, (which is certainly a considerable sum,) but only to 383 ecus 2 livres, and that is not much, for it is frightful to see how quickly a dollar goes here! I am not at all surprised that so little is thought of a louis-d'or in Paris, for it does not go far. Four dollars, or a louis-d'or, which are the same, are gone in no time. Adieu!

104. Paris, May 29, 1778.

I AM pretty well, thank God! but still I am often puzzled to know what to make of it all. I feel neither hot nor cold, and don't take much pleasure in anything. What, however, cheers and strengthens me most is the thought that you, dearest papa, and my dear sister, are well; that I am an honest German, and though I cannot SAY, I may at all events THINK what I please, and, after all, that is the chief thing. Yesterday I was for the second time at Count Sickingen's, ambassador from the Elector Palatine; (I dined there once before with Wendling and Ramm.) I don't know whether I told you what a charming man he is, and a great connoisseur and devoted lover of music. I passed eight hours quite alone with him. The whole forenoon, and afternoon too, till ten o'clock at night, we were at the piano, playing all kind of music, praising, admiring, analyzing, discussing, and criticizing. He has nearly thirty scores of operas. I must not forget to tell you that I had the satisfaction of seeing your "School for the Violin" translated into French; I believe it is about eight years since the translation appeared. I have just returned from a music-shop where I went to buy a sonata of Schobert's for one of my pupils, and I mean to go again soon to examine the book more closely, that I may write to you about it minutely, for to-day I have not time to do this.

105. Paris, June 12, 1778.

I MUST now write something that concerns our Raaff. [Footnote: Mozart wrote the part of Idomeneo for Raaff in the year 1781.] You no doubt remember that I did not write much in his favor from Mannheim, and was by no means satisfied with his singing—in short, that he did not please me at all. The cause, however, was that I can scarcely say I really heard him at Mannheim. The first time was at the rehearsal of Holzbauer's "Gunther," when he was in his every-day clothes, his hat on his head, and a stick in his hand. When he was not singing, he stood looking like a sulky child. When he began to sing the first recitative, it went tolerably well, but every now and then he gave a kind of shriek, which I could not bear. He sang the arias in a most indolent way, and yet some of the notes with too much emphasis, which is not what I like. This has been an invariable habit of his, which the Bernacchi school probably entails; for he is a pupil of Bernacchi's. At court, too, he used to sing all kinds of airs which, in my opinion, by no means suited his voice; so he did not at all please me. When at length he made his debut here in the Concert Spirituel, he sang Bach's scena, "Non so d' onde viene" which is, besides, my great favorite, and then for the first time I really heard him sing, and he pleased me—that is, in this class of music; but the style itself, the Bernacchi school, is not to my taste. He is too apt to fall into the cantabile. I admit that, when he was younger and in his prime, this must have made a great impression and taken people by surprise; I could like it also, but there is too much of it, and it often seems to me positively ludicrous. What does please me in him is when he sings short pieces—for instance, andantinos; and he has likewise certain arias which he gives in a manner peculiar to himself. Let each occupy his proper place. I fancy that bravura singing was once his forte, which is even still perceptible in him, and so far as age admits of it he has a good chest and a long breath; and then his andantino! His voice is fine and very pleasing; if I shut my eyes and listen to him, I think his singing very like Meissner's, only Raaffs voice seems to me more agreeable. I speak of the present time, for I never heard either in his best days. I can therefore only refer to their style or method of singing, for this a singer always retains. Meissner, as you know, had the bad habit of purposely making his voice tremble at times,—entire quavers and even crotchets, when marked sostenuto, —and this I never could endure in him. Nothing can be more truly odious; besides, it is a style of singing quite contrary to nature. The human voice is naturally tremulous, but only so far as to be beautiful; such is the nature of the voice, and it is imitated not only on wind instruments, but on stringed instruments, and even on the piano. But the moment the proper boundary is passed it is no longer beautiful, because it becomes unnatural. It seems to me then just like an organ when the bellows are panting. Now Raaff never does this,—in fact, he cannot bear it. Still, so far as a genuine cantabile goes, Meissner pleases me (though not altogether, for he also exaggerates) better than Raaff. In bravura passages and roulades, Raaff is indeed a perfect master, and he has such a good and distinct articulation, which is a great charm; and, as I already said, his andantinus and canzonetti are delightful. He composed four German songs, which are lovely. He likes me much, and we are very intimate; he comes to us almost every day. I have dined at least six times with Count von Sickingen, and always stay from one o'clock till ten. Time, however, flies so quickly in his house that it passes quite imperceptibly. He seems fond of me, and I like very much being with him, for he is a most friendly, sensible person, possessing excellent judgment and a true insight into music, I was there again to-day with Raaff. I took some music with me, as the Count (long since) asked me to do so. I brought my newly completed symphony, with which, on Corpus Christi day, the Concert Spirituel is to commence. The work pleased them both exceedingly, and I am also well satisfied with it. Whether it will be popular here, however, I cannot tell, and, to say the truth, I care very little about it. For whom is it to please? I can answer for its pleasing the few intelligent Frenchmen who may be there; as for the numskulls—

why, it would be no great misfortune if they were dissatisfied. I have some hope, nevertheless, that even the dunces among them may find something to admire. Besides, I have been careful not to neglect le premier coup d'archet; and that is sufficient. All the wiseacres here make such a fuss on that point! Deuce take me if I can see any difference! Their orchestra begins all at one stroke, just as in other places. It is too laughable! Raaff told me a story of Abaco on this subject. He was asked by a Frenchman, in Munich or elsewhere,—"Monsieur, vous avez ete a Paris?" "Oui." "Est-ce que vous etiez au Concert Spirituel?" "Oui." "Que dites-vous du premier coup d'archet? avez-vous entendu le premier coup d'archet?" "Oui, j'ai entendu le premier et le dernier." "Comment le dernier? que veut dire cela?" "Mais oui, le premier et le dernier; et le dernier meme m'a donne plus de plaisir." [Footnote: The imposing impression produced by the first grand crash of a numerous orchestra, commencing with precision, in tutti, gave rise to this pleasantry.] A few days afterwards his kind mother was taken ill. Even in her letters from Mannheim she often complained of various ailments, and in Paris also she was still exposed to the discomfort of cold dark lodgings, which she was obliged to submit to for the sake of economy; so her illness soon assumed the worst aspect, and Mozart experienced the first severe trial of his life. The following letter is addressed to his beloved and faithful friend, Abbe Bullinger, tutor in Count Lodron's family in Salzburg.

(Private.)

106. Paris, July 3, 1778.

MY VERY DEAR FRIEND,—

Mourn with me! This has been the most melancholy day of my life; I am now writing at two o'clock in the morning. I must tell you that my mother, my darling mother, is no more. God has called her to Himself; I clearly see that it was His will to take her from us, and I must learn to submit to the will of God. The Lord giveth, and the Lord taketh away. Only think of all the distress, anxiety, and care I have endured for the last fourteen days. She died quite unconscious, and her life went out like a light. She confessed three days before, took the sacrament, and received extreme unction. The last three days, however, she was constantly

delirious, and to-day, at twenty minutes past five o'clock, her features became distorted, and she lost all feeling and perception. I pressed her hand, I spoke to her, but she did not see me, she did not hear me, and all feeling was gone. She lay thus till the moment of her death, five hours after, at twenty minutes past ten at night. There was no one present but myself, Herr Heiner, a kind friend whom my father knows, and the nurse. It is quite impossible for me to describe the whole course of the illness to-day. I am firmly convinced that she must have died, and that God had so ordained it. All I would ask of you at present is to act the part of a true friend, by preparing my father by degrees for this sad intelligence. I have written to him by this post, but only that she is seriously ill; and now I shall wait for your answer and be guided by it. May God give him strength and courage! My dear friend, I am consoled not only now, but have been so for some time past. By the mercy of God I have borne it all with firmness and composure. When the danger became imminent, I prayed to God for only two things—a happy death for my mother, and strength and courage for myself; and our gracious God heard my prayer and conferred these two boons fully on me. I entreat you, therefore, my best friend, to watch over my father for me; try to inspire him with courage, that the blow may not be too hard and heavy on him when he learns the worst. I also, from my heart, implore you to comfort my sister. Pray go straight to them, but do not tell them she is actually dead—only prepare them for the truth. Do what you think best, say what you please; only act so that my mind may be relieved, and that I may not have to dread another misfortune. Support and comfort my dear father and my dear sister. Answer me at once, I entreat. Adieu! Your faithful
    W. A. M.

107. Paris, July 3, 1778.

MONSIEUR MON TRES-CHER PERE,—

I have very painful and sad news to give you, which has, in fact, been the cause of my not having sooner replied to your letter of the 11th. My dearest mother is very ill. She has been bled according to her usual custom, which was indeed very necessary; it did her much good, but a few days afterwards she complained of shivering and feverishness; then

107. Paris, July 3, 1778.

diarrhoea came on and headache. At first we only used our home remedies, antispasmodic powders; we would gladly have had recourse to the black powder, but we had none, and could not get it here. As she became every moment worse, could hardly speak, and lost her hearing, so that we were obliged to shout to her, Baron Grimm sent his doctor to see her. She is very weak, and still feverish and delirious. They do give me some hope, but I have not much. I hoped and feared alternately day and night for long, but I am quite reconciled to the will of God, and hope that you and my sister will be the same. What other resource have we to make us calm? More calm, I ought to say; for altogether so we cannot be. Whatever the result may be, I am resigned, knowing that it comes from God, who wills all things for our good, (however unaccountable they may seem to us;) and I do firmly believe (and shall never think otherwise) that no doctor, no man living, no misfortune, no casualty, can either save or take away the life of any human being—none but God alone. These are only the instruments that He usually employs, but not always; we sometimes see people swoon, fall down, and be dead in a moment. When our time does come, all means are vain,— they rather hurry on death than retard it; this we saw in the case of our friend Hefner. I do not mean to say by this that my mother will or must die, or that all hope is at an end; she may recover and be restored to health, but only if the Lord wills it thus. After praying to God with all my strength for health and life for my darling mother, I like to indulge in such consolatory thoughts, and, after doing so, I feel more cheerful and more calm and tranquil, and you may easily imagine how much I require comfort. Now for another subject. Let us put aside these sad thoughts, and still hope, but not too much; we must place our trust in the Lord, and console ourselves by the thought that all must go well if it be in accordance with the will of the Almighty, as he knows best what is most profitable and beneficial both for our temporal and spiritual welfare.

I have composed a symphony for the opening of the Concert Spirituel, which was performed with great applause on Corpus Christi day. I hear, too, that there is a notice of it in the "Courrier de l'Europe," and that it has given the greatest satisfaction. I was very nervous during the rehearsal, for in my life I never heard anything go so badly. You can have no idea of the way in which they scraped and scrambled through my symphony twice over; I was really very uneasy, and would gladly have had it rehearsed again, but so many things had been tried over that there was no time left. I therefore went to bed with an aching heart and in a discontented and angry spirit. Next day I resolved not to go to the concert at all; but in the evening, the weather being fine, I made up my mind at last to go, determined that if it went as badly as at the rehearsal, I would go into the orchestra, take the violin out of the hands of M. La Haussaye, the first violin, and lead myself. I prayed to God that it might go well, for all is to His greater honor and glory; and ecce, the symphony began, Raaff was standing beside me, and just in the middle of the allegro a passage occurred which I felt sure must please, and there was a burst of applause; but as I knew at the time I wrote it what effect it was sure to produce, I brought it in once more at the close, and then rose shouts of "Da capo!" The andante was also liked, but the last allegro still more so. Having observed that all last as well as first allegros here begin together with all the other instruments, and generally unisono, mine commenced with only two violins, piano for the first eight bars, followed instantly by a forte; the audience, as I expected, called out "hush!" at the soft beginning, and the instant the forte was heard began to clap their hands. The moment the symphony was over I went off in my joy to the Palais Royal, where I took a good ice, told over my beads, as I had vowed, and went home, where I am always happiest, and always shall be happiest, or in the company of some good, true, upright German, who, so long as he is unmarried, lives a good Christian life, and when he marries loves his wife, and brings up his children properly.

I must give you a piece of intelligence that you perhaps already know—namely, that the ungodly arch-villain Voltaire has died miserably like a dog—just like a brute. This is his reward! You must long since have remarked that I do not like being here, for many reasons, which, however, do not signify as I am actually here. I never fail to do my very best, and to do so with all my strength. Well, God will make all things right. I have a project in my head, for the success of which I daily pray to God. If it be His almighty will, it must come to pass; but, if not, I am quite contented. I shall then at all events have done my part. When this is in train, and if it turns out as I wish, you must then do your part also, or the whole work would be incomplete. Your kindness leads me to hope that you will certainly do so. Don't trouble yourself by any useless thoughts on the subject; and one favor I must beg of you beforehand, which is, not to ask me to reveal my thoughts more clearly till the time comes. It is very difficult at present to find a good libretto for an opera. The old ones, which are the best, are not written in the modern style, and the new ones are all good for nothing; for poetry, which was the only thing of which France had reason to be proud, becomes every day worse, and poetry is the only thing which requires to be good here, for music they do not understand. There are now two operas in aria which I could write, one in two acts, and the other in three. The two-act one is "Alexandra et Roxane," but the author of the libretto is still in the country; the one in three acts is "Demofonte" (by Metastasio). It is a translation interspersed with choruses and dancing, and specially adapted to the French stage. But this one I have not yet got a sight of. Write to me whether you have Schroter's concertos in Salzburg, or Hullmandell's sonatas. I should like to buy them to send to you. Both of them are beautiful. With regard to Versailles, it never was my intention to go there. I asked the advice of Baron Grimm and other kind friends on the point, and they all thought just as I did. The salary is not much, and I should be obliged to live a dreary life for six months in a place where nothing is to be gained, and my talents completely buried. Whoever enters the king's service is forgotten in Paris; and then to become an organist! A good appointment would be most welcome to me, but only that of a Capellmeister, and a well-paid one too.

Now, farewell! Be careful of your health; place your trust in God, and then you will find consolation. My dearest mother is in the hands of the Almighty. If He still spares her to us, as I wish He may, we will thank Him for this blessing, but if He takes her to Himself, all our anguish, misery, and despair can be of no avail. Let us rather submit with firmness to His almighty will, in the full conviction that it will prove for our good, as he does nothing without a cause. Farewell, dearest papa! Do what you can to preserve your health for my sake.

108. Paris, July 9, 1778.

I HOPE you are prepared to receive with firmness most melancholy and painful intelligence. My last letter of the 3d must have shown you that no good news could be hoped for. That very same day, the 3d, at twenty minutes past ten at night, my mother fell asleep peacefully in the Lord; indeed, when I wrote to you she was already in the enjoyment of heavenly bliss, for all was then over. I wrote to you in the night, and I hope you and my dear sister will forgive me for this slight but very necessary deception; for, judging of your grief and sorrow by my own, I could not prevail on myself to startle you suddenly by such dreadful intelligence; but I hope you have now summoned up courage to hear the worst, and that, after at first giving way to natural and only too just anguish and tears, you will eventually submit to the will of God, and adore His inscrutable, unfathomable, and all-wise providence. You can easily conceive what I have had to endure, and what courage and fortitude I required to bear with composure seeing her become daily worse and worse; and yet our gracious God bestowed this boon on me. I have, indeed, suffered and wept, but what did it avail? So I strove to be comforted, and I do hope, my dear father, that my dear sister and you will do likewise. Weep, weep, as you cannot fail to weep, but take comfort at last; remember that God Almighty has ordained it, and how can we rebel against Him? Let us rather pray to Him and thank Him for His goodness, for she died a happy death. Under these heart-rending circumstances there were three things that consoled me—my entire and steadfast submission to the will of God, and the sight of her easy and blessed death, which made me feel that in a moment she had become so happy; for how far happier is she now than we are! Indeed, I would fain at that moment have gone with her. From this wish and longing proceeded my third source of consolation—namely, that she is not lost to us forever, that we shall see her again, and live to-gether far more happily and blessedly than in this world. The time as yet we know not, but that does not disturb me; when God wills it I am ready. His heavenly and holy will has been fulfilled. Let us therefore pray a pious Vater unser for her soul, and turn our thoughts to other matters, for there is a time for everything.

I write this in the house of Madame d'Epinay and M. Grimm, with whom I now live; I have a pretty little room with a very agreeable prospect, and am as happy as it is possible to be under my present circumstances. It will be a great aid in restoring my tranquillity, to hear that my dear father and sister submit with calmness and fortitude to the will of God, and trust Him with their whole heart, in the entire belief that He orders all for the best. My dearest father, do not give way! My dearest sister, be firm! You do not as yet know your brother's kind heart, because he has not yet had an opportunity to prove it. Remember, my loved ones both, that you have a son and a brother anxious to devote all his powers to make you happy, knowing well that the day must come when you will not be hostile to his wish and his desire,—not certainly such as to be any discredit to him,—and that you will do all that lies in your power to

108. Paris, July 9, 1778.

make him happy. Oh! then we shall all live together as peacefully, honorably, and contentedly as it is possible to do in this world, and at last in God's good time all meet again above—the purpose for which we were destined and created.

I received your last letter of the 29th, and see with pleasure that you are both, thank God! in good health. I could not help laughing heartily at Haydn's tipsy fit. Had I been there, I certainly should have whispered in his ear "Adlgasser!" It is really disgraceful in so clever a man to render himself incapable by his own folly of performing his duties at a festival instituted in honor of God; when the Archbishop too and his whole court were present, and the church full of people, it was quite abominable.[Footnote: The father had written, "Haydn (organist of the church of the Holy Trinity) played the organ in the afternoon at the Litany, and the Te Deum laudamus, but in such a dreadful manner that we were quite startled, and thought he was about to undergo the fate of the deceased Adlgasser [who was seized with paralysis when playing the organ] It turned out, however, that he was only rather intoxicated, so his head and hands did not agree"] This is one of my chief reasons for detesting Salzburg— those coarse, slovenly, dissipated court musicians, with whom no honest man of good breeding could possibly live! instead of being glad to associate with them, he must feel ashamed of them. It is probably from this very cause that musicians are neither loved nor respected with us. If the orchestra were only organised like that at Mannheim! I wish you could see the subordination that prevails there— the authority Cannabich exercises; where all is done in earnest. Cannabich, who is the best director I ever saw, is both beloved and feared by his subordinates, who, as well as himself, are respected by the whole town. But certainly they behave very differently, have good manners, are well dressed (and do not go to public-houses to get drunk). This can never be the case in Salzburg, unless the Prince will place confidence either in you or me and give us full powers, which are indispensable to a conductor of music; otherwise it is all in vain. In Salzburg every one is master—so no one is master. If I were to undertake it, I should insist on exercising entire authority. The Grand Chamberlain must have nothing to say as to musical matters, or on any point relating to music. Not every person in authority can become a Capellmeister, but a Capellmeister must become a person of authority.

By the by, the Elector is again in Mannheim. Madame Cannabich and also her husband correspond with me. If what I fear were to come to pass, and it would be a sad pity if it did,—namely, that the orchestra were to be much diminished,—I still cherish one hope. You know that there is nothing I desire more than a good appointment,—good in reputation, and good in money,—no matter where, provided it be in a Catholic country. You fenced skilfully indeed with Count Stahremberg [FOOTNOTE: A prebendary of Salzburg, to whom the father had "opened his heart," and told him all that had occurred in Salzburg. Wolfgang's reinstatement in his situation was being negotiated at the time.] throughout the whole affair; only continue as you have begun, and do not allow yourself to be deluded; more especially be on your guard if by any chance you enter into conversation with that silly goose——; [FOOTNOTE: He probably alludes to the Archbishop's sister, Countess Franziska von Walles, who did the honors of her brother's court, and who, no doubt, also interfered in this matter.] I know her, and believe me, though she may have sugar and honey on her lips, she has gall and wormwood in her head and in her heart. It is quite natural that the whole affair should still be in an unsettled state, and many things must be conceded before I could accept the offer; and even if every point were favorably adjusted, I would rather be anywhere than at Salzburg. But I need not concern myself on the matter, for it is not likely that all I ask should be granted, as I ask a great deal. Still it is not impossible; and if all were rightly organized, I would no longer hesitate, but solely for the happiness of being with you. If the Salzburgers wish to have me, they must comply with my wishes, or they shall never get me.

So the Prelate of Baumburg has died the usual prelatical death; but I had not heard that the Prelate of the Holy Cross [in Augsburg] was also dead. I grieve to hear it, for he was a good, honest, upright man. So you had no faith in Deacon Zeschinger [see No. 68] being made prelate? I give you my honor I never conjectured anything else; indeed, I do not know who else could have got it; and what better prelate could we have for music?

My friend Raaff leaves this to-morrow; he goes by Brussels to Aix-la-Chapelle and Spa, and thence to Mannheim, when he is to give me immediate notice of his arrival, for we mean to correspond. He sends numerous greetings to you and to my sister. You write that you have heard nothing for a very long time of my pupil in composition; very true, but what can I say about her? She will never be a composer; all labor is vain with her, for she is not only vastly stupid, but also vastly lazy.

108. Paris, July 9, 1778.

I had previously answered you about the opera. As to Noverre's ballet, I only wrote that he might perhaps arrange a new one. He wanted about one half to complete it, and this I set to music. That is, six pieces are written by others, consisting entirely of old trumpery French airs; the symphony and contre-danses, and about twelve more pieces, are contributed by me. This ballet has already been given four times with great applause. I am now positively determined to write nothing more without previously knowing what I am to get for it: but this was only a friendly act towards Noverre. Herr Wendling left this last May. If I were to see Baron Bach, I must have very good eyes, for he is not here but in London. Is it possible that I did not tell you this? You shall find that, in future, I will answer all your letters minutely. It is said that Baron Bach will soon return here; I should be glad of that for many reasons, especially because at his house there will be always opportunity to try things over in good earnest. Capellmeister Bach will also soon be here; I believe he is writing an opera. The French are, and always will be, downright donkeys; they can do nothing themselves, so they must have recourse to foreigners. I talked to Piccini at the Concert Spirituel; he is always most polite to me and I to him when we do by chance meet. Otherwise I do not seek much acquaintance, either with him or any of the other composers; they understand their work and I mine, and that is enough. I already wrote to you of the extraordinary success my symphony had in the Concert Spirituel. If I receive a commission to write an opera, I shall have annoyance enough, but this I shall not much mind, being pretty well accustomed to it—if only that confounded French language were not so detestable for music! It is, indeed, too provoking; even German is divine in comparison. And then the singers—but they do not deserve the name, for they do not sing, but scream and bawl with all their might through their noses and throats. I am to compose a French oratorio for the ensuing Lent, to be given at the Concert Spirituel. M. Le Gros (the director) is amazingly well-disposed towards me. You must know that (though I used to see him every day) I have not been near him since Easter; I felt so indignant at his not having my symphony performed. I was often in the same house visiting Raaff, and thus passed his rooms constantly. His servants often saw me, when I always sent him my compliments. It is really a pity he did not give the symphony—it would have been a good hit; and now he has no longer the opportunity to do so, for how seldom are four such performers to be found together! One day, when I went to call on Raaff, I was told that he was out, but would soon be home; so I waited. M. Le Gros came into the room and said, "It is really quite a marvel to have the pleasure of seeing you once more." "Yes; I have a great deal to do." "I hope you will stay and dine with us to-day?" "I regret that I cannot, being already engaged." "M. Mozart, we really must soon spend a day together." "It will give me much pleasure." A long pause; at length, "A propos, are you disposed to write a grand symphony for me for Corpus Christi day?" "Why not?" "May I then rely on this?" "Oh, yes! if I may, with equal confidence, rely on its being performed, and that it will not fare like the sinfonie concertante." This opened the flood-gates; he excused himself in the best way he could, but did not find much to say. In short, the symphony [Kochel, No. 297] was highly approved of; and Le Gros is so satisfied with it that he says it is his very best symphony. The andante, however, has not the good fortune to please him; he declares that it has too many modulations, and is too long. He derives this opinion from the audience forgetting to clap their hands as loudly, and to be as vociferous, as at the end of the first and last movements. But this andante is a great favorite WITH MYSELF, as well as with all connoisseurs, amateurs, and the greater part of those who heard it. It is the exact reverse of what Le Gros says, for it is both simple and short. But in order to satisfy him (and no doubt some others) I have written a fresh one. Each good in its own way— each having a different character. The last pleases me the best. The first good opportunity I have, I will send you this sinfonie concertante, and also the "School for the Violin," some pieces for the piano, and Vogler's book ("Ton Wissenschaft und Kunst"), and then I hope to have your opinion of them. On August l5th, Ascension Day, my sinfonie, with the new andante, is to be performed for the second time. The sinfonie is in Re, the an- dante in Sol, for here one must not say in D or in G. Le Gros is now all for me.

Take comfort and pray without ceasing; this is the only resource we have. I hope you will cause a holy mass to be said in Maria Plain and in Loretto. I have done so here. As for the letter to Herr Bahr, I don't think it is necessary to send it to me; I am not as yet acquainted with him; I only know that he plays the clarionet well, but is in other respects no desirable companion, and I do not willingly associate with such people; no credit is derived from them, and I really should feel positively ashamed to give him a letter recommending me to him—even if he could be of service to me; but it so happens that he is by no means in good repute here. Many do not know him at all. Of the two Staunitz, the junior only is here [Mannheim composer]. The elder of the two (the veritable Hafeneder composer) is in London. They are wretched scribblers, gamblers, and drunkards, and not the kind of people for me. The one now here has scarcely a coat to his back. By the by, if Brunetti should ever be dismissed, I would be glad to recommend a friend of mine to the Archbishop as first violin; he is a most worthy man, and very steady. I think he is about forty years of age, and a widower; his name is Rothfischer. He is Concertmeister at Kirchheim-Boland, with the Princess of Nassau- Weilberg [see No. 91]. Entre nous, he is dissatisfied, for he is no favorite with his Prince—that is, his music is not. He urged me to forward his interests, and it would cause me real pleasure to be of use to him, for never was there such a kind man.

109. Paris, July 18,1778.

I HOPE you got my last two letters. Let us allude no more to their chief purport. All is over; and were we to write whole pages on the subject, we could not alter the fact.

The principal object of this letter is to congratulate my dear sister on her name-day. I think I wrote to you that M. Raaff had left this, but that he is my very true and most particular friend, and I can entirely depend on his regard. I could not possibly write to you, because I did not myself know that he had so much affection for me. Now, to write a story properly, one ought to begin from the beginning. I ought to tell you, first, that Raaff lodged with M. Le Gros. It just occurs to me that you already know this; but what am I to do? It is written, and I can't begin the letter again, so I proceed. When he arrived, we happened to be at dinner. This, too, has nothing to do with the matter; it is only to let you know that people do dine in Paris, as elsewhere. When I went home I found a letter for me from Herr Weber, and the bearer of it was Raaff. If I wished to deserve the name of a historian, I ought here to insert the contents of this letter; and I can with truth say that I am very reluctant to decline giving them. But I must not be too prolix; to be concise is a fine thing, which you can see by my letter. The third day I found him at home and thanked him; it is always advisable to be polite. I no longer remember what we talked about. An historian must be unusually dull who cannot forthwith supply some falsehood—I mean some romance. Well! we spoke of the fine weather; and when we had said our say, we were silent, and I went away. Some days after—though what day it was I really forget, but one day in the week assuredly—I had just seated myself, at the piano of course; and Ritter, the worthy Holzbeisser, was sitting beside me. Now, what is to be deduced from that? A great deal. Raaff had never heard me at Mannheim except at a concert, where the noise and uproar was so great that nothing could be heard; and HE had such a miserable piano that I could not have done myself any justice on it. Here, however, the instrument was good, and I saw Raaff sitting opposite me with a speculative air; so, as you may imagine, I played some preludes in the Fischietti method, and also played a florid sonata in the style and with the fire, spirit, and precision of Haydn, and then a fugue with all the skill of Lipp, Silber, and Aman. [Footnote: Fischietti was Capellmeister in Salzburg; Michael Haydn and Lipp, organists.] My fugue-playing has everywhere gained me the greatest applause. When I had quite finished, (Raaff all the time calling out Bravo! while his countenance showed his true and sincere delight,) I entered into conversation with Ritter, and among other things said that I by no means liked being here; adding, "The chief cause of this is music; besides, I can find no resources here, no amusement, no agreeable or sociable intercourse with any one,—especially with ladies, many of whom are disreputable, and those who are not so are deficient in good breeding." Ritter could not deny that I was right. Raaff at last said, smiling, "I can quite believe it, for M. Mozart is not WHOLLY here to admire the Parisian beauties; one half of him is elsewhere—where I have just come from." This of course gave rise to much laughing and joking; but Raaff presently said, in a serious tone, "You are quite right, and I cannot blame you; she deserves it, for she is a sweet, pretty, good girl, well educated, and a superior person with considerable talent." This gave me an excellent opportunity strongly to recommend my beloved Madlle. Weber to him; but there was no occasion for me to say much, as he was already quite fascinated by her. He promised me, as soon as he returned to Mannheim, to give her lessons, and to interest himself in her favor. I ought, by rights, to insert something here, but I must first finish the history of our friendship; if there is still room, I may do so. He was in my eyes only an every-day acquaintance, and no more; but I often sat with him in his room, so by degrees I began to place more confidence in him, and at last told him all my Mannheim history,—how I had been bamboozled and made a fool of, adding that perhaps I might still get an appointment there. He neither said yes nor no; and on every occasion when I alluded to it he seemed

109. Paris, July 18, 1778.

each time more indifferent and less interested in the matter. At last, however, I thought I remarked more complacency in his manner, and he often, indeed, began to speak of the affair himself. I introduced him to Herr Grimm and to Madame d'Epinay. On one occasion he came to me and said that he and I were to dine with Count Sickingen some day soon; adding, "The Count and I were conversing together, and I said to him, 'A propos, has your Excellency heard our Mozart?' 'No; but I should like very much both to see and to hear him, for they write me most astonishing things about him from Mannheim.' 'When your Excellency does hear him, you will see that what has been written to you is rather too little than too much.' 'Is it possible?' 'Beyond all doubt, your Excellency.'" Now, this was the first time that I had any reason to think Raaff interested in me. Then it went on increasing, and one day I asked him to come home with me; and after that he often came of his own accord, and at length every day. The day after he left this, a good-looking man called on me in the forenoon with a picture, and said, "Monsieur, je viens de la part de ce Monsieur," showing me a portrait of Raaff, and an admirable likeness. Presently he began to speak German; and it turned out that he was a painter of the Elector's, whom Raaff had often mentioned to me, but always forgot to take me to see him. I believe you know him, for it must be the very person Madame Urspringer, of Mayence, alludes to in her letter, because he says he often met us at the Urspringers'. His name is Kymli. He is a most kind, amiable man, well-principled, honorable, and a good Christian; one proof of which is the friendship between him and Raaff. Now comes the best evidence of Raaff's regard for me, and the sincere interest he takes in my welfare: it is, that he imparts his intentions rather to those whom he can trust than to those more immediately concerned, being unwilling to promise without the certainty of a happy result. This is what Kymli told me. Raaff asked him to call on me and to show me his portrait, to see me often, and to assist me in every way, and to establish an intimate friendship with me. It seems he went to him every morning, and repeatedly said to Kymli, "I was at Herr Mozart's again yesterday evening; he is, indeed, a wonderful little fellow; he is an out-and-outer, and no mistake!" and was always praising me. He told Kymli everything, and the whole Mannheim story—in short, all. The fact is, that high-principled, religious, and well-conducted people always like each other. Kymli says I may rest assured that I am in good hands. "Raaff will certainly do all he can for you, and he is a prudent man who will set to work cleverly; he will not say that it is your wish, but rather your due. He is on the best footing with the Oberststallmeister. Rely on it, he will not be beat; only you must let him go his own way to work." One thing more. Father Martini's letter to Raaff, praising me, must have been lost. Raaff had, some time since, a letter from him, but not a word about me in it. Possibly it is still lying in Mannheim; but this is unlikely, as I know that, during his stay in Paris, all his letters have been regularly forwarded to him. As the Elector justly entertains a very high opinion of the Padre Maestro, I think it would be a good thing if you would be so kind as to apply to him to write again about me to Raaff; it might be of use, and good Father Martini would not hesitate to do a friendly thing twice over for me, knowing that he might thus make my fortune. He no doubt would express the letter in such a manner that it could be shown, if need be, to the Elector. Now enough as to this; my wish for a favorable issue is chiefly that I may soon have the happiness of embracing my dear father and sister. Oh! how joyously and happily we shall live together! I pray fervently to God to grant me this favor; a new leaf will at last be turned, please God! In the fond hope that the day will come, and the sooner the better, when we shall all be happy, I mean, in God's name, to persevere in my life here, though so totally opposed to my genius, inclinations, knowledge, and sympathies. Believe me, this is but too true,—I write you only the simple truth. If I were to attempt to give you all my reasons, I might write my fingers off and do no good. For here I am, and I must do all that is in my power. God grant that I may not thus impair my talents; but I hope it will not continue long enough for that. God grant it! By the by, the other day an ecclesiastic called on me. He is the leader of the choir at St. Peter's, in Salzburg, and knows you very well; his name is Zendorff; perhaps you may not remember him? He gives lessons here on the piano—in Paris. N. B., have not you a horror of the very name of Paris? I strongly recommend him as organist to the Archbishop; he says he would be satisfied with three hundred florins. Now farewell! Be careful of your health, and strive to be cheerful. Remember that possibly you may ere long have the satisfaction of tossing off a good glass of Rhenish wine with your son—your truly happy son. Adieu!

20th.—Pray forgive my being so late in sending you my congratulations, but I wished to present my sister with a little prelude. The mode of playing it I leave to her own feeling. This is not the kind of prelude to pass from one key to another, but merely a capriccio to try over a piano. My sonatas [Kochel, Nos. 301-306] are soon to be

109. Paris, July 18, 1778.

published. No one as yet would agree to give me what I asked for them, so I have been obliged at last to give in, and to let them go for 15 louis-d'or. It is the best way too to make my name known here. As soon as they appear I will send them to you by some good opportunity (and as economically as possible) along with your "School for the Violin," Vogler's book, Hullmandel's sonatas, Schroter's concertos, some of my pianoforte sonatas, the sinfonie concertante, two quartets for the flute, and a concerto for harp and flute [Kochel, No. 298, 299].

Pray, what do you hear about the war? For three days I was very depressed and sorrowful; it is, after all, nothing to me, but I am so sensitive that I feel quickly interested in any matter. I heard that the Emperor had been defeated. At first it was reported that the King of Prussia had surprised the Emperor, or rather the troops commanded by Archduke Maximilian; that two thousand had fallen on the Austrian side, but fortunately the Emperor had come to his assistance with forty thousand men, but was forced to retreat. Secondly, it was said that the King had attacked the Emperor himself, and entirely surrounded him, and that if General Laudon had not come to his relief with eighteen hundred cuirassiers, he would have been taken prisoner; that sixteen hundred cuirassiers had been killed, and Laudon himself shot dead. I have not, however, seen this in any newspaper, but to-day I was told that the Emperor had invaded Saxony with forty thousand troops. Whether the news be true I know not. This is a fine griffonage, to be sure! but I have not patience to write prettily; if you can only read it, it will do well enough. A propos, I saw in the papers that, in a skirmish between the Saxons and Croats, a Saxon captain of grenadiers named Hopfgarten had lost his life, and was much lamented. Can this be the kind, worthy Baron Hopfgarten whom we knew at Paris with Herr von Bose? I should grieve if it were, but I would rather he died this glorious death than have sacrificed his life, as too many young men do here, to dissipation and vice. You know this already, but it is now worse than ever.

N. B. I hope you will be able to decipher the end of the prelude; you need not be very particular about the time; it is the kind of thing that may be played as you feel inclined. I should like to inflict twenty-five stripes on the sorry Vatel's shoulders for not having married Katherl. Nothing is more shameful, in my opinion, than to make a fool of an honest girl, and to play her false eventually; but I hope this may not be the case. If I were her father, I would soon put a stop to the affair.

110. Paris, July 31, 1778.

I HOPE you have got my two letters of the 11th and 18th. Meantime I have received yours of the 13th and 20th. The first brought tears of sorrow to my eyes, as I was reminded by it of the sad death of my darling mother, and the whole scene recurred vividly to me. Never can I forget it while I live. You know that (though I often wished it) I had never seen any one die, and the first time I did so it was fated to be my own mother! My greatest misery was the thoughts of that hour, and I prayed earnestly to God for strength. I was heard, and strength was given to me. Melancholy as your letter made me, still I was inexpressibly happy to find that you both bear this sorrow as it ought to be borne, and that my mind may now be at ease about my beloved father and sister. As soon as I read your letter, my first impulse was to throw myself on my knees, and fervently to thank our gracious God for this blessing. I am now comparatively happy, because I have no longer anything to dread on account of the two persons who are dearest to me in this world; had it been otherwise, such a terrible misfortune would have utterly overwhelmed me. Be careful therefore of your precious health for my sake, I entreat, and grant to him who flatters himself that he is now what you love most in the world the joy and felicity soon to embrace you.

Your last letter also caused my tears to flow from joy, as it convinced me more than ever of your fatherly love and care. I shall strive with all my might still more to deserve your affection. I thank you for the powder, but am sure you will be glad to hear that I do not require to use it. During my dear mother's illness it would have been very useful, but now, thank God! I am perfectly well and healthy. At times I have fits of melancholy, but the best way to get rid of them is by writing or receiving letters, which always cheers me; but, believe me, these sad feelings never recur without too good cause. You wish to have an account of her illness and every detail connected with it; that you shall have; but I must ask you to let it be short, and I shall only allude to the principal facts, as the event is over, and cannot, alas! now be altered, and I require some space to write on business topics.

In the first place, I must tell you that NOTHING could have saved my mother. No doctor in the world could have restored her to health. It was the manifest will of God; her time was come, and God chose to take

110. Paris, July 31, 1778.

her to Himself. You think she put off being bled too long? it may be so, as she did delay it for a little, but I rather agree with the people here, who dissuaded her from being bled at all. The cause of my mother's illness was internal inflammation. After being bled she rallied for some days, but on the 19th she complained of headache, and for the first time stayed in bed the whole day. On the 20th she was seized first with shivering and then with fever, so I gave her an anti- spasmodic powder. I was at that time very anxious to send for another doctor, but she would not allow me to do so, and when I urged her very strongly, she told me that she had no confidence in any French medical man. I therefore looked about for a German one. I could not, of course, go out and leave her, but I anxiously waited for M. Heina, who came regularly every day to see us; but on this occasion two days passed without his appearing. At last he came, but as our doctor was prevented paying his usual visit next day, we could not consult with him; in fact, he did not come till the 24th. The previous day, when I had been expecting him so eagerly, I was in great trouble, for my mother suddenly lost her sense of hearing. The doctor, an old German about seventy, gave her rhubarb in wine. I could not understand this, as wine is usually thought heating; but when I said so, every one exclaimed, "How can you say so? Wine is not heating, but strengthening; water is heating." And all the time the poor invalid was longing for a drink of fresh water. How gladly would I have complied with her wish! My dear father, you cannot conceive what I went through, but nothing could be done, except to leave her in the hands of the physician. All that I could do with a good conscience, was to pray to God without ceasing, that He would order all things for her good. I went about as if I had altogether lost my head. I had ample leisure then to compose, but I was in such a state that I could not have written a single note. The 25th the doctor did not come; on the 26th he visited her again. Imagine my feelings when he all at once said to me, "I fear she will scarcely live through the night; she may die at any moment. You had better see that she receives the sacrament." So I hurried off to the end of the Chaussee d'Antin, and went on beyond the Barriere to find Heina, knowing that he was at a concert in the house of some count. He said that he would bring a German priest with him next morning. On my way back I looked in on Madame d'Epinay and M. Grimm for a moment as I passed. They were distressed that I had not spoken sooner, as they would at once have sent their doctor. I did not tell them my reason, which was, that my mother would not see a French doctor. I was hard put to it, as they said they would send their physician that very evening. When I came home, I told my mother that I had met Herr Heina with a German priest, who had heard a great deal about me and was anxious to hear me play, and that they were both to call on me next day. She seemed quite satisfied, and though I am no doctor, still seeing that she was better I said nothing more. I find it impossible not to write at full length—indeed, I am glad to give you every particular, for it will be more satisfactory to you; but as I have some things to write that are indispensable, I shall continue my account of the illness in my next letter. In the mean time you must have seen from my last letter, that all my darling mother's affairs and my own are in good order. When I come to this point, I will tell you how things were arranged. Heina and I regulated everything ourselves.

Now for business. Do not allow your thoughts to dwell on what I wrote, asking your permission not to reveal my ideas till the proper time arrived. Pray do not let it trouble you. I cannot yet tell you about it, and if I did, I should probably do more harm than good; but, to tranquillize you, I may at least say that it only concerns myself. Your circumstances will be made neither better nor worse, and until I see you in a better position I shall think no more about the matter. If the day ever arrives when we can live together in peace and happiness, (which is my grand object),—when that joyful time comes, and God grant it may come soon!—then the right moment will have arrived, and the rest will depend on yourself. Do not, therefore, discompose yourself on the subject, and be assured that in every case where I know that your happiness and peace are involved, I shall invariably place entire confidence in you, my kind father and true friend, and detail everything to you minutely. If in the interim I have not done so, the fault is not solely mine. [FOOTNOTE: He had evidently in his thoughts, what was indeed manifest in his previous letters, a speedy marriage with his beloved Aloysia.] M. Grimm recently said to me, "What am I to write to your father? What course do you intend to pursue? Do you remain here, or go to Mannheim?" I really could not help laughing: "What could I do at Mannheim now? would that I had never come to Paris! but so it is. Here I am, and I must use every effort to get forward." "Well," said he, "I scarcely think that you will do much good here." "Why? I see a number of wretched bunglers who make a livelihood, and why, with my talents, am I to fail? I assure you that I like being at Mannheim, and wish very much to get some appointment there, but it must be one that is honorable and of good repute. I must have entire certainty on the subject before I move a step." "I fear," said he,

110. Paris, July 31, 1778.

"that you are not sufficiently active here— you don't go about enough." "Well," said I, "that is the hardest of all for me to do." Besides, I could go nowhere during my mother's long illness, and now two of my pupils are in the country, and the third (the Duke de Guines's daughter) is betrothed, and means no longer to continue her lessons, which, so far as my credit is concerned, does not distress me much. It is no particular loss to me, for the Duke only pays me what every one else does. Only imagine! I went to his house every day for two hours, being engaged to give twenty-four lessons, (but it is the custom here to pay after each twelve lessons.) They went into the country, and when they came back ten days afterwards, I was not apprised of it; had I not by chance inquired out of mere curiosity, I should not have known that they were here. When I did go, the governess took out her purse and said to me, "Pray excuse my only paying you at present for twelve lessons, for I have not enough money." This is a noble proceeding! She then gave me three louis-d'or, adding, "I hope you are satisfied; if not, I beg you will say so." M. le Duc can have no sense of honor, or probably thinks that I am only a young man and a thick-headed German, (for this is the way in which the French always speak of us,) and that I shall be quite contented. The thick-headed German, however, was very far from being contented, so he declined receiving the sum offered. The Duke intended to pay me for one hour instead of two, and all from economy. As he has now had a concerto of mine for harp and flute, for the last four months, which he has not yet paid me for, I am only waiting till the wedding is over to go to the governess and ask for my money. What provokes me most of all is that these stupid Frenchmen think I am still only seven years old, as they saw me first when I was that age. This is perfectly true, for Madame d'Epinay herself told me so quite seriously. I am therefore treated here like a beginner, except by the musicians, who think very differently; but most votes carry the day!

After my conversation with Grimm, I went the very next day to call on Count Sickingen. He was quite of my opinion that I ought to have patience and wait till Raaff arrives at his destination, who will do all that lies in his power to serve me. If he should fail, Count Sickingen has offered to procure a situation for me at Mayence. In the mean time my plan is to do my utmost to gain a livelihood by teaching, and to earn as much money as possible. This I am now doing, in the fond hope that some change may soon occur; for I cannot deny, and indeed at once frankly confess, that I shall be delighted to be released from this place.

Giving lessons is no joke here, and unless you wear yourself out by taking a number of pupils, not much money can be made. You must not think that this proceeds from laziness. No! it is only quite opposed to my genius and my habits. You know that I am, so to speak, plunged into music,—that I am occupied with it the whole day,—that I like to speculate, to study, and to reflect. Now my present mode of life effectually prevents this. I have, indeed, some hours at liberty, but those few hours are more necessary for rest than for work.

I told you already about the opera. One thing is certain—I must compose a great opera or none. If I write only smaller ones, I shall get very little, for here everything is done at a fixed price, and if it should be so unfortunate as not to please the obtuse French, it is all up with it. I should get no more to write, have very little profit, and find my reputation damaged. If, on the other hand, I write a great opera, the remuneration is better, I am working in my own peculiar sphere, in which I delight, and I have a greater chance of being appreciated, because in a great work there is more opportunity to gain approval. I assure you that if I receive a commission to write an opera, I have no fears on the subject. It is true that the devil himself invented their language, and I see the difficulties which all composers have found in it. But, in spite of this, I feel myself as able to surmount these difficulties as any one else. Indeed, when I sometimes think in my own mind that I may look on my opera as a certainty, I feel quite a fiery impulse within me, and tremble from head to foot, through the eager desire to teach the French more fully how to know, and value, and fear the Germans. Why is a great opera never intrusted to a Frenchman? Why is it always given to a foreigner? To me the most insupportable part of it will be the singers. Well, I am ready. I wish to avoid all strife, but if I am challenged I know how to defend myself. If it runs its course without a duel, I should prefer it, for I do not care to wrestle with dwarfs.

God grant that some change may soon come to pass! In the mean time I shall certainly not be deficient in industry, trouble, and labor. My hopes are centred on the winter, when every one returns from the country. My heart beats with joy at the thought of the happy day when I shall once more see and embrace you.

The day before yesterday my dear friend Weber, among other things, wrote to me that the day after the Elector's arrival it was publicly announced that he was to take up his residence in Munich, which came like a thunder-clap on Mannheim, wholly, so to say, extinguishing the universal illumination by which the inhabitants had testified their joy on the previous day. The fact was also communicated to all the court musicians, with the addition that each was at liberty to follow the court to Munich or to remain in Mannheim, (retaining the same salaries,) and in a fortnight each was to give a written and sealed decision to the Intendant. Weber, who is, as you know, in the most miserable circumstances, wrote as follows:—"I anxiously desire to follow my gracious master to Munich, but my decayed circumstances prevent my doing so." Before this occurred there was a grand court concert, where poor Madlle. Weber felt the fangs of her enemies; for on this occasion she did not sing! It is not known who was the cause of this. Afterwards there was a concert at Herr von Gemmingen's, where Count Seeau also was. She sang two arias of mine, and was so fortunate as to please, in spite of those Italian scoundrels [the singers of Munich], those infamous charlatans, who circulated a report that she had very much gone off in her singing. When her songs were finished, Cannabich said to her, "Mademoiselle, I hope you will always continue to fall off in this manner; tomorrow I will write to M. Mozart in your praise." One thing is certain; if war had not already broken out, the court would by this time have been transferred to Munich. Count Seeau, who is quite determined to engage Madlle. Weber, would have left nothing undone to insure her coming to Munich, so that there was some hope that the family might have been placed in better circumstances; but now that all is again quiet about the Munich journey, these poor people may have to wait a long time, while their debts daily accumulate. If I could only help them! Dearest father, I recommend them to you from my heart. If they could even for a few years be in possession of 1000 florins!

111. Paris, August 7, 1778.

To HERR BULLINGEB.
Paris, August 7, 1778.

MY VERY DEAR FRIEND,—

Allow me above all to thank you most warmly for the proof of friendship you gave me by your interest in my dear father—first in preparing, and then kindly consoling him for his loss [see No. 106]. You played your part admirably. These are my father's own words. My kind friend, how can I sufficiently thank you? You saved my father for me. I have you to thank that I still have him. Permit me to say no more on the subject, and not to attempt to express my gratitude, for I feel too weak and incompetent to do so. My best friend, I am forever your debtor; but patience! It is too true that I am not yet in a position to repay what I owe you, but rely on it God will one day grant me the opportunity of showing by deeds what I am unable to express by words. Such is my hope; till that happy time, however, arrives, allow me to beg you to continue your precious and valued friendship to me, and also to accept mine afresh, now and forever; to which I pledge myself in all sincerity of heart. It will not, indeed, be of much use to you, but not on that account less sincere and lasting. You know well that the best and truest of all friends are the poor. The rich know noth-ing of friendship, especially those who are born to riches, and even those whom fate enriches often become very different when fortunate in life. But when a man is placed in favorable circumstances, not by blind, but reasonable good fortune and merit, who during his early and less prosperous days never lost courage, remaining faithful to his religion and his God, striving to be an honest man and good Christian, knowing how to value his true friends,—in short, one who really deserves better fortune,—from such a man no ingratitude is to be feared.

I must now proceed to answer your letter. You can be under no further anxiety as to my health, for you must have ere this received three letters from me. The first, containing the sad news of my mother's death, was enclosed, my dear friend, to you. You must forgive my silence on the subject, but my thoughts recur to it constantly. You write that I should now think only of my father, tell him frankly all my thoughts, and place entire confidence in him. How unhappy should I be if I required this injunction! It was expedient that you should suggest it, but I am happy to say (and you will also be glad to hear it) that I do not need this advice. In my last letter to my dear father, I wrote to him all that I myself know up to this time, assuring him that I would always keep him minutely informed of everything, and candidly tell him my intentions, as I place entire faith in him, being confident of his fatherly care, love, and goodness. I feel assured that at a future day he will not deny me a request on which my whole happiness in life depends, and which (for he cannot expect anything else from me) will certainly be quite fair and reasonable.

111. Paris, August 7, 1778.

My dear friend, do not let my father read this. You know him; he would only fancy all kinds of things, and to no purpose.

Now for our Salzburg affair. You, my dear friend, are well aware how I do hate Salzburg, not only on account of the injustice shown to my father and myself there, which was in itself enough to make us wish to forget such a place, and to blot it out wholly from our memory. But do not let us refer to that, if we can contrive to live respectably there. To live respectably and to live happily, are two very different things; but the latter I never could do short of witchcraft,—it would indeed be supernatural if I did,—so this is impossible, for in these days there are no longer any witches. Well, happen what may, it will always be the greatest possible pleasure to me to embrace my dear father and sister, and the sooner the better. Still I cannot deny that my joy would be twofold were this to be elsewhere, for I have far more hope of living happily anywhere else. Perhaps you may misunderstand me, and think that Salzburg is on too small a scale for me. If so, you are quite mistaken. I have already written some of my reasons to my father. In the mean time, let this one suffice, that Salzburg is no place for my talent. In the first place, professional musicians are not held in much consideration; and, secondly, one hears nothing. There is no theatre, no opera there; and if they really wished to have one, who is there to sing? For the last five or six years the Salzburg orchestra has always been rich in what is useless and superfluous, but very poor in what is useful and indispensable; and such is the case at the present moment. Those cruel French are the cause of the band there being without a Capellmeister. [FOOTNOTE: The old Capellmeister, Lolli, had died a short time previously.] I therefore feel assured that quiet and order are now reigning in the orchestra. This is the result of not making provision in time. Half a dozen Capellmeisters should always be held in readiness, that, if one fails, another can instantly be substituted. But where, at present, is even ONE to be found? And yet the danger is urgent. It will not do to allow order, quiet, and good-fellowship to prevail in the orchestra, or the mischief would still further increase, and in the long run become irremediable. Is there no ass-eared old periwig, no dunderhead forthcoming, to restore the concern to its former disabled condition? I shall certainly do my best in the matter. To-morrow I intend to hire a carriage for the day, and visit all the hospitals and infirmaries, to see if I can't find a Capellmeister in one of them. Why were they so improvident as to allow Misliweczeck to give them the slip, and he so near too? [See

No. 64.] He would have been a prize, and one not so easy to replace,-- freshly emerged, too, from the Duke's Clementi Conservatorio. He was just the man to have awed the whole court orchestra by his presence. Well, we need not be uneasy: where there is money there are always plenty of people to be had. My opinion is that they should not wait too long, not from the foolish fear that they might not get one at all,—for I am well aware that all these gentlemen are expecting one as eagerly and anxiously as the Jews do their Messiah,—but simply because things cannot go on at all under such circumstances. It would therefore be more useful and profitable to look out for a Capellmeister, there being NONE at present, than to write in all directions (as I have been told) to secure a good female singer.

[FOOTNOTE: In order the better to conciliate Wolfgang, Bullinger had been desired to say that the Archbishop, no longer satisfied with Madlle. Haydn, intended to engage another singer; and it was hinted to Mozart, that he might be induced to make choice of Aloysia Weber; (Jahn, ii. 307.) Madlle. Haydn was a daughter of Lipp, the organist, and sent by the Archbishop to Italy to cultivate her voice. She did not enjoy a very good reputation.]

I really can scarcely believe this. Another female singer, when we have already so many, and all admirable! A tenor, though we do not require one either, I could more easily understand—but a prima donna, when we have still Cecarelli! It is true that Madlle. Haydn is in bad health, for her austere mode of life has been carried too far. There are few of whom this can be said. I wonder that she has not long since lost her voice from her perpetual scourgings and flagellations, her hair-cloth, unnatural fasts, and night-prayers! But she will still long retain her powers, and instead of becoming worse, her voice will daily improve. When at last, however, she departs this life to be numbered among the saints, we still have five left, each of whom can dispute the palm with the other. So you see how superfluous a new one is. But, knowing how much changes and novelty and variety are liked with us, I see a wide field before me which may yet form an epoch.

[FOOTNOTE: Archbishop Hieronymus, in the true spirit of Frederick the Great, liked to introduce innovations with an unsparing hand; many, however, being both necessary and beneficent.] Do your best that the orchestra may have a leg to stand on, for that is what is most wanted. A head they have [the Archbishop], but that is just the misfortune; and till a change is made in this respect, I will never come to Salzburg. When it does take place, I am willing to come and to turn over the leaf as often as I see V. S. [volti subito] written. Now as to the war [the Bavarian Succession]. So far as I hear, we shall soon have peace in Germany. The King of Prussia is certainly rather alarmed. I read in the papers that the Prussians had surprised an Imperial detachment, but that the Croats and two Cuirassier regiments were near, and, hearing the tumult, came at once to their rescue, and attacked the Prussians, placing them between two fires, and capturing five of their cannon. The route by which the Prussians entered Bohemia is now entirely cut up and destroyed. The Bohemian peasantry do all the mischief they can to the Prussians, who have besides constant desertions among their troops; but these are matters which you must know both sooner and better than we do. But I must write you some of our news here. The French have forced the English to retreat, but it was not a very hot affair. The most remarkable thing is that, friends and foes included, only 100 men were killed. In spite of this, there is a grand jubilation here, and nothing else is talked of. It is also reported that we shall soon have peace. It is a matter of indifference to me, so far as this place is concerned; but I should indeed be very glad if we were soon to have peace in Germany, for many reasons. Now farewell! Your true friend and obedient servant,

WOLFGANG ROMATZ.

112. St. Germains, August 27, 1778.

I WRITE to you very hurriedly; you will see that I am not in Paris. Herr Bach, from London [Johann Christian], has been here for the last fortnight. He is going to write a French opera, and is only come for the purpose of hearing the singers, and afterwards goes to London to complete the opera, and returns here to put it on the stage. You may easily imagine his joy and mine when we met again; perhaps his delight may not be quite as sincere as mine, but it must be admitted that he is an honorable man and willing to do justice to others. I love him from my heart (as you know), and esteem him; and as for him, there is no doubt that he praises me warmly, not only to my face, but to others also, and not in the exaggerated manner in which some speak, but in earnest. Tenducci is also here, Bach's dearest friend, and he expressed the greatest delight at seeing me again. I must now tell you how I happen to be at St. Germains. The Marechal de Noailles lives here, as you no doubt know, (for I am told I was here fifteen years ago, though I don't remember it.) Tenducci is a great favorite of his, and as he is exceedingly partial to me, he was anxious to procure me this acquaintance. I shall gain nothing here, a trifling present perhaps, but at the same time I do not lose, for it costs me nothing; and even if I do not get anything, still I have made an acquaintance that may be very useful to me. I must make haste, for I am writing a scena for Tenducci, which is to be given on Sunday; it is for pianoforte, hautboy, horn, and bassoon, the performers being the Marechal's own people—Germans, who play very well. I should like to have written to you long since, but just as I had begun the letter (which is now lying in Paris) I was obliged to drive to St. Germains, intending to return the same day, and I have now been here a week. I shall return to Paris as soon as I can, though I shall not lose much there by my absence, for I have now only one pupil, the others being in the country. I could not write to you from here either, because we were obliged to wait for an opportunity to send a letter to Paris. I am quite well, thank God, and trust that both of you are the same. You must have patience—all goes on slowly; I must make friends. France is not unlike Germany in feeding people with encomiums, and yet there is a good hope that, by means of your friends, you may make your fortune. One lucky thing is, that food and lodging cost me nothing. When you write to the friend with whom I am staying [Herr Grimm], do not be too obsequious in your thanks. There are some reasons for this which I will write to you some other time. The rest of the sad history of the illness will follow in the next letter. You desire to have a faithful portrait of Rothfischer? He is an attentive, assiduous director, not a great genius, but I am very much pleased with him, and, best of all, he is the kindest creature, with whom you can do anything—if you know how to set about it, of course. He directs better than Brunetti, but is not so good in solo-playing. He has more execution, and plays well in his way, (a little in the old-fashioned Tartini mode,) but Brunetti's style is more agreeable. The concertos which he writes for himself are pretty and pleasant to listen to, and also to play occasionally. Who can tell whether he may not please? At all events, he plays a thousand million times better than Spitzeger, and, as I already said, he directs well, and is active in his calling. I recommend him to you heartily, for he is the most good-natured man! Adieu!

113. Paris, Sept. 11, 1778.

I HAVE received your three letters. I shall only reply to the last, being the most important. When I read it, (Heina was with me and sends you his regards,) I trembled with joy, for I fancied myself already in your arms. True it is (and this you will yourself confess) that no great stroke of good fortune awaits me; still, when I think of once more embracing you and my dear sister, I care for no other advantage. This is indeed the only excuse I can make to the people here, who are vociferous that I should remain in Paris; but my reply invariably is, "What would you have? I am content, and that is everything; I have now a place I can call my home, and where I can live in peace and quiet with my excellent father and beloved sister. I can do what I choose when not on duty. I shall be my own master, and have a certain competency; I may leave when I like, and travel every second year. What can I wish for more?" The only thing that disgusts me with Salzburg, and I tell you of it just as I feel it, is the impossibility of having any satisfactory intercourse with the people, and that musicians are not in good repute there, and—that the Archbishop places no faith in the experience of intelligent persons who have seen the world. For I assure you that people who do not travel (especially artists and scientific men) are but poor creatures. And I at once say that if the Archbishop is not prepared to allow me to travel every second year, I cannot possibly accept the engagement. A man of moderate talent will never rise above mediocrity, whether he travels or not, but a man of superior talents (which, without being unthankful to Providence, I cannot deny that I possess) deteriorates if he always remains in the same place. If the Archbishop would only place confidence in me, I could soon make his music celebrated; of this there can be no doubt. I also maintain that my journey has not been unprofitable to me—I mean, with regard to composition, for as to the piano, I play it as well as I ever shall. One thing more I must settle about Salzburg, that I am not to take up the violin as I formerly did. I will no longer conduct with the violin; I intend to conduct, and also accompany airs, with the piano. It would have been a good thing to have got a written agreement about the situation of Capellmeister, for otherwise I may have the honor to discharge a double duty, and be paid only for one, and at last be superseded by some stranger. My dear father, I must decidedly say that I really could not make up my mind to take this step were it not for the pleasure of seeing you both again; I wish also to get away from Paris, which I detest, though my affairs here begin to improve, and I don't doubt that if I could bring myself to endure this place for a few years, I could not fail to succeed. I am now pretty well known—that is, the people all know ME, even if I don't know them. I acquired considerable fame by my two symphonies; and (having heard that I was about to leave) they now really want me to write an opera, so I said to Noverre, "If you will be responsible for its BEING PERFORMED as soon as it is finished, and will name the exact sum that I am to receive for it, I will remain here for the next three months on purpose," for I could not at once decline, or they would have thought that I distrusted myself. This was not, however, done; and I knew beforehand that they could not do it, for such is not the custom here. You probably know that in Paris it is thus:—When the opera is finished it is rehearsed, and if these stupid Frenchmen do not think it good it is not given, and the composer has had all his trouble for nothing; if they approve, it is then put on the stage; as its popularity increases, so does the rate of payment. There is no certainty. I reserve the discussion of these matters till we meet, but I must candidly say that my own affairs begin to prosper. It is no use trying to hurry matters—chi va piano, va sano. My complaisance has gained me both friends and patrons; were I to write you all, my fingers would ache. I will relate it to you personally and place it clearly before you. M. Grimm may be able to help CHILDREN, but not grown-up people; and—but no, I had better not write on the subject. Yet I must! Do not imagine that he is the same that he was; were it not for Madame d'Epinay, I should be no longer in this house. And he has no great cause to be so proud of his good deeds towards me, for there were four houses where I could have had both board and lodging. The worthy man does not know that, if I had remained in Paris, I intended to have left him next month to go to a house that, unlike his, is neither stupid nor tiresome, and where a man has not constantly thrown in his face that a kindness has been done him. Such conduct is enough to cause me to forget a benefit, but I will be more generous than he is. I regret not remaining here only because I should have liked to show him that I do not require him, and that I can do as much as his Piccini, although I am only a German! The

113. Paris, Sept. 11, 1778.

greatest service he has done me consists in fifteen louis-d'or which he lent me bit by bit during my mother's life and at her death. Is he afraid of losing them? If he has a doubt on the subject, then he deserves to be kicked, for in that case he must mistrust my honesty (which is the only thing that can rouse me to rage) and also my talents; but the latter, indeed, I know he does, for he once said to me that he did not believe I was capable of writing a French opera. I mean to repay him his fifteen louis-d'or, with thanks, when I go to take leave of him, accompanied by some polite expressions. My poor mother often said to me, "I don't know why, but he seems to me somehow changed." But I always took his part, though I secretly felt convinced of the very same thing. He seldom spoke of me to any one, and when he did, it was always in a stupid, injudicious, or disparaging way. He was constantly urging me to go to see Piccini, and also Caribaldi,—for there is a miserable opera buffa here,—but I always said, "No, I will not go a single step," In short, he is of the Italian faction; he is insincere himself, and strives to crush me. This seems incredible, does it not? But still such is the fact, and I give you the proof of it. I opened my whole heart to him as a true friend, and a pretty use he made of this! He always gave me bad advice, knowing that I would follow it; but he only succeeded in two or three instances, and latterly I never asked his opinion at all, and if he did advise me to do anything, I never did it, but always appeared to acquiesce, that I might not subject myself to further insolence on his part.

But enough of this; we can talk it over when we meet. At all events, Madame d'Epinay has a better heart. The room I inhabit belongs to her, not to him. It is the invalid's room—that is, if any one is ill in the house, he is put there; it has nothing to recommend it except the view,—only four bare walls, no chest of drawers—in fact, nothing. Now you may judge whether I could stand it any longer. I would have written this to you long ago, but feared you would not believe me. I can, however, no longer be silent, whether you believe me or not; but you do believe me, I feel sure. I have still sufficient credit with you to persuade you that I speak the truth. I board too with Madame d'Epinay, and you must not suppose that he pays anything towards it, but indeed I cost her next to nothing. They have the same dinner whether I am there or not, for they never know when I am to be at home, so they can make no difference for me; and at night I eat fruit and drink one glass of wine. All the time I have been in their house, now more than two months, I have not dined with them more than fourteen times at most, and with the exception of the fifteen louis-d'or, which I mean to repay with thanks, he has no outlay whatever on my account but candles, and I should really be ashamed of myself more than of him, were I to offer to supply these; in fact I could not bring myself to say such a thing. This is my nature. Recently, when he spoke to me in such a hard, senseless, and stupid way, I had not nerve to say that he need not be alarmed about his fifteen louis-d'or, because I was afraid of offending him; I only heard him calmly to the end, when I asked whether he had said all he wished—and then I was off! He presumes to say that I must leave this a week hence—IN SUCH HASTE IS HE. I told him it was impossible, and my reasons for saying so. "Oh! that does not matter; it is your father's wish." "Excuse me, in his last letter he wrote that he would let me know in his next when I was to set off." "At all events hold yourself in readiness for your journey." But I must tell you plainly that it will be impossible for me to leave this before the beginning of next month, or at the soonest the end of the present one, for I have still six arias to write, which will be well paid. I must also first get my money from Le Gros and the Duc de Guines; and as the court goes to Munich the end of this month, I should like to be there at the same time to present my sonatas myself to the Electress, which perhaps might bring me a present. I mean to sell my three concertos to the man who has printed them, provided he gives me ready money for them; one is dedicated to Jenomy, another to Litzau; the third is in B. I shall do the same with my six difficult sonatas, if I can; even if not much, it is better than nothing. Money is much wanted on a journey. As for the symphonies, most of them are not according to the taste of the people here; if I have time, I mean to arrange some violin concertos from them, and curtail them; in Germany we rather like length, but after all it is better to be short and good. In your next letter I shall no doubt find instructions as to my journey; I only wish you had written to me alone, for I would rather have nothing more to do with Grimm. I hope so, and in fact it would be better, for no doubt our friends Geschwender and Heina can arrange things better than this upstart Baron. Indeed, I am under greater obligations to Heina than to him, look at it as you will by the light of a farthing-candle. I expect a speedy reply to this, and shall not leave Paris till it comes. I have no reason to hurry away, nor am I here either in vain or fruitlessly, because I shut myself up and work, in order to make as much money as possible. I have still a request, which I hope you will not refuse. If it should so happen, though I hope and believe it is not so, that the Webers are not in Munich, but still at Mannheim, I wish to have the pleasure of going there to visit them. It takes me, I own, rather out of my way, but not much—at all events it does not appear much to me. I don't believe, after all, that it will be necessary, for I think I shall meet them in Munich; but I shall ascertain this to-morrow by a letter. If it is not the case, I feel beforehand that you will not deny me this happiness. My dear father, if the Archbishop wishes to have a new singer, I can, by heavens! find none better than her. He will never get a Teyberin or a De' Amicis, and the others are assuredly worse. I only lament that when people from Salzburg flock to the next Carnival, and "Rosamunde" is given, Madlle. Weber will not please, or at all events they will not be able to judge of her merits as they deserve, for she has a miserable part, almost that of a dumb personage, having only to sing some stanzas between the choruses. She has one aria where something might be expected from the ritournelle; the voice part is, however, alla Schweitzer, as if dogs were yelping. There is only one air, a kind of rondo in the second act, where she has an opportunity of sustaining her voice, and thus showing what she can do. Unhappy indeed is the singer who falls into Schweitzer's hands; for never while he lives will he learn how to write for the voice. When I go to Salzburg I shall certainly not fail to plead zealously for my dear friend; in the mean time you will not neglect doing all you can in her favor, for you cannot cause your son greater joy. I think of nothing now but the pleasure of soon embracing you. Pray see that everything the Archbishop promised you is made quite secure, and also what I stipulated, that my place should be at the piano. My kind regards to all my friends, and to Herr Bullinger in particular. How merry shall we be together! I have all this already in my thoughts, already before my eyes. Adieu!

114. Nancy, Oct. 3, 1778.

PRAY excuse my not having told you of my journey previous to leaving Paris. But I really cannot describe to you the way in which the whole affair was hurried forward, contrary to my expectations, wish, or will. At the very last moment I wanted to send my luggage to Count Sickingen's, instead of to the bureau of the diligence, and to remain some days longer in Paris. This, I give you my honor, I should at once have done had I not thought of you, for I did not wish to displease you. We can talk of these matters better at Salzburg. But one thing more—only fancy how Herr Grimm deceived me, saying that I was going by the diligence, and should arrive at Strassburg in five days; and I did not find out till the last day that it was quite another carriage, which goes at a snail's pace, never changes horses, and is ten days on the journey. You may easily conceive my rage; but I only gave way to it when with my intimate friends, for in his presence I affected to be quite merry and pleased. When I got into the carriage, I received the agreeable information that we should be travelling for twelve days. So this is an instance of Grimm's good sense! It was entirely to save money that he sent me by this slow conveyance, not adverting to the fact that the expense would amount to the same thing from the constant living at inns. Well, it is now past. What vexed me most in the whole affair was his not being straightforward with me. He spared his own money, but not mine, as he paid for my journey, but not for my board. If I had stayed eight or ten days longer in Paris, I could have paid my own journey, and made it comfortably.

I submitted to this conveyance for eight days, but longer I could not stand it—not on account of the fatigue, for the carriage was well hung, but from want of sleep. We were off every morning at four o'clock, and thus obliged to rise at three. Twice I had the satisfaction of being forced to get up at one o'clock in the morning, as we were to set off at two. You know that I cannot sleep in a carriage, so I really could not continue this without the risk of being ill. I would have taken the post, but it was not necessary, for I had the good fortune to meet with a person who quite suited me—a German merchant who resides in Paris, and deals in English wares. Before getting into the carriage we exchanged a few words, and from that moment we remained together. We did not take our meals with the other passengers, but in our own room, where we also slept. I was glad to meet this man, for, being a great traveller, he understands it well. He also was very much disgusted with our carriage; so we proceed to-morrow by a good conveyance, which does not cost us much, to Strassburg. You must excuse my not writing more, but when I am in a town where I know no one, I am never in a good humor; though I believe that if I had friends here I should like to remain, for the town is indeed charming—handsome houses, spacious streets, and superb squares.

I have one request to make, which is to give me a large chest in my room that I may have all my things within my reach. I should like also to have the little piano that Fischietti and Rust had, beside my writing-table, as it suits me better than the small one of Stein. I don't bring many new things of my own with me, for I have not composed much. I have not yet got the three quartets and the flute concerto I wrote for M. de Jean; for when he went to Paris he packed them in the wrong trunk, so they are left at Mannheim. I can therefore bring nothing finished with me except my sonatas [with violin]; M. Le Gros purchased the two overtures from me and the sinfonie concertante, which he thinks exclusively his own; but this is not the case, for I have it still fresh in my head, and mean to write it out again as soon as I am at home.

The Munich company of comedians are, I conclude, now acting? [in Salzburg.] Do they give satisfaction? Do people go to see them? I suppose that, as for the operettas, the "Fischermadchen" ("La Pescatrice" of Piccini), or "Das Bauernmadchen bei Hof" ("La Contadina in Corte," by Sacchini), will be given first? The prima donna is, no doubt, Madlle. Keiserin, whom I wrote to you about from Munich. I have heard her, but do not know her. At that time it was only her third appearance on any stage, and she had only learned music three weeks [see No. 62]. Now farewell! I shall not have a moment's peace till I once more see those I love.

115. Strassburg, Oct. 15, 1778.

I GOT your three letters safely, but could not possibly answer them sooner. What you write about M. Grimm, I, of course, know better than you can do. That he was all courtesy and civility I do not deny; indeed, had this not been the case, I would not have stood on such ceremony with him. All that I owe M. Grimm is fifteen louis-d'or, and he has only himself to blame for their not being repaid, and this I told him. But what avails any discussion? We can talk it over at Salzburg. I am very much obliged to you for haing put my case so strongly before Father Martini, and also for having written about me to M. Raaff. I never doubted your doing so, for I am well aware that it rejoices you to see your son happy and pleased, and you know that I could never be more so than in Munich; being so near Salzburg, I conld constantly visit you. That Madlle. Weber, or rather MY DEAR WEBERIN, should now receive a salary, and justice be at last done to her merits, rejoices me to a degree natural in one who feels such deep interest in all that concerns her. I still warmly recommend her to you; though I must now, alas! give up all hope of what I so much wished,—her getting an engagement in Salzburg,—for the Archbishop would never give her the salary she now has. All we can now hope for is that she may sometimes come to Salzburg to sing in an opera. I had a hurried letter from her father the day before they went to Munich, in which he also mentions this news. These poor people were in the greatest distress about me, fearing that I must be dead, a whole month having elapsed without any letter from me, (owing to the last one being lost;) an idea that was confirmed by a report in Mannheim that my poor dear mother had died of a contagious disease. So they have been all praying for my soul. The poor girl went every day for this purpose into the Capuchin church. Perhaps you may laugh at this? I did not; on the contrary, I could not help being much touched by it.

To proceed. I think I shall certainly go by Stuttgart to Augsburg, because I see by your letter that nothing, or at least not much, is to be made in Donaueschingen; but I will apprise you of all this before leaving Strassburg. Dearest father, I do assure you that, were it not for the pleasure of soon embracing you, I would never come to Salzburg; for, with the exception of this commendable and delightful impulse, I am really committing the greatest folly in the world. Rest assured that these are my own thoughts, and not borrowed from others. When my resolution to leave Paris was known, certain facts were placed before me, and the sole weapons I had to contend against or to conquer these, were my true and tender love for my kind father, which could not be otherwise than laudable in their eyes, but with the remark that if my father had known my present circumstances and fair prospects, (and had not got different and false impressions by means of a kind friend,) he certainly would not have written to me in such a strain as to render me wholly incapable of offering the least resistance to his wish; and in my own mind I thought, that had I not been exposed to so much annoyance in the house where I lived, and the journey come on me like a sudden thunder-clap, leaving me no time to reflect coolly on the subject, I should have earnestly besought you to have patience for a time, and to let me remain a little longer in Paris. I do assure you that I should have succeeded in gaining fame, honor, and wealth, and been thus enabled to defray your debts. But now it is settled, and do not for a moment suppose that I regret it; but you alone, dearest father, you alone can sweeten the bitterness of Salzburg for me; and that you will do so, I feel convinced. I must also candidly say that I should arrive in Salzburg with a lighter heart were it not for my official capacity there, for this thought is to me the most intolerable of all. Reflect on it yourself, place yourself in my position. At Salzburg I never know how I stand; at one time I am everything, at another absolutely nothing. I neither desire SO MUCH nor SO LITTLE, but still I wish to be SOMETHING—if indeed I am something! In every other place I know what my duties are. Elsewhere those who undertake the violin stick to it,—the same with the piano, I trust this will be regulated hereafter, so that all may turn out well and for my happiness and satisfaction. I rely wholly on you.

Things here are in a poor state; but the day after to-morrow, Saturday the 17th, I MYSELF ALONE, (to save expense,) to please some kind friends, amateurs, and connoisseurs, intend to give a subscription concert. If I engaged an orchestra, it would with the lighting cost me more than three louis-d'or, and who knows whether we shall get as much? My sonatas are not yet published, though promised for the end of September. Such is the effect of not looking after things yourself, for which that obstinate Grimm is also to blame. They will probably be full of mistakes, not being able to revise them myself, for I was obliged to devolve the task on another, and I shall be without my sonatas in Munich. Such an occurrence, though apparently a trifle, may often bring success, honor, and wealth, or, on the other hand, misfortune.

116. Strassburg, Oct. 20, 1778.

You will perceive that I am still here, by the advice of Herr Frank and other Strassburg magnates, but I leave this to-morrow. In my last letter I mentioned that on the 17th I was to give a kind of sample of a concert, as concerts here fare worse than even at Salzburg. It is, of course, over. I played quite alone, having engaged no musicians, so that I might at least lose nothing; briefly, I took three louis-d'or. The chief receipts consisted in the shouts of Bravo! and Bravissimo! which echoed on every side. Prince Max of Zweibrucken also honored the concert by his presence. I need not tell you that every one was pleased. I intended then to pursue my journey, but was advised to stay till the following Saturday, in order to give a grand concert in the theatre. I did so, and, to the surprise, indignation, and disgrace of all the Strassburgers, my receipts were exactly the same. The Director, M. de Villeneuve, abused the inhabitants of this most detestable town in the most unmeasured terms. I took a little more money, certainly, but the cost of the band (which is very bad, but its pay very good), the lighting, printing, the guard at the door, and the check-takers at the entrances, made up a considerable sum. Still I must tell you that the applause and clapping of hands almost deafened me, and made my ears ache; it was as if the whole theatre had gone crazy. Those who were present, loudly and publicly denounced their fellow- citizens, and I told them all that if I could have reasonably supposed so few people would have come, I would gladly have given the concert gratis, merely for the pleasure of seeing the theatre well filled. And in truth I should have preferred it, for, upon my word, I don't know a more desolate sight than a long table laid for fifty, and only three at dinner. Besides, it was so cold; but I soon warmed myself, for, to show the Strassburg gentlemen how little I cared, I played a very long time for my own amusement, giving a concerto more than I had promised, and, at the close, extemporizing. It is now over, but at all events I gained honor and fame.

I have drawn on Herr Scherz for eight louis-d'or, as a precaution, for no one can tell what may happen on a journey; and I HAVE is better than I MIGHT HAVE HAD. I have read the fatherly well-meaning letter which you wrote to M. Frank when in such anxiety about me. [Footnote: "Your sister and I confessed, and took the Holy Communion," writes the father, "and prayed to God fervently for your recovery. Our excellent Bullinger prays daily for you also."] When I wrote to you from Nancy, not knowing myself, you of course could not know, that I should have to wait so long for a good opportunity. Your mind may be quite at ease about the merchant with whom I am travelling; he is the most upright man in the world, takes more care of me than of himself, and, entirely to oblige me, is to go with me to Augsburg and Munich, and possibly even to Salzburg. We actually shed tears when we think that we must separate. He is not a learned man, but a man of experience, and we live together like children. When he thinks of his wife and family whom he has left in Paris, I try to comfort him, and when I think of my own people he speaks comfort to me.

On the 31st of October, my name-day, I amused myself (and, better still, others) for a couple of hours. At the repeated entreaties of Herr Frank, de Berger, I gave another concert, by which, after paying the expenses, (not heavy this time,) I actually cleared a louis-d'or! Now you see what Strassburg is! I wrote at the beginning of this letter that I was to

116. Strassburg, Oct. 20, 1778.

leave this on the 27th or 28th, but it proved impossible, owing to a sudden inundation here, when the floods caused great damage. You will probably see this in the papers. Of course travelling was out of the question, which was the only thing that induced me to consent to give another concert, being obliged to remain at all events.

To-morrow I go by the diligence to Mannheim. Do not be startled at this. In foreign countries it is expedient to follow the advice of those who know from experience what ought to be done. Most of the strangers who go to Stuttgart (N.B., by the diligence) do not object to this detour of eight hours, because the road is better and also the conveyance. I must now, dearest father, cordially wish you joy of your approaching name-day. My kind father, I wish you from my heart all that a son can wish for a good father, whom he so highly esteems and dearly loves. I thank the Almighty that He has permitted you again to pass this day in the enjoyment of perfect health, and implore from Him the boon, that during the whole of my life (and I hope to live for a good many years to come) I may be able to congratulate you every year. However strange, and perhaps ridiculous, this wish may seem to you, I do assure you it is both sincere and well-intended.

I hope you received my last letter from Strassburg. I wish to write nothing further of M. Grimm, but it is entirely owing to his stupidity in pressing forward my departure so much, that my sonatas are not yet engraved, or at all events that I have not got them, and when I do I shall probably find them full of mistakes. If I had only stayed three days longer in Paris, I could have revised them myself and brought them with me. The engraver was desperate when I told him that I could not correct them, but must commission someone else to do so. Why? Because, being resolved not to be three days longer in the same house with Grimm, I told him that on account of the sonatas I was going to stay with Count Sickingen, when he replied, his eyes sparkling with rage, "If you leave my house before you leave Paris, I will never in my life see you again. In that case do not presume ever to come near me, and look on me as your bitterest enemy." Self- control was indeed very necessary. Had it not been for your sake, who knew nothing about the matter, I certainly should have replied, "Be my enemy; by all means be so. You are so already, or you would not have prevented me putting my affairs in order here, which would have enabled me to keep my word, to preserve my honor and reputation, and also to make money, and probably a lucky hit; for if I present my sonatas to the Electress when I go to Munich, I shall thus keep my promise, probably receive a present, and make my fortune besides." But as it was, I only bowed, and left the room without saying a syllable. Before quitting Paris, however, I said all this to him, but he answered me like a man totally devoid of sense, or rather like a malicious man who affects to have none. I have written twice to Herr Heina, but have got no answer. The sonatas ought to have appeared by the end of September, and M. Grimm was to have forwarded the promised copies immediately to me, so I expected to have found them in Strassburg; but M. Grimm writes to me that he neither hears nor sees anything of them, but as soon as he does they are to be forwarded, and I hope to have them ere long.

Strassburg can scarcely do without me. You cannot think how much I am esteemed and beloved here. People say that I am disinterested as well as steady and polite, and praise my manners. Every one knows me. As soon as they heard my name, the two Herrn Silbermann and Herr Hepp (organist) came to call on me, and also Capellmeister Richter. He has now restricted himself very much; instead of forty bottles of wine a day, he only drinks twenty! I played publicly on the two best organs that Silbermann has here, in the Lutheran and New Churches, and in the Thomas Church. If the Cardinal had died, (and he was very ill when I arrived,) I might have got a good situation, for Herr Richter is seventy-eight years of age. Now farewell! Be cheerful and in good spirits, and remember that your son is, thank God! well, and rejoicing that his happiness daily draws nearer. Last Sunday I heard a new mass of Herr Richter's, which is charmingly written.

117. Mannheim, November 12, 1778.

I arrived here safely on the 6th, agreeably surprising all my kind friends. God be praised that I am once more in my beloved Mannheim! I assure you, if you were here you would say the same. I am living at Madame Cannabich's, who, as well as her family and all my good friends here, was quite beside herself with joy at seeing me again. We have not yet done talking, for she tells me of all the events and changes that have taken place during my absence. I have not been able to dine once at home since I came, for people are fighting to have me; in a word, just as I love Mannheim, so Mannheim loves me; and, though of course I don't

117. Mannheim, November 12, 1778.

know it positively, still I do think it possible that I may get an appointment here. But HERE, not in Munich, for my own belief is that the Elector will soon once more take up his residence in Mannheim, for he surely cannot long submit to the coarseness of the Bavarian gentlemen. You know that the Mannheim company is in Munich. There they hissed the two best actresses, Madame Toscani and Madame Urban. There was such an uproar that the Elector himself leant over his box and called out, "Hush!" To this, however, no one paid any attention; so he sent down Count Seeau, who told some of the officers not to make such a noise, as the Elector did not like it; but the only answer he got was, that they had paid their money, and no man had a right to give them any orders. But what a simpleton I am! You no doubt have heard this long ago through our....

I have now something to say. I may PERHAPS make forty louis-d'or here. To be sure, I should have to stay six weeks, or at most two months, in Mannheim. Seiler's company is here, whom you no doubt already know by reputation. Herr von Dalberg is the director. He will not hear of my leaving this till I have written a duodrama for him, and indeed I did not long hesitate, for I have often wished to write this style of drama. I forget if I wrote to you about it the first time that I was here. Twice at that time I saw a similar piece performed, which afforded me the greatest pleasure; in fact, nothing ever surprised me so much, for I had always imagined that a thing of this kind would make no effect. Of course you know that there is no singing in it, but merely recitation, to which the music is a sort of obligato recitativo. At intervals there is speaking while the music goes on, which produces the most striking effect. What I saw was Benda's "Medea." He also wrote another, "Ariadne auf Naxos," and both are truly admirable. You are aware that of all the Lutheran Capellmeisters Benda was always my favorite, and I like those two works of his so much that I constantly carry them about with me. Conceive my joy at now composing the very thing I so much wished! Do you know what my idea is?—that most operatic recitatives should be treated in this way, and the recitative only occasionally sung WHEN THE WORDS CAN BE THOROUGHLY EXPRESSED BY THE MUSIC. An Academie des Amateurs is about to be established here, like the one in Paris, where Herr Franzl is violin leader, and I am at this moment writing a concerto for violin and piano. I found my dear friend Raaff still here, but he leaves this on the 8th. He has sounded my praises here, and shown sincere interest in me, and I hope he will do the same in Munich. Do you know what that confounded fellow Seeau said here?—that my opera buffa had been hissed at Munich! Fortunately he said so in a place where I am well known; still, his audacity provokes me; but the people, when they go to Munich, will hear the exact reverse. A whole flock of Bavarians are here, among others Fraulein de Pauli (for I don't know her present name). I have been to see her because she sent for me immediately. Oh! what a difference there is between the people of the Palatinate and those of Bavaria! What a language it is! so coarse! and their whole mode of address! It quite annoys me to hear once more their hoben and olles (haben and alles), and their WORSHIPFUL SIR. Now good-bye! and pray write to me soon. Put only my name, for they know where I am at the post-office. I am so well known here that it is impossible a letter for me can be lost. My cousin wrote to me, and by mistake put Franconian Hotel instead of Palatine Hotel. The landlord immediately sent the letter to M. Serrarius's, where I lodged when I was last here. What rejoices me most of all in the whole Mannheim and Munich story is that Weber has managed his affairs so well. They have now 1600 florins; for the daughter has 1000 florins and her father 400, and 200 more as prompter. Cannabich did the most for them. It is quite a history about Count Seeau; if you don't know it, I will write you the details next time.

I beg, dearest father, that you will make use of this affair at Salzburg, and speak so strongly and so decidedly, that the Archbishop may think it possible I may not come after all, and thus be induced to give me a better salary, for I declare I cannot think of it with composure. The Archbishop cannot pay me sufficiently for the slavery of Salzburg. As I said before, I feel the greatest pleasure at the thought of paying you a visit, but only annoyance and misery in seeing myself once more at that beggarly court. The Archbishop must no longer attempt to play the great man with me as he used to do, or I may possibly play him a trick,—this is by no means unlikely,—and I am sure that you would participate in my satisfaction.

118. Mannheim, Nov. 24, 1778.

MY DEAR BARON VON DALBERG,—

I called on you twice, but had not the good fortune to find you at home; yesterday you were in the house, but engaged, so I could not see you. I hope you will therefore excuse my troubling you with these few lines, as it is very important to me to explain myself fully. Herr Baron, you are well aware that I am not an interested man, particularly when I know that it is in my power to do a service to so great a connoisseur and lover of music as yourself. On the other hand, I also know that you certainly would not wish that I should be a loser on this occasion; I therefore take the liberty to make my final stipulations on the subject, as it is impossible for me to remain here longer in uncertainty. I agree to write a monodrama for the sum of twenty-five louis-d'or, and to stay here for two months longer to complete everything, and to attend all the rehearsals, but on this condition, that, happen what may, I am to be paid by the end of January. Of course I shall also expect free admission to the theatre. Now, my dear Baron, this is all that I can do, and if you consider, you will admit that I certainly am acting with great discretion. With regard to your opera, I do assure you I should rejoice to compose music for it, but you must yourself perceive that I could not undertake such a work for twenty-five louis-d'or, as it would be twice the labor of a monodrama (taken at the lowest rate). The chief obstacle would be your having told me that Gluck and Schweitzer are partially engaged to write this work. But were you even to give me fifty louis-d'or, I would still as an honest man dissuade you from it. An opera without any singers! what is to be done in such a case? Still, if on this occasion there is a prospect of its being performed, I will not hesitate to undertake the work to oblige you; but it is no trifling one—of that I pledge you my word. I have now set forth my ideas clearly and candidly, and request your decision.

119. Mannheim, Dec. 3, 1778.

I MUST ask your forgiveness for two things,—first, that I have not written to you for so long; and secondly, that this time also I must be brief. My not having answered you sooner is the fault of no one but yourself, and your first letter to me at Mannheim. I really never could have believed—but silence! I will say no more on the subject. Lot us have done with it. Next Wednesday, the 9th, I leave this; I cannot do so sooner, because, thinking that I was to be here for a couple of months, I accepted some pupils, and of course wish to make out the twelve lessons. I assure you that you have no idea what kind and true friends I have here, which time will prove. Why must I be so brief? Because my hands are more than full. To please Herr Gemmingen and myself, I am writing the first act of the melodramatic opera (that I was commissioned to write), but now do so gratis; I shall bring it with me and finish it at home. You see how strong my inclination must be for this kind of composition. Of course Herr von Gemmingen is the poet. The duodrama is called "Semiramis."

Next Wednesday I set off, and do you know how I travel? With the worthy prelate, the Bishop of Kaisersheim. When a kind friend of mine mentioned me to him, he at once knew my name, expressing the pleasure it would be to him to have me as a travelling companion. He is (though a priest and prelate) a most amiable man. I am therefore going by Kaisersheim and not by Stuttgart; but it is just the same to me, for I am very lucky in being able to spare my purse a little (as it is slender enough) on the journey. Be so good as to answer me the following questions. How do the comedians please at Salzburg? Is not the young lady who sings, Madlle. Keiserin? Does Herr Feiner play the English horn? Ah! if we had only clarionets too! You cannot imagine the splendid effect of a symphony with flutes, hautboys, and clarionets. At my first audience of the Archbishop I shall tell him much that is new, and also make some suggestions. Oh, how much finer and better our orchestra might be if the Archbishop only chose! The chief cause why it is not so, is that there are far too many performances. I make no objection to the chamber-music, only to the concerts on a larger scale.

A propos, you say nothing of it, but I conclude you have received the trunk; if not, Herr von Grimm is responsible for it. You will find in it the aria I wrote for Madlle. Weber. You can have no idea of the effect of that aria with instruments; you may not think so when you see it, but it ought to be sung by a Madlle. Weber! Pray, give it to no one, for that would be most unfair, as it was written solely for her, and fits her like a well-fitting glove.

120. Kaisersheim, Dec. 18, 1778.

I ARRIVED here safely on Sunday the 13th, God be praised! I travelled in the most agreeable way, and had likewise the inexpressible pleasure to find a letter from you here. The reason that I did not forthwith answer it was, because I wished to give you sure and precise information as to my departure, for which I had not fixed any time; but I have at length resolved, as the prelate goes to Munich on the 26th or 27th, to be again his companion. I must tell you, however, that he does not go by Augsburg. I lose nothing by this; but if you have anything to arrange or transact where my presence is wanted, I can at any time, if you wish it, (being so near,) make a little expedition from Munich. My journey from Mannheim to this place would have been most agreeable to a man, leaving a city with a light heart. The prelate and his Chancellor, an honest, upright, and amiable man, drove together in one carriage, and Herr Kellermeister, Father Daniel, Brother Anton, the Secretary, and I, preceded them always half an hour, or an hour. But for me, to whom nothing could be more painful than leaving Mannheim, this journey was only partly agreeable, and would not have been at all so, but rather very tiresome, if I had not from my early youth been so much accustomed to leave people, countries, and cities, and with no very sanguine hope of soon or ever again seeing the kind friends I left. I cannot deny, but at once admit, that not only I myself, but all my intimate friends, particularly the Cannabichs, were in the most pitiable distress during the last few days after my departure was finally settled. We felt as if it were not possible for us to part. I set off at half-past eight o'clock in the morning, and Madame Cannabich did not leave her room; she neither would nor could take leave of me. I did not wish to distress her, so left the house without seeing her. My very dear father, I can safely say that she is one of my best and truest friends, for I only call those friends who are so in every situation, who, day and night, think how they can best serve the interests of their friend, applying to all influential persons, and toiling to secure his happiness. Now I do assure you such is the faithful portrait of Madame Cannabich. There may indeed be an alloy of self-interest in this, for where does anything take place—indeed, how can anything be done in this world—without some alloy of selfishness? What I like best in Madame Cannabich is, that she never attempts to deny this. I will tell you when we meet in what way she told me so, for when we are alone, which, I regret to say, is very seldom, we become quite confidential. Of all the intimate friends who frequent her house, I alone possess her entire confidence; for I alone know all her domestic and family troubles, concerns, secrets, and circumstances. We were not nearly so well acquainted the first time I was here, (we have agreed on this point,) nor did we mutually under stand each other so well; but living in the same house affords greater facilities to know a person. When in Paris I first began fully to appreciate the sincere friendship of the Cannabichs, having heard from a trustworthy source the interest both she and her husband took in me. I reserve many topics to explain and to discuss personally, for since my return from Paris the scene has undergone some remarkable changes, but not in all things. Now as to my cloister life. The monastery itself made no great impression on me, after having seen the celebrated Abbey of Kremsmunster. I speak of the exterior and what they call here the court square, for the most renowned part I have yet to see. What appears to me truly ridiculous is the formidable military. I should like to know of what use they are. At night I hear perpetual shouts of "Who goes there?" and I invariably reply, "Guess!" You know what a good and kind man the prelate is, but you do not know that I may class myself among his favorites, which, I believe, does me neither good nor harm, but it is always pleasant to have one more friend in the world. With regard to the monodrama, or duodrama, a voice part is by no means necessary, as not a single note is sung, but entirely spoken; in short, it is a recitative with instruments, only the actor speaks the words instead of singing them. If you were to hear it even with the piano, it could not fail to please you, but properly performed, you would be quite transported. I can answer for this; but it requires a good actor or actress.

I shall really feel quite ashamed if I arrive in Munich without my sonatas. I cannot understand the delay; it was a stupid trick of Grimm's, and I have written to him to that effect. He will now see that he was in rather too great a hurry. Nothing ever provoked me so much. Just reflect

120. Kaisersheim, Dec. 18, 1778.

on it. I know that my sonatas were published in the beginning of November, and I, the author, have not yet got them, therefore cannot present them to the Electress, to whom they are dedicated. I have, however, taken measures in the mean time which will insure my getting them. I hope that my cousin in Augsburg has received them, or that they are lying at Josef Killiau's for her; so I have written to beg her to send them to me at once.

Until I come myself, I commend to your good offices an organist, and also a good pianist, Herr Demmler, from Augsburg. I had entirely forgotten him, and was very glad when I heard of him here. He has considerable genius; a situation in Salzburg might be very useful in promoting his further success, for all he requires is a good leader in music; and I could not find him a better conductor than you, dear father, and it would really be a pity if he were to leave the right path. [See No. 68.] That melancholy "Alceste" of Schweitzer's is to be performed in Munich. The best part (besides some of the openings, middle passages, and the finales of some arias) is the beginning of the recitative "0 Jugendzeit," and this was made what it is by Raaff's assistance; he punctuated it for Hartig (who plays Admet), and by so doing introduced the true expression into the aria. The worst of all, however, (as well as the greater part of the opera,) is certainly the overture.

As for the trifles that are not to be found in the trunk, it is quite natural that under such circumstances something should be lost, or even stolen. The little amethyst ring I felt I ought to give to the nurse who attended my dear mother, whose wedding-ring was left on her finger. [A large blot.] The ink-bottle is so full, and I am too hasty in dipping in my pen, as you will perceive. As for the watch, you have guessed rightly. I sold it, but only got five louis-d'or for it, and that in consideration of the works, which were good; for the shape, as you know, was old-fashioned and quite out of date. Speaking of watches, I must tell you that I am bringing one with me—a genuine Parisian. You know what sort of thing my jewelled watch was—how inferior all the so-called precious stones were, how clumsy and awkward its shape; but I would not have cared so much about that, had I not been obliged to spend so much money in repairing and regulating it, and after all the watch would one day gain a couple of hours, and next day lose in the same proportion. The one the Elector gave me did just the same, and, moreover, the works were even worse and more fragile. I exchanged these two watches and their chains for a Parisian one which is worth twenty louis-d'or. So now at last I know what o'clock it is; with my five watches I never got so far as that before! At present, out of four, I have, at all events, one on which I can depend.

121. Kaisersheim, Dec. 23, 1778.

MA TRES-CHERE COUSINE,—

I write to you in the greatest haste, and in the deepest sorrow and remorse, and with the determined purpose to tell you that it is my intention to set off to-morrow to Munich. I would, I assure you, gladly have gone to Augsburg, but the prelate was resolved to claim me, for which you cannot blame me. It is my loss, so don't be cross. I may perhaps make an escapade from Munich to Augsburg, but this is by no means certain. If you will be as glad to see me, as I shall be to see you, do come to the good town of Munich. Be sure you come by the new year, that I may see your face so dear, and escort you far and near. One thing I very much regret, which is that I cannot give you house-room, because I am not at an hotel, but am living with—whom do you think? I should like to know this myself [with the Webers]. But now Spassus apart. For that very reason, and for my sake, it would be advisable you should come; perhaps you may have a great part to play, but at all events come. I can then pay you in my own mighty person all proper compliments. Now adieu, angel of piety! I await you with anxiety. Your sincere cousin,

W. A. MOZART.

P.S.—Write to me forthwith to Munich, Poste Restante, a little note of twenty-four pages, but do not mention where you are to lodge, that I may not find you out nor you me.

122. Munich, Dec. 29, 1778.

I WRITE from the house of M. Becke [flute-player; see No. 60]. I arrived here safely, God be praised! on the 25th, but have been unable to write to you till now. I reserve everything till our glad, joyous meeting, when I can once more have the happiness of conversing with you, for to-day I can only weep. I have far too sensitive a heart. In the mean time, I must tell you that the day before I left Kaisersheim I received the sonatas; so I shall be able to present them myself to the Electress. I only delay leaving this till the opera [Footnote: Schweitzer's "Alceste." (See No. 120.)] is given, when I intend immediately to leave Munich, unless I were to find that it would be very beneficial and useful to me to remain here for some time longer. In which case I feel convinced, quite convinced, that you would not only be satisfied I should do so, but would yourself advise it. I naturally write very badly, for I never learned to write; still, in my whole life I never wrote worse than this very day, for I really am unfit for anything—my heart is too full of tears. I hope you will soon write to me and comfort me. Address to me, Poste Restante, and then I can fetch the letter myself. I am staying with the Webers. I think, after all, it would be better, far better, to enclose your letter to me to our friend Becke.

I intend (I mention it to you in the strictest secrecy) to write a mass here; all my best friends advise my doing so. I cannot tell you what friends Cannabich and Raaff have been to me. Now farewell, my kindest and most beloved father! Write to me soon.

A happy new-year! More I cannot bring myself to write to-day. This letter is scrawled hurriedly, quite unlike the others, and betrays the most violent agitation of mind. During the whole journey there was nothing to which Mozart looked forward with such joy as once more seeing his beloved Madlle. Weber in Munich. He had even destined "a great part" for the Basle (his cousin) in the affair; but he was now to learn that Aloysia had been faithless to him. Nissen relates: "Mozart, being in mourning for his mother, appeared dressed, according to the French custom, in a red coat with black buttons; but soon discovered that Aloysia's feelings towards him had undergone a change. She seemed scarcely to recognize one for whose sake she had once shed so many tears. On which Mozart quickly seated himself at the piano and sang,

"Ich lass das Madel gern das mich nicht will," ["I gladly give up the girl who slights me."] His father, moreover, was displeased in the highest degree by Wolfgang's protracted absence, fearing that the Archbishop might recall his appointment; so Wolfgang became very uneasy lest he should not meet with a kind reception from his father on his return home.

123. Munich, Dec. 31, 1778.

I HAVE this instant received your latter from my friend Becke. I wrote to you from his house two days ago, but a letter such as I never wrote before; for this kind friend said so much to me about your tender paternal love, your indulgence towards me, your complaisance and discretion in the promotion of my future happiness, that my feelings were softened even to tears. But, from your letter of the 28th, I see only too clearly that Herr Becke, in his conversation with me, rather exaggerated. Now, distinctly, and once for all, as soon as the opera ("Alceste") is given, I intend to leave this, whether the diligence goes the day after or the same night. If you had spoken to Madame Robinig, I might have travelled home with her. But be that as it may, the opera is to be given on the 11th, and on the 12th (if the diligence goes) I set off. It would be more for my interest to stay here a little longer, but I am willing to sacrifice this to you, in the hope that I shall have a twofold reward for it in Salzburg. I don't think your idea about the sonatas at all good; even if I do not get them, I ought to leave Munich forthwith. Then you advise my not being seen at court; to a man so well known as I am here such a thing is impossible. But do not be uneasy. I received my sonatas at Kaisersheim; and, as soon as they are bound, I mean to present them to the Electress. A. propos, what do you mean by DREAMS OF PLEASURE? I do not wish to give up dreaming, for what mortal on the whole compass of the earth does not often dream? above all DREAMS OF PLEASURE— peaceful dreams, sweet, cheering dreams if you will—dreams which, if realized, would have rendered my life (now far rather sad than pleasurable) more endurable.

The 1st.—I have this moment received, through a Salzburg vetturino, a letter from you, which really at first quite startled me. For Heaven's sake tell me, do you really think that I can at once fix a day for my journey; or is it your belief that I don't mean to come at all? When I am so very near, I do think you might be at ease on that point. When the fellow had explained his route to me, I felt a strong inclination to go with him, but at present I really cannot; to-morrow or next day I intend to present the sonatas to the Electress, and then (no matter how strongly I may be urged) I must wait a few days for a present. Of one thing I give you my word, that to please you I have resolved not to wait to see the opera, but intend to leave this the day after I receive the present I expect. At the same time I confess I feel this to be very hard on me; but if a few days more or less appear of such importance to you, so let it be. Write to me at once on this point. The 2d.—I rejoice at the thoughts of conversing with you, for then you will first comprehend how my matters stand here. You need have neither mistrust nor misgivings as to Raaff, for he is the most upright man in the world, though no lover of letter-writing. The chief cause of his silence, however, is no doubt that he is unwilling to make premature promises, and yet is glad to hold out some hope too; besides, like Cannabich, he has worked for me with might and main.

124. Munich, Jan. 8, 1779.

[Footnote: The second grand aria that Mozart wrote for Aloysia, bears the same date.]

I HOPE you received my last letter, which I meant to have given to the vetturino, but having missed him I sent it by post. I have, in the mean time, got all your letters safely through Herr Becke. I gave him my letter to read, and he also showed me his. I assure you, my very dear father, that I am now full of joy at returning to you, (but not to Salzburg,) as your last letter shows that you know me better than formerly. There never was any other cause for my long delay in going home but this doubt, which gave rise to a feeling of sadness that I could no longer conceal; so I at last opened my heart to my friend Becke. What other cause could I possibly have? I have done nothing to cause me to dread reproach from you; I am guilty of no fault; (by a fault I mean that which does not become a Christian, and a man of honor;) in short, I now rejoice, and already look forward to the most agreeable and happy days, but only in the society of yourself and my dear sister. I give you my solemn word of honor that I cannot endure Salzburg or its inhabitants, (I speak of the natives of Salzburg.) Their language, their manners, are to me quite intolerable. You cannot think what I suffered during Madame Robinig's visit here, for it is long indeed since I met with such a fool; and, for my still further annoyance, that silly, deadly dull Mosmayer was also there.

But to proceed. I went yesterday, with my dear friend Cannabich, to the Electress to present my sonatas. Her apartments are exactly what I should like mine one day to be, very pretty and neat, just like those of a private individual, all except the view, which is miserable. We were there fully an hour and a half, and she was very gracious. I have managed to let her know that I must leave this in a few days, which will, I hope, expedite matters. You have no cause to be uneasy about Count Seeau; I don't believe the thing will come through his hands, and even if it does, he will not venture to say a word. Now, once for all, believe that I have the most eager longing to embrace you and my beloved sister. If it were only not in Salzburg! But as I have not hitherto been able to see you without going to Salzburg, I do so gladly. I must make haste, for the post is just going.

My cousin is here. Why? To please me, her cousin; this is, indeed, the ostensible cause. But—we can talk about it in Salzburg; and, on this account, I wished very much that she would come with me there. You will find a few lines, written by her own hand, attached to the fourth page of this letter. She is quite willing to go; so if it would really give you pleasure to see her, be so kind as to write immediately to her brother, that the thing may be arranged. When you see her and know her, she is certain to please you, for she is a favorite with every one.

Wolfgang's pleasantries, in the following; letter to his cousin, show that his good humor was fully restored. He was received at home with very great rejoicings, and his cousin soon followed him.

125. Salzburg, May 10, 1779.

DEAREST, sweetest, most beauteous, fascinating, and charming of all cousins, most basely maltreated by an unworthy kinsman! Allow me to strive to soften and appease your just wrath, which only heightens your charms and winning beauty, as high as the heel of your slipper! I hope to soften you, Nature having bestowed on me a large amount of softness, and to appease you, being fond of sweet pease. As to the Leipzig affair, I can't tell whether it may be worth stooping to pick up; were it a bag of ringing coin, it would be a very different thing, and nothing less do I mean to accept, so there is an end of it.

Sweetest cousin, such is life! One man has got a purse, but another has got the money, and he who has neither has nothing; and nothing is even less than little; while, on the other hand, much is a great deal more than nothing, and nothing can come of nothing. Thus has it been from the beginning, is now, and ever shall be; and as I can make it neither worse nor better, I may as well conclude my letter. The gods know I am sincere. How does Probst get on with his wife? and do they live in bliss or in strife? most silly questions, upon my life! Adieu, angel! My father sends you his uncle's blessing, and a thousand cousinly kisses from my sister. Angel, adieu!

A TENDER ODE.
TO MY COUSIN.

[Footnote: A parody of Klopstock's "Dein susses Bild, Edone"]

THY sweet image, cousin mine,
 Hovers aye before me;
Would the form indeed were thine!
 How I would adore thee!
I see it at the day's decline;
I see it through the pale moonshine,
And linger o'er that form divine
By all the flowers of sweet perfume
 I'll gather for my cousin,—
By all the wreaths of myrtle-bloom

I'll wreathe her by the dozen,—
I call upon that image there
To pity my immense despair,
And be indeed my cousin fair

[Footnote: These words are written round the slightly sketched caricature of a face.]

FORTH PART. MUNICH.—IDOMENEO. NOVEMBER 1780 TO JANUARY 1781.

MOZART now remained stationary at Salzburg till the autumn of 1780, highly dissatisfied at being forced to waste his youthful days in inactivity, and in such an obscure place, but still as busy as ever. A succession of grand instrumental compositions were the fruits of this period: two masses, some vespers, the splendid music for "Konig Thamos," and the operetta "Zaide" for Schikaneder. At length, however, to his very great joy, a proposal was made to him from Munich to write a grand opera for the Carnival of 1781. It was "Idomeneo, Konig von Greta." At the beginning of Novemher he once more set off to Munich in order to "prepare an exact fit," on the spot, of the different songs in the opera for the singers, and to rehearse and practise everything with them. The Abbate Varesco in Salzburg was the author of the libretto, in which many an alteration had yet to be made, and these were all to be effected through the intervention of the father.

126. Munich, Nov. 8, 1780.

FORTUNATE and pleasant was my arrival here,—fortunate, because no mishap occurred during the journey; and pleasant, because we had scarcely patience to wait for the moment that was to end this short but disagreeable journey. I do assure you it was impossible for us to sleep for a moment the whole night. The carriage jolted our very souls out, and the seats were as hard as stone! From Wasserburg I thought I never could arrive in Munich with whole bones, and during two stages I held on by the straps, suspended in the air and not venturing to sit down. But no matter; it is past now, though it will serve me as a warning in future rather to go on foot than drive in a diligence.

Now as to Munich. We arrived here at one o'clock in the forenoon, and the same evening I called on Count Seeau [the Theatre Intendant], but as he was not at home I left a note for him. Next morning I went there with Becke. Seeau has been moulded like wax by the Mannheim people. I have a request to make of the Abbate [Gianbattista Varesco].

The aria of Ilia in the second act and second scene must be a little altered for what I require,—"Se il padre perdei, in te lo ritrovo" This verse could not be better; but now comes what always appeared unnatural to me,— N.B. in an aria,—I mean, to speak aside. In a dialogue these things are natural enough, for a few words can be hurriedly said aside, but in an aria, where the words must be repeated, it has a bad effect; and even were this not the case, I should prefer an uninterrupted aria. The beginning may remain if he chooses, for it is charming and quite a natural flowing strain, where, not being fettered by the words, I can write on quite easily; for we agreed to bring in an aria andantino here in concert with four wind instruments, viz. flute, hautboy, horn, and bassoon; and I beg that you will let me have the air as soon as possible.

Now for a grievance. I have not, indeed, the honor of being acquainted with the hero Del Prato [the musico who was to sing Idamante], but from description I should say that Cecarelli is rather the better of the two, for often in the middle of an air our musico's breath entirely fails; nota bene, he never was on any stage, and Raaff is like a statue. Now only for a moment imagine the scene in the first act! But there is one good thing, which is, that Madame Dorothea Wendlincr is arci-contentissima with her scena, and insisted on hearing it played three times in succession. The Grand Master of the Teutonic Order arrived yesterday. "Essex" was given at the Court Theatre, and a magnificent ballet. The theatre was all illuminated. The beginning was an overture by Cannabich, which, as it is one of his last, I did not know. I am sure, if you had heard it you would have been as much pleased and excited as I was, and if you had not previously known the fact, you certainly could not have believed that it was by Cannabich. Do come soon to hear it, and to admire the orchestra. I have no more to say. There is to be a grand concert this evening, where Mara is to sing three airs. Tell me whether it snows as heavily in Salzburg as here. My kind regards to Herr Schikaneder [impresario in Salzburg], and beg him to excuse my not yet sending him the aria, for I have not been able to finish it entirely.

127. Munich, Nov. 13, 1780.

I WRITE in the greatest haste, for I am not yet dressed, and must go off to Count Seeau's. Cannabich, Quaglio, and Le Grand, the ballet-master, also dine there to consult about what is necessary for the opera. Cannabich and I dined yesterday with Countess Baumgarten, [Footnote: He wrote an air for her, the original of which is now in the State Library at Munich.] nee Lerchenteld. My friend is all in all in that family, and now I am the same. It is the best and most serviceable house here to me, for owing to their kindness all has gone well with me, and, please God, will continue to do so. I am just going to dress, but must not omit the chief thing of all, and the principal object of my letter,— to wish you, my very dearest and kindest father, every possible good on this your name-day. I also entreat the continuance of your fatherly love, and assure you of my entire obedience to your wishes. Countess la Rose sends her compliments to you and my sister, so do all the Cannabichs and both Wendling families, Ramm, Eck father and son, Becke, and Herr del Prato, who happens to be with me. Yesterday Count Seeau presented me to the Elector, who was very gracious. If you were to speak to Count Seeau now, you would scarcely recognize him, so completely have the Mannheimers transformed him.

I am ex commissione to write a formal answer in his name to the Abbate Varesco, but I have no time, and was not born to be a secretary. In the first act (eighth scene) Herr Quaglio made the same objection that we did originally,—namely, that it is not fitting the king should be quite alone in the ship. If the Abbe thinks that he can be reasonably represented in the terrible storm forsaken by every one, WITHOUT A SHIP, exposed to the greatest peril, all may remain as it is; but, N. B., no ship—for he cannot be alone in one; so, if the other mode be adopted, some generals or confidants (mates) must land from the ship with him. Then the king might address a few words to his trusty companions, and desire them to leave him alone, which in his melancholy situation would be quite natural.

The second duet is to be omitted altogether, and indeed with more profit than loss to the opera; for if you will read the scene it evidently becomes cold and insipid by the addition of an air or a duet, and very irksome to the other actors, who must stand, by all the time unoccupied;

besides, the noble contest between Ilia and Idamante would become too long, and thus lose its whole interest.

Mara has not the good fortune to please me. She does too little to be compared to a Bastardella [see No. 8], (yet this is her peculiar style,) and too much to touch the heart like a Weber [Aloy-sia], or any judicious singer.

P.S.—A propos, as they translate so badly here, Count Seeau would like to have the opera translated in Salzburg, and the arias alone to be in verse. I am to make a contract that the payment of the poet and the translator should be made in one sum. Give me an answer soon about this. Adieu! What of the family portraits? Are they good likenesses? Is my sister's begun yet? The opera is to be given for the first time on the 26th of January. Be so kind as to send me the two scores of the masses that I have with me, and also the mass in B. Count Seeau is to mention them soon to the Elector; I should like to be known here in this style also. I have just heard a mass of Gruan's; it would be easy to compose half a dozen such in a day. Had I known that this singer, Del Prato, was so bad, I should certainly have recommended Cecarelli.

128. Munich, Nov. 15, 1780.

The aria is now admirable, but there is still an alteration to be made recommended by Raaff; he is, however, right, and even were he not, some courtesy ought to be shown to his gray hairs. He was with me yesterday, and I played over his first aria to him, with which he was very much pleased. The man is old, and can no longer show off in an aria like that in the second art,—"Fuor del mar ho un mare in seno," As, moreover, in the third act he has no aria, (the one in the first act not being so cantabile as he would like, owing to the expression of the words,) he wishes after his last speech, "0 Creta fortuiiata, 0 me felice," to have a pretty aria to sing instead of the quartet; in this way a superfluous air would be got rid of, and the third act produce a far better effect. In the last scene also of the second act, Idomeneo has an aria, or rather a kind of cavatina, to sing between the choruses. For this it would be better to substitute a mere recitative, well supported by the instruments. For in this scene, (owing to the action and grouping which have been recently settled with Le Grand,) the finest of the whole opera, there cannot fail to be such a noise and confusion in the theatre, that an aria, would make a very bad figure in this place, and moreover there is a thunderstorm which is not likely to subside during Raaff's aria! The effect, therefore, of a recitative between the choruses must be infinitely better. Lisel Wendling has also sung through her two arias half a dozen times, and is much pleased with them. I heard from a third person that the two Wendlings highly praised their arias, and as for Raaff he is my best and dearest friend. I must teach the whole opera myself to Del Prato. He is incapable of singing even the introduction to any air of importance, and his voice is so uneven! He is only engaged for a year, and at the end of that time (next September) Count Seeau will get another. Cecarelli might try his chance then serieusement.

I nearly forgot the best of all. After mass last Sunday, Count Seeau presented me, en passant, to H.S.H. the Elector, who was very gracious. He said, "I am happy to see you here again;" and on my replying that I would strive to deserve the good opinion of His Serene Highness, he clapped me on the shoulder, saying, "Oh! I have no doubt whatever that all will go well—a piano piano si va lontano."

Deuce take it! I cannot write everything I wish. Raaff has just left me; he sends you his compliments, and so do the Cannabichs, and Wendlings, and Ramm. My sister must not be idle, but practise steadily, for every one is looking forward with pleasure to her coming here. My lodging is in the Burggasse at M. Fiat's [where the marble slab to his memory is now erected].

129. Munich, Nov. 22, 1780.

I SEND herewith, at last, the long-promised aria for Herr Schikaneder. During the first week that I was here I could not entirely complete it, owing to the business that caused me to come here. Besides, Le Grand, the ballet-master, a terrible talker and bore, has just been with me, and by his endless chattering caused me to miss the diligence. I hope my sister is quite well. I have at this moment a bad cold, which in such weather is quite the fashion here. I hope and trust, however, that it will soon take its departure,—indeed, both phlegm and cough are gradually disappearing. In your last letter you write repeatedly, "Oh! my poor eyes! I du not wish to write myself blind—half-past eight at night, and no spectacles!" But why do you write at night, and without spectacles? I cannot understand it. I have not yet had an opportunity of speaking to Count Seeau, but hope to do so to-day, and shall give you any information I can gather by the next post. At present all will, no doubt, remain as it is. Herr Raaff paid me a visit yesterday morning, and I gave him your regards, which seemed to please him much. He is, indeed, a worthy and thoroughly respectable man. The day before yesterday Del Frato sang in the most disgraceful way at the concert. I would almost lay a wager that the man never manages to get through the rehearsals, far less the opera; he has some internal disease.

Come in!—Herr Panzacchi! [who was to sing Arbace]. He has already paid me three visits, and has just asked me to dine with him on Sunday. I hope the same thing won't happen to me that happened to us with the coffee. He meekly asks if, instead of se la sa, he may sing se co la, or even ut, re, mi, fa, sol, la.

I am so glad when you often write to me, only not at night, and far less without spectacles. You must, however, forgive me if I do not say much in return, for every minute is precious; besides, I am obliged chiefly to write at night, for the mornings are so very dark; then I have to dress, and the servant at the Weiser sometimes admits a troublesome visitor. When Del Prato comes I must sing to him, for I have to teach him his whole part like a child; his method is not worth a farthing. I will write more fully next time. What of the family portraits? My sister, if she has nothing better to do, might mark down the names of the best comedies that have been performed during my absence. Has Schikaneder still good receipts? My compliments to all my friends, and to Gilofsky's Katherl. Give a pinch of Spanish snuff from me to Pimperl [the dog], a good wine-sop, and three kisses. Do you not miss me at all? A thousand compliments to all—all! Adieu! I embrace you both from my heart, and hope my sister will soon recover. [Nannerl, partly owing to her grief in consequence of an unfortunate love-affair, was suffering from pains in the chest, which threatened to turn to consumption.]

130. Munich, Nov. 24, 1780.

I beg you will convey to Madlle. Katharine Gilofsky de Urazowa my respectful homage. Wish her in my name every possible happiness on her name-day; above all, I wish that this may be the last time I congratulate her as Mademoiselle. What you write to me about Count Seinsheim is done long ago; they are all links of one chain. I have already dined with, him once, and with Baumgarten twice, and once with Lerchenfeld, father of Madlle. Baumgarten. Not a single day passes without some of these people being at Cannabich's. Do not be uneasy, dearest father, about my opera; I do hope that all will go well. No doubt it will be assailed by a petty cabal, which will in all probability be defeated with ridicule; for the most respected and influential families among the nobility are in my favor, and the first-class musicians are one and all for me. I cannot tell you what a good friend Cannabich is—so busy and active! In a word, he is always on the watch to serve a friend. I will tell you the whole story about Mara. I did not write to you before on the subject, because I thought that, even if you knew nothing of it, you would be sure to hear the particulars here; but now it is high time to tell you the whole truth, for probably additions have been made to the story,—at least, in this town, it has been told in all sorts of different ways. No one can know about it better than I do, as I was present, so I heard and witnessed the whole affair. When the first symphony was over, it was Madame Mara's turn to sing. I then saw her husband come sneaking in behind her with his violoncello in his hand; I thought she was going to sing an aria obligato with violoncello accompaniment. Old Danzi, the first violoncello, also accompanies well. All at once Toeschi (who is a director, but has no authority when Cannabich is present) said to Danzi (N. B., his son-in-law), "Rise, and give Mara your place." When Cannabich saw and heard this, he called out, "Danzi, stay where you are; the Elector prefers his own people playing the accompaniments." Then the air began, Mara standing behind his wife, looking very sheepish, and still holding his violoncello. The instant they entered the concert-room, I took a dislike to both, for you could not well see two more insolent-looking people, and the sequel will convince you of this. The aria had a second part, but Madame Mara did not think proper to inform the orchestra of the fact previously, but after the last ritournelle came down into the room with her usual air of effrontery to pay her respects to the nobility. In the mean time her husband attacked Cannabich. I cannot write every detail, for it would be too long; but, in a word, he insulted both the orchestra and Cannabich's character, who, being naturally very much irritated, laid hold of his arm, saying, "This is not the place to answer you." Mara wished to reply, but Cannabich threatened that if he did not hold his tongue he would have him removed by force. All were indignant at Mara's impertinence. A concerto by Ramm was then given, when this amiable couple proceeded to lay their complaint before Count Seeau; but from him, also, as well as from every one else, they heard that they were in the wrong. At last Madame Mara was foolish enough to speak to the Elector himself on the subject, her husband in the mean time saying in an arrogant tone, "My wife is at this moment complaining to the Elector—an unlucky business for Cannabich; I am sorry for him." But people only burst out laughing in his face. The Elector, in reply to Madame Mara's complaint, said, "Madame, you sang like an angel, although your husband did not accompany you;" and when she wished to press her grievance, he said, "That is Count Seeau's affair, not mine." When they saw that nothing was to be done, they left the room, althouoh she had still two airs to sing. This was nothing short of an insult to the Elector, and I know for certain that, had not the Archduke and other strangers been present, they would have been very differently treated; but on this account Count Seeau was annoyed, so he sent after them immediately, and they came back. She sang her two arias, but was not accompanied by her husband. In the last one (and I shall always believe that Herr Mara did it on purpose) two bars were wanting—N. B., only in the copy from which Cannabich was playing. When this occurred, Mara seized Cannabich's arm, who quickly got right, but struck his bow on the desk, exclaiming audibly, "This copy is all wrong." When the aria was at an end, he said, "Herr Mara, I give you one piece of advice, and I hope you will profit by it: never seize the arm of the director of an orchestra, or lay your account with getting at least half a dozen sound boxes ou the ear." Mara's tone was now, however, entirely lowered; he begged to be forgiven, and excused himself as he best could. The most shameful part of the affair was that Mara (a miserable violoncellist, all here declare) would never have been heard at court at all but for Cannabich, who had taken considerable trouble about it. At the first concert before my arrival he played a concerto, and accompanied his wife, taking Danzi's place without saying a word either to Danzi or any one else, which was

130. Munich, Nov. 24, 1780.

allowed to pass. The Elector was by no means satisfied with his mode of accompanying, and said he preferred his own people. Cannabich, knowing this, mentioned to Count Seeau, before the concert began, that he had no objection to Mara's playing, but that Danzi must also play. When Mara came he was told this, and yet he was guilty of this insolence. If you knew these people, you would at once see pride, arrogance, and unblushing effrontery written on their faces.

My sister is now, I hope, quite recovered. Pray do not write me any more melancholy letters, for I require at this time a cheerful spirit, a clear head, and inclination to work, and these no one can have who is sad at heart. I know, and, believe me, deeply feel, how much you deserve rest and peace, but am I the obstacle to this? I would not willingly be so, and yet, alas! I fear I am. But if I attain my object, so that I can live respectably here, you must instantly leave Salzburg. You will say, that may never come to pass; at all events, industry and exertion shall not be wanting on my part. Do try to come over soon to see me. We can all live together. I have a roomy alcove on my first room in which two beds stand. These would do capitally for you and me. As for my sister, all we can do is to put a stove into the next room, which will only be an affair of four or five florins; for in mine we might heat the stove till it is red-hot, and leave the stove-door open into the bargain, yet it would not make the room endurable—it is so frightfully cold in it. Ask the Abbate Varesco if we could not break off at the chorus in the second act, "Placido e il mare" after Elettra's first verse, when the chorus is repeated,—at all events after the second, for it is really far too long. I have been confined to the house two days from my cold, and, luckily for me, I have very little appetite, for in the long run it would be inconvenient to pay for my board. I have, however, written a note to the Count on the subject, and received a message from him that he would speak to me about it shortly. By heavens! he ought to be thoroughly ashamed of himself. I won't pay a single kroutzer.

131. Munich, Dec. 1, 1780.

THE rehearsal went off with extraordinary success; there were only six violins in all, but the requisite wind-instruments. No one was admitted but Count Seeau's sister and young Count Seinsheim. This day week we are to have another rehearsal, with twelve violins for the first act, and then the second act will be rehearsed (like the first on the previous occasion). I cannot tell you how delighted and surprised all were; but I never expected anything else, for I declare I went to this rehearsal with as quiet a heart as if I had been going to a banquet. Count Seinsheim said to me, "I do assure you that though I expected a great deal from you, I can truly say this I did not expect."

The Cannabichs and all who frequent their house are true friends of mine. After the rehearsal, (for we had a great deal to discuss with the Count,) when I went home with Cannabich, Madame Cannabich came to meet me, and hugged me from joy at the rehearsal having passed off so admirably; then came Ramm and Lang, quite out of their wits with delight. My true friend the excellent lady, who was alone in the house with her invalid daughter Rose, had been full of solicitude on my account. When you know him, you will find Ramm a true German, saying exactly what he thinks to your face. He said to me, "I must honestly confess that no music ever made such an impression on me, and I assure you I thought of your father fifty times at least, and of the joy he will feel when he hears this opera. But enough of this subject. My cold is rather worse owing to this rehearsal, for it is impossible not to feel excited when honor and fame are at stake, however cool you may be at first. I did everything you prescribed for my cold, but it goes on very slowly, which is particularly inconvenient to me at present; but all my writing about it will not put an end to my cough, and yet write I must. To-day I have begun to take violet syrup and a little almond oil, and already I feel relieved, and have again stayed two days in the house. Yesterday morning Herr Raaff came to me again to hear the aria in the second act. The man is as much enamored of his aria as a young passionate lover ever was of his fair one. He sings it the last thing before he goes to sleep, and the first thing in the morning when he awakes. I knew already, from a sure source, but now from himself, that he said to Herr von Viereck (Oberststallmeister) and to Herr von Kastel, "I am accustomed constantly to change my parts, to suit me better, in recitative as well as in arias, but this I have left just as it was, for every single note is in accordance with my voice." In short, he is as happy as a king. He wishes the interpolated aria to be a little altered, and so do I. The part commencing with the word era he does not like, for what we want here is a calm tranquil aria; and if consisting of only one part, so much the better, for a second subject would have to be brought in about the middle, which leads me out of my way. In "Achill in Sciro" there is an air of this kind, "or che mio figlio sei." I thank my sister very much for the list of comedies she sent me. It is singular enough about the comedy "Rache fur Rache"; it was frequently given here with much applause, and quite lately too, though I was not there myself. I beg you will present my devoted homage to Madlle. Therese von Barisani; if I had a brother, I would request him to kiss her hand in all humility, but having a sister only is still better, for I beg she will embrace her in the most affectionate manner in my name. A propos, do write a letter to Cannabich; he deserves it, and it will please him exceedingly. What does it matter if he does not answer you? You must not judge him from his manner; he is the same to every one, and means nothing. You must first know him well.

132. Munich, Dec. 5, 1780.

The death of the Empress [Maria Theresa] does not at all affect my opera, for the theatrical performances are not suspended, and the plays go on as usual. The entire mourning is not to last more than six weeks, and my opera will not be given before the 20th of January. I wish you to get my black suit thoroughly brushed to make it as wearable as possible, and forward it to me by the first diligence; for next week every one must be in mourning, and I, though constantly on the move, must cry with the others.

With regard to Raaff's last aria, I already mentioned that we both wish to have more touching and pleasing words. The word era is constrained; the beginning good, but gelida massa is again hard. In short, far-fetched or pedantic expressions are always inappropriate in a pleasing aria. I should also like the air to express only peace and contentment; and one part would be quite as good—in fact, better, in my opinion. I also wrote about Panzacchi; we must do what we can to oblige the good old man. He wishes to have his recitative in the third act lengthened a couple of lines, which, owing to the chiaro oscuro and his being a good actor, will have a capital effect. For example, after the strophe, "Sei la citta del pianto, e questa reggia quella del duol," comes a slight glimmering of hope, and then, "Madman that I am! whither does my grief lead me?" "Ah! Creta tutta io vedo." The Abbato Varesco is not obliged to rewrite the act on account of these things, for they can easily be interpolated. I have also written that both I and others think the oracle's subterranean speech too long to make a good effect. Reflect on this. I must now conclude, having such a mass of writing to do. I have not seen Baron Lehrbach, and don't know whether he is here or not; and I have no time to run about. I may easily not know whether he is here, but he cannot fail to know positively that I am. Had I been a girl, no doubt he would have come to see me long ago. Now adieu!

I have this moment received your letter of the 4th December. You must begin to accustom yourself a little to the kissing system. You can meanwhile practise with Maresquelli, for each time that you come to Dorothea Wendling's (where everything is rather in the French style) you will have to embrace both mother and daughter, but—N. B., on the chin, so that the paint may not be rubbed off. More of this next time. Adieu!

P.S.—Don't forget about my black suit; I must have it, or I shall be laughed at, which is never agreeable.

133. Munich, Dec. 13, 1780.

Your last letters seemed to me far too short, so I searched all the pockets in my black suit to see if I could not find something more. In Vienna and all the Imperial dominions, the gayeties are to be resumed six weeks hence,—a very sensible measure, for mourning too long is not productive of half as much good to the deceased as of injury to the living. Is Herr Schikaneder to remain in Salzburg? If so, he might still see and hear my opera. Here people, very properly, cannot comprehend why the mourning should last for three months, while that for our late Elector was only six weeks. The theatre, however, goes on as usual. You do not write to me how Herr Esser accompanied my sonatas—ill, or well? The comedy, "Wie man sich die Sache deutet," is charming, for I saw it—no, not saw it, but read it, for it has not yet been performed;

besides, I have been only once in the theatre, having no leisure to go, the evening being the time I like best to work. If her Grace, the most sensible gracious Frau von Robinig, does not on this occasion change the period of her gracious journey to Munich, her Grace will be unable to hear one note of my opera. My opinion, however, is, that her Grace in her supreme wisdom, in order to oblige your excellent son, will graciously condescend to stay a little longer. I suppose your portrait is now begun, and my sister's also, no doubt. How is it likely to turn out? Have you any answer yet from our plenipotentiary at Wetzlar? I forget his name—Fuchs, I think. I mean, about the duets for two pianos. It is always satisfactory to explain a thing distinctly, and the arias of Esopus are, I suppose, still lying on the table? Send them to me by the diligence, that I may give them myself to Herr von Dummhoff, who will then remit them post-free. To whom? Why, to Heckmann—a charming man, is he not? and a passionate lover of music. My chief object comes to-day at the close of my letter, but this is always the case with me. One day lately, after dining with Lisel Wendling, I drove with Le Grand to Cannabich's (as it was snowing heavily). Through the window they thought it was you, and that we had come together. I could not understand why both Karl and the children ran down the steps to meet us, and when they saw Le Grand, did not say a word, but looked quite discomposed, till they explained it when we went up-stairs. I shall write nothing more, because you write so seldom to me—nothing, except that Herr Eck, who has just crept into the room to fetch his sword which he forgot the last time he was here, sends his best wishes to Thresel, Pimperl, Jungfer Mitzerl, Gilofsky, Katherl, my sister, and, last of all, to yourself. Kiss Thresel for me; a thousand kisses to Pimperl.

134. Munich, Dec. 16, 1780.

HERR ESSER came to call on me yesterday for the first time. Did he go about on foot in Salzburg, or always drive in a carriage, as he does here? I believe his small portion of Salzburg money will not remain long in his purse. On Sunday we are to dine together at Cannabich's, and there he is to let us hear his solos, clever and stupid. He says he will give no concert here, nor does he care to appear at court; he does not intend to seek it, but if the Elector wishes to hear him,—"Eh, bien! here am I; it would be a favor, but I shall not announce myself." But, after all, he may be a worthy fool—deuce take it! cavalier, I meant to say. He asked me why I did not wear my Order of the Spur. I said I had one in my head quite hard enough to carry. He was so obliging as to dust my coat a little for me, saying, "One cavalier may wait upon another." In spite of which, the same afternoon—from forgetfulness, I suppose—he left his spur at home, (I mean the outward and visible one,) or at all events contrived to hide it so effectually that not a vestige of it was to be seen. In case I forget it again, I must tell you that Madame and Madlle. Cannabich both complain that their throats are daily becoming larger owing to the air and water here, which might at last become regular goitres. Heaven forbid! They are indeed taking a certain powder—how do I know what? Not that this is its name; at all events, it seems to do them no good. For their sakes, therefore, I took the liberty to recommend what we call goitre pills, pretending (in order to enhance their value) that my sister had three goitres, each larger than the other, and yet at last, by means of these admirable pills, had got entirely rid of them! If they can be made up here, pray send me the prescription; but if only to be had at Salzburg, I beg you will pay ready money for them, and send a few cwt. of them by the next diligence. You know my address.

There is to be another rehearsal this afternoon of the first and second acts in the Count's apartments; then we shall only have a chamber rehearsal of the third, and afterwards go straight to the theatre. The rehearsal has been put off owing to the copyist, which enraged Count Seinsheim to the uttermost. As for what is called the popular taste, do not be uneasy, for in my opera there is music for every class, except for the long-eared. A propos, how goes on the Archbishop? Next Monday I shall have been six weeks away from Salzburg. You know, dear father, that I only stay there to oblige you, for, by heavens! if I followed my own inclinations, before coming here I would have torn up my last diploma; for I give you my honor that not Salzburg itself, but the Prince and his proud nobility, become every day more intolerable to me. I should rejoice were I to be told that my services were no longer required, for with the great patronage that I have here, both my present and future circumstances would be secure, death excepted, which no one can guard against, though no great misfortune to a single man. But anything in the world to please you. It would be less trying to me if I could only occasionally escape from time to time, just to draw my breath. You know how difficult it was to get away on this occasion; and without some very urgent cause, there would not be the faintest hope of such a thing. It is enough to make one weep to think of it, so I say no more. Adieu! Come soon to see me at Munich and to hear my opera, and then tell me whether I have not a right to feel sad when I think of Salzburg. Adieu!

135. Munich, Dec. 19, 1780.

THIS last rehearsal has been as successful as the first, and satisfactorily proved to the orchestra and all those who heard it, their mistake in thinking that the second act could not possibly excel the first in expression and novelty. Next Saturday both acts are again to be rehearsed, but in a spacious apartment in the palace, which I have long wished, as the room at Count Seeau's is far too small. The Elector is to be in an adjoining room (incognito) to hear the music. "It must be a life-and-death rehearsal," said Cannabich to me. At the last one he was bathed in perspiration.

Cannabich, whose name-day this is, has just left me, reproaching me for discontinuing this letter in his presence. As to Madame Duschek, the thing is impossible at present, but I will do what I can with pleasure after my opera is given. I beg you will write to her and say, with my compliments, that next time she comes to Salzburg we can square accounts. It would delight me if I could get a couple of cavaliers like old Czernin,—this would be a little yearly help; but certainly not for less than 100 florins a year, in which case it might be any style of music they pleased. I trust that you are now quite recovered; indeed, after the friction performed by a Barisani Theres, you cannot be otherwise. You have no doubt seen by my letters that I am well and happy. Who would not feel happy to have completed such a great and laborious work—and completed it, too, with honor and renown? Three arias alone are wanting—the last chorus in the third act, and the overture and ballet; and then—Adieu partie!

One more indispensable remark, and I have done. The scene between father and son in the first act, and the first scene in the second act between Idomenco and Arbace, are both too long, and sure to weary the audience, particularly as in the first the actors are both bad, and in the second one of them is also very inferior; besides, the whole details are only a narrative of what the spectators have already seen with their own eyes. The scenes will be printed just as they are. I only wish the Abbate would point out to me how not only to curtail them, but very considerably to curtail them; otherwise I must do it myself, for the scenes cannot remain as they are—I mean, so far as the music is concerned. I have just got your letter, which, being begun by my sister, is without a date. A thousand compliments to Thresel— my future upper and under nursery-maid to be. I can easily believe that Katherl would gladly come to Munich, if (independent of the journey) you would allow her to take my place at meals. Eh! bien. I can contrive it, for she can occupy the same room with my sister.

136. Munich, Dec 27, 1780.

I HAVE received the entire opera, Schachtner's letter, your note, and the pills. As for the two scenes to be curtailed, it was not my own suggestion, but one to which I consented—my reason being that Raaff and Del Prato spoil the recitative by singing it quite devoid of all spirit and fire, and so monotonously. They are the most miserable actors that ever trod the stage. I had a desperate battle royal with Seeau as to the inexpediency, unfitness, and almost impossibility of the omissions in question. However, all is to be printed as it is, which at first he positively refused to agree to, but at last, on rating him soundly, he gave way. The last rehearsal was splendid. It took place in a spacious apartment in the palace. The Elector was also within hearing. On this occasion it was rehearsed with the whole orchestra, (of course I mean those who belong to the opera.) After the first act the Elector called out Bravo! rather too audibly, and when I went into the next room to kiss his hand he said, "Your opera is quite charming, and cannot fail to do you honor." As he was not sure whether he could remain for the whole performance, we played the concerted aria and the thunderstorm at the beginning of the second act, by his desire, when he again testified his approbation in the kindest manner, and said, laughing, "Who could believe that such great things could be hidden in so small a head?" Next day, too, at his reception, he extolled my opera much. The ensuing rehearsal will probably take place in the theatre. A propos, Becke told me, a day or two ago, that he had written to you about the last rehearsal but one, and among other things had said that Raaff's aria in the second act is not composed in accordance with the sense of the words, adding, "So I am told, for I understand Italian too little to be able to judge." I replied, "If you had only asked me first and written afterwards! I must tell you that

136. Munich, Dec 27, 1780.

whoever said such a thing can understand very little Italian. The aria is quite adapted to the words. You hear the mare, and the mare funesto; and the passages dwell on the minacciar, and entirely express minacciar (threatening). Moreover, it is the most superb aria in the opera, and has met with universal approbation."

Is it true that the Emperor is ill? Is it true that the Archbishop intends to come to Munich? Raaff is the best and most upright man alive, but—so addicted to old-fashioned routine that flesh and blood cannot stand it; so that it is very difficult to write for him, but very easy if you choose to compose commonplace arias, as for instance the first one, "Vedromi intorno." When you hear it, you will say that it is good and pretty, but had I written it for Zonca it would have suited the words better. Raaff likes everything according to rule, and does not regard expression. I have had a piece of work with him about the quartet. The more I think of the quartet as it will be on the stage, the more effective I consider it, and it has pleased all those who have heard it on the piano. Raaff alone maintains that it will not be successful. He said to me confidentially, "There is no opportunity to expand the voice; it is too confined." As if in a quartet the words should not far rather be spoken, as it were, than sung! He does not at all understand such things. I only replied, "My dear friend, if I were aware of one single note in this quartet which ought to be altered, I would change it at once; but there is no single thing in my opera with which I am so pleased as with this quartet, and when you have once heard it sung in concert you will speak very differently. I took every possible pains to conform to your taste in your two arias, and intend to do the same with the third, so I hope to be successful; but with regard to trios and quartets, they should be left to the composer's own discretion." On which he said that he was quite satisfied. The other day he was much annoyed by some words in his last aria—rinvigorir and ringiovenir, and especially vienmi a rinvigorir—five i's! It is true, this is very disagreeable at the close of an air.

137. Munich, Dec. 30. 1780.

A HAPPY New-Year! Excuse my writing much, for I am over head and ears in my work. I have not quite finished the third act; and as there is no extra ballet, but only an appropriate divertissement in the opera, I have the honor to write that music also, but I am glad of it, for now the music will be all by the same master. The third act will prove at least as good as the two others,—in fact, I believe, infinitely better, and that it might fairly be said, finis coronat opus. The Elector was so pleased at the rehearsal that, as I already wrote to you, he praised it immensely next morning at his reception, and also in the evening at court. I likewise know from good authority that, on the same evening after the final rehearsal, he spoke of my music to every one he conversed with, saying, "I was quite surprised; no music ever had such an effect on me; it is magnificent music." The day before yesterday we had a recitative rehearsal at Wendling's, and tried over the quartet all together. We repeated it six times, and now it goes well. The stumbling-block was Del Prato; the wretch can literally do nothing. His voice is not so bad, if he did not sing from the back of the throat; besides, he has no intonation, no method, no feeling. He is only one of the best of the youths who sing in the hope of getting a place in the choir of the chapel. Raaff was glad to find himself mistaken about the quartet, and no longer doubts its effect. Now I am in a difficulty with regard to Raaff's last air, and you must help me out of it. He cannot digest the rinvigorir and ringiovenir, and these two words make the whole air hateful to him. It is true that mostrami and vienmi are also not good, but the worst of all are the two final words; to avoid the shake on the i in the first word rinvigorir, I was forced to transfer it to the o. Raaff has now found, in the "Natal di Giove," which is in truth very little known, an aria quite appropriate to this situation. I think it is the ad libitum aria, "Bell' alme al ciel diletto" and he wishes me to write music for these words. He says, "No one knows it, and we need say nothing." He is quite aware that he cannot expect the Abbate to alter this aria a third time, and he will not sing it as it is written. I beg you will send me an immediate reply. I shall conclude, for I must now write with all speed; the composing is finished, but not the writing out.

My compliments to dear Thresel: the maid who waits on me here is also named Thresel, but, heavens! how inferior to the Linz Thresel in beauty, virtue, charms—and a thousand other merits! You probably know that the worthy musico Marquesi, the Marquessius di Milano, has been poisoned in Naples, but how? He was enamored of a Duchess, whose rightful lover became jealous, and sent three or four fellows to give him his choice between drinking poison out of a cup and being assassinated. He chose the former, but being an Italian poltroon he died ALONE, and allowed his murderers to live on in peace and quiet. I would at least (in my own room) have taken a couple with me into the next world, if absolutely obliged to die myself. Such an admirable singer is a great loss. Adieu!

138. Munich, Jan. 3, 1780.

MY head and my hands are so fully occupied with my third act, that it would not be wonderful if I turned into a third act myself, for it alone has cost me more trouble than the entire opera; there is scarcely a scene in it which is not interesting to the greatest degree. The accompaniment of the underground music consists merely of five instruments, namely, three trombones and two French horns, which are placed on ths spot whence the voice proceeds. The whole orchestra is silent at this part.

The grand rehearsal positively takes place on the 20th, and the first performance on the 22d. All you will both require is to bring one black dress, and another for every-day wear, when you are only visiting intimate friends where there is no ceremony, and thus save your black dress a little; and if my sister likes, one pretty dress also, that she may go to the ball and the Academie Masquee.

Herr von Robinig is already here, and sends his regards to you. I hear that the two Barisanis are also coming to Munich; is this true? Heaven be praised that the cut on the finger of the Archbishop was of no consequence! Good heavens! how dreadfully I was alarmed at first! Cannabich thanks you for your charming letter, and all his family beg their remembrances. He told me you had written very humorously. You must have been in a happy mood.

No doubt we shall have a good many corrections to make in the third act when on the stage; as for instance scene sixth, after Arbace's aria, the personages are marked, "Idomeneo, Arbace, How can the latter so instantly reappear on the spot? Fortunately he might stay away altogether. In order to make the matter practicable, I have written a somewhat longer introduction to the High Priest's recitative. After the mourning chorus the King and his people all go away, and in the following scene the directions are, "Idomeneo kneels down in the Temple." This is impossible; he must come accompanied by his whole suite. A march must necessarily be introduced here, so I have composed a very simple one for two violins, tenor, bass, and two hautboys, to be played a mezza voce, and during this time the King appears, and the Priests prepare the offerings for the sacrifice. The King then kneels down and begins the prayer.

In Elettra's recitative, after the underground voice has spoken, there ought to be marked exeunt. I forgot to look at the copy written for the press to see whether it is there, and whereabouts it comes. It seems to me very silly that they should hurry away so quickly merely to allow Madlle. Elettra to be alone.

I have this moment received your few lines of January 1st. When I opened the letter I chanced to hold it in such a manner that nothing but a blank sheet met my eyes. At last I found the writing. I am heartily glad that I have got an aria for Raaff, as he was quite resolved to introduce the air he had discovered, and I could not possibly (N. B., with a Raaff) have arranged in any other way than by having Varesco's air printed, but Raaff's sung. I must stop, or I shall waste too much time. Thank my sister very much for her New-Year's wishes, which I heartily return. I hope we shall soon be right merry together. Adieu! Remembrances to friends, not forgetting Ruscherle. Young Eck sends her a kiss, a sugar one of course.

139. Munich, Jan. 10, 1780.

My greatest piece of news is that the opera is put off for a week. The grand rehearsal is not to take place till the 27th—N. B., my birthday—and the opera itself on the 29th. Why? Probably to save Count Seeau two hundred gulden. I, indeed, am very glad, because we can now rehearse frequently and more carefully. You should have seen the faces of the Robinigs when I told them this news. Louisa and Sigmund are delighted to stay; but Lise, that SNEAKING MISERY, has such a spiteful Salzburg tongue that it really drives me distracted. Perhaps they may still remain, and I hope so on Louisa's account. In addition to many other little altercations with Count Seeau, I have had a sharp contention with him about the trombones. I call it so, because I was obliged to be downright rude, or I never should have carried my point. Next Saturday the three acts are to be rehearsed in private. I got your letter of the 8th, and read it with great pleasure; the burlesque, too, I like very much. Excuse my writing more at this time; for, in the first place, as you see, my pen and ink are bad, and, in the second, I have still a couple of airs to write for the last ballet. I hope you will send no more such letters as the last, of only three or four lines.

140. Munich, Jan. 18, 1780.

PRAY forgive a short letter, for I must go this very moment, ten o'clock (in the forenoon of course), to the rehearsal. There is to be a recitative rehearsal for the first time to-day in the theatre. I could not write before, having been so incessantly occupied with those confounded dances. Laus Deo, I have got rid of them at last, but only of what was most pressing. The rehearsal of the third act went off admirably. It was considered very superior to the second act. The poetry is, however, thought far too long, and of course the music likewise, (which I always said it was.) On this account the aria of Idamante, "No la morte io non pavento" is to be omitted, which was, indeed, always out of place there; those who have heard it with the music deplore this. Raaff's last air, too, is still more regretted, but we must make a virtue of necessity. The prediction of the oracle is still far too long, so I have shortened it; but Varesco need know nothing of this, because it will all be printed just as he wrote it. Madame von Robinig will bring with her the payment both for him and Schachtner. Herr Geschwender declined taking any money with him. In the meantime say to Varesco in my name, that he will not get a farthing from Count Seeau beyond the contract, for all the alterations were made FOR ME and not for the Count, and he ought to be obliged to me into the bargain, as they were indispensable for his own reputation. There is a good deal that might still be altered; and I can tell him that he would not have come off so well with any other composer as with me. I have spared no trouble in defending him.

The stove is out of the question, for it costs too much. I will have another bed put up in the room that adjoins the alcove, and we must manage the best way we can. Do not forget to bring my little watch with you. We shall probably make an excursion to Augsburg, where we could have the little silly thing regulated. I wish you also to bring Schachtner's operetta. There are people who frequent Cannabich's house, who might as well hear a thing of the kind. I must be off to the rehearsal. Adieu!

The father and sister arrived on the 25th of January, and the first performance of the opera took place a few days afterwards; then the family amused themselves for some little time with the gayeties of the Carnival. The Archbishop had gone to Vienna; and, desiring to appear in the Imperial city in the full splendor of a spiritual prince, he had taken with him, in addition to fine furniture and a large household, some of his most distinguished musicians. On this account, therefore, Mozart, in the middle of March, also received the command to go to Vienna. He set off immediately.

END OF VOL. I.

The End.